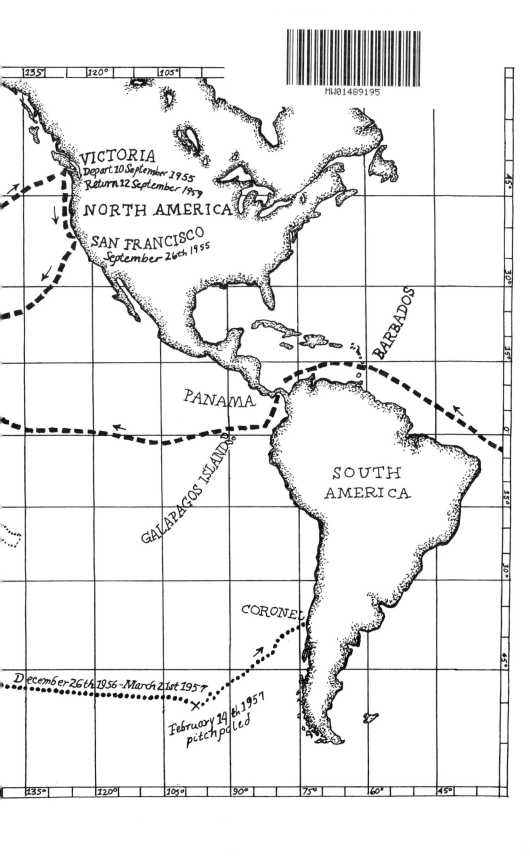

135° 120° 105°

VICTORIA
Depart 10 September 1955
Return 12 September 1957

NORTH AMERICA

SAN FRANCISCO
September 26th 1955

BARBADOS

PANAMA

GALAPAGOS ISLANDS

SOUTH
AMERICA

CORONEL

December 26th 1956 ~ March 21st 1957

February 14th 1957
pitchpoled

45°

30°

15°

0°

15°

30°

45°

135° 120° 105° 90° 75° 60° 45°

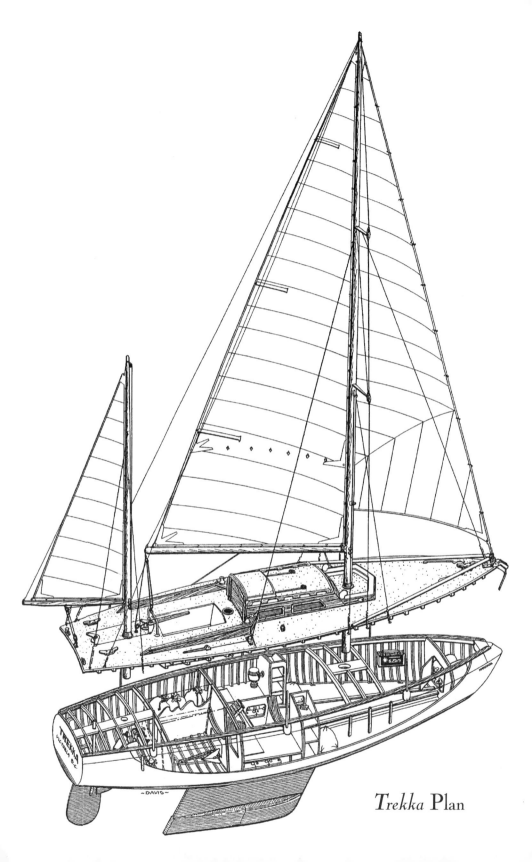

Trekka Plan

TREKKA

Round the World

JOHN GUZZWELL

FOREWORD BY HAL ROTH

FINE EDGE
Productions
FineEdge.com

Cover design by Melanie Haage
Back cover photos by the author and Réanne Hemingway-Douglass
Frontispiece drawing of *Trekka* by Steve Davis
Book design and production by Melanie Haage and Molly Cadranell
Inside cover maps by Faith Rumm after the author's originals
Photos by the author except where noted
Inside maps by the author
Illustration on page 139 courtesy of *Yachting Magazine*
Copyediting by Cindy Kamler

Library of Congress Cataloging-in-Publication Data

Guzzwell, John.
    Trekka round the world / John Guzzwell ; foreword by Hal Roth. — 1st ed.
        p.   cm.
    ISBN 0-938665-56-1
    1. Trekka (Yawl)   2. Voyages around the world.
  G440..T77G89   1998
  910.4'1 — dc21
                                          98-44068
                                                  CIP

ISBN ISBN 0-938665-56-1

Publisher's note: The spelling used in this book follows the author's preference for
Canadian English. Use of "we" in text generally refers to the author and his boat *Trekka*.

Address requests for permission to Fine Edge Productions,
Route 2, Box 303, Bishop, CA 93514
www.fineedge.com

Printed in the United States of America
First Edition

For Dorothy

Contents

Maritime Museum of British Columbia Society

28 Bastion Square, Victoria, British Columbia V8W 1H9   Fax: (250) 382-2869   ☎ (250) 385-4222

21 September 1998

Mr. Don Douglass
Fine Edge Productions
Route 2, Box 303
Bishop, CA   93514

RE: *Trekka Rround the World*

John Guzzwell's epic adventure, *Trekka Round the World*, continues to be an inspiration to all people interested in sailing. Victorians hold *Trekka* dear to their heart, since John built her and sailed her from this fair city.

Almost twenty years ago a Victoria based heritage group– the Thermopylae Club initiated a campaign to purchase *Trekka* from her then owner Eric Abranovich in Hawaii and place her in a public collection. After an intensive fundraising campaign, the club succeeded in making the purchase and donating her to this museum. Since December 29, 1981 she has been on public display with us.

Nothing in this world remains static, even in museums. Over the past two years the Maritime Museum of British Columbia has been engaged in a major redevelopment of its galleries. The museum occupies a classic Victorian-styled building built in 1888. As beautiful as it is, we have severe limitations on public display space. Another famous vessel, John Voss's *Tilikum*, is already on display, and in order to tell a complete history of the Pacific Northwest, we have had to remove *Trekka* from our main floor gallery.

At the time of writing this letter, we are engaged in finding a new exhibition location for *Trekka*. We are working with the Thermopylae Club to find a site that provides public access and protection to *Trekka* to ensure her long term preservation.

For readers of this book who want to view *Trekka*, we suggest contacting the museum at the above address to determine her new location. *Trekka's* story is an inspiration to all, she will always remain one of our finest treasures.

Kindest regards,

Guy Mathias
Executive Director, MMBC

Foreword

by Hal Roth

EVERY GENERATION HAS ITS HEROES, and in the long-distance sailing world it's people like Miles and Beryl Smeeton, Peter and Anne Pye, Eric and Susan Hiscock, and the famous single-handers Bernard Moitessier, Francis Chichester, and John Guzzwell. All these sailors have made voyage after voyage to distant corners of the world, and they've made these passages not once or twice but year after year—in fact, for most of their lives. Unfortunately their names are probably strange to most yachtsmen of today because the books of these sailors are largely out of print and forgotten. And regrettably, all these men and women have passed from the scene. All, that is, except John Guzzwell who, at the age of sixty-eight, completed the 1998 Singlehanded TransPac Race from San Francisco to Hawaii in a sleek wooden yacht of his own design that he built himself.

Trekka Round the World is the story of John's first great voyage. He had completed his apprenticeship as a yacht joiner (a specialist carpenter), and entirely by himself built *Trekka*, a jewel-like 20-foot 6-inch, light-displacement wooden yawl designed by Laurent Giles. At the age of twenty-five he set out to see the world. The year was 1955.

John sailed round the world by way of Hawaii, New Zealand, Australia, South Africa, Panama, and back to Victoria, stopping en route at several remote islands. He started out with cotton sails. He navigated with a sextant. This was long before the days of satellite navigation, single side-band radios, compulsory life rafts, VHF radios, watermakers, auxiliary charging plants, etc. Instead of an inboard diesel engine, John had a four-horsepower outboard and four gallons of fuel that he kept in a locker. In those days there were no marinas or specialized yacht harbors. You anchored with the fishing boats or by yourself. That was it.

It's a remarkable achievement to make a sailing trip around the world in a smart and seamanlike fashion by yourself. To even manage such a small yacht in storms and calms is a wonder. To have anchors and warps and spare sails, clothing, plenty of food, charts, navigational equipment, books to read, Band-Aids, sail needles, and a thousand other things requires a very orderly person and miracles of stowage. And to make the journey in a twenty-footer that you've constructed yourself is the ultimate capstone. I salute John on his wonderful voyage.

John's sailing was simple and uncluttered, but wonderfully satisfying with a purity that most of today's overladen and overpriced yachts fail to achieve. Outgoing and affable, John made friends everywhere, and his account sparkles with humor and good fellowship.

But what gives this book a kicker was John's chance meeting with a yacht named *Tzu Hang*, a 46-foot wooden ketch owned by two keen sailors named Miles and Beryl Smeeton. John and the Smeetons saw one another in various harbors, occasionally sailed in company, and became fast friends as they worked their way across the Pacific. The Smeetons decided to sail from Melbourne, Australia to the Falkland Islands via Cape Horn. They wanted a third person as crew to make the watches easier.

"Will you hold up your trip and come along with us for a few months?" asked the Smeetons. "Of course," said John. It was a fateful decision.

So halfway through his trip around the world, John stored his yacht ashore, moved aboard *Tzu Hang*, and used his skills to help prepare the big ketch for the Cape Horn adventure. At the end of 1956 the threesome set off on the 6,700-mile run to the Falkland Islands. However, about 1,000 miles west of the western entrance to the Strait of Magellan, they had an experience that was to change their lives.

While Beryl Smeeton was steering, a colossal wave waterfalled onto the yacht and capsized and pitchpoled the vessel. Not only did *Tzu Hang* lose her masts, bowsprit, and rudder, but the huge wave stripped the decks clean and even tore off the stout wooden doghouse. This left a great hole in the deck through which water poured below. Beryl was injured, over the side, and thirty yards away. The yacht was flooded. It looked like the end of the affair. Beryl managed to swim back to *Tzu Hang*. The men pulled her on board.

"I know where the buckets are," she said, and set everyone to work.

John tacked sails and bits of wood torn from below over the opening in the deck. Meanwhile the Smeetons bailed from below. In the days that followed, John used his boatbuilding skills and constructed new masts from the inside woodwork that he took down. The threesome cut smaller sails from the spare sails. They built a steering oar, gradually converted the wreck into a seagoing proposition, and somehow managed to sail to Coronel, Chile with the jury rig. It was an incredible achievement, and one that you read with tears in your eyes. They had literally come back from the dead. It's a story that all explorers and sailors and adventurers know—or should know.

"There was a wonderful feeling of comradeship between the three of us," writes John. "We all realised that without the other two we would never have survived and though we all wanted to get into Coronel, I think we also realised that we would never be this close again."

These modest words belie the greatest adventure of his life.

Hal Roth, author of seven books including *Two Against Cape Horn*, *Two on a Big Ocean*, *Always a Distant Anchorage*, and *Chasing the Long Rainbow*, holds the prestigious Blue Water Medal of the Cruising Club of America.

Preface and Acknowledgements

I N LOOKING BACK over the years to the times recounted in these pages, I realise what a profound effect little *Trekka* has had upon my life.

Like many young people caught up in the turmoil of war, my education in a normal-school system ended at twelve years of age, yet with a knowledge of the basics, encouragement from my parents, and by listening to and observing others, I acquired a good dose of common sense which has served me well in the intervening years.

Certainly the building and sailing of *Trekka* was a wonderfully stimulating time for me. At sea, I read voraciously, devouring all manner of books from the classics to what my father would have called "penny dreadfulls." The skills I learned during my five-year apprenticeship as a joiner have been a wonderful asset and have provided the means to sustain my family in various locations about the globe. I have remained very involved in the marine field having built vessels, mainly yachts, in several different countries.

In rewriting this entirely new edition of *Trekka*'s voyage almost forty years after the original version was first published in England, I have added new material and photographs, plus a few anecdotes which I hope will enhance the story. It has been an enjoyable task gathering up many of the mementos of the voyage, and I am indeed grateful for the help received from several friends. I would like to thank, in particular, Molly Cadranell who helped organize and design a draft layout from my fumbling printouts, Steve Davis who produced the line drawing of *Trekka*, Don Douglass for convincing me to reissue the book, and my editor, Réanne Hemingway-Douglass, for her help in pulling it all together. I reserve a special thanks to Dorothy for her assistance in guiding me through the complexities of a personal computer program and for allowing me space in her life, as well as to my four sons James, John, Jonothan and Stephen for their encouragement and support over the years.

It is my hope that indeed all who read this book will find the vision and initiative to bring the world of sailing into their lives. A little boat can go a long way!

Prologue

SHIPS AND THE SEA have always been familiar and well-loved friends to me. I inherited this love from my father, also John, who hailed from the English fishing port of Grimsby which is the home of several hundred deep-sea trawlers. At Grimsby my grandfather's red-sailed smacks were gathering a silvery harvest of codfish from the Dogger Bank long before the era of steam trawlers and mechanized fishing.

When my father was a boy, steam trawling was still in its infancy, but when the time came for him to decide what profession he would follow, he chose to become a marine engineer; the first ship he went to sea in was one of his father's new steam trawlers. After years of wandering about the world, from gold mining in the frozen wastes of Alaska to pearl fishing in the South Seas, he eventually met my mother and settled down in Jersey, one of the Channel Islands which lie within sight of the French coast.

Although I was born in England, it was in Jersey that I grew up, and my earliest recollections are of living in a small cottage close to a beach of golden sand with white fishing boats pulled up near by and bronzed fishermen in blue jerseys making nets and repairing lobster pots. I was only three years old when the call of the sea became too much for my father; shore life, though easy, was very unsatisfying to him and it was not long before he decided to have a small yacht built and make a long voyage in her.

The yacht was built by Uphams of Brixham, a well known West Country firm who had built many fishing vessels for my great grand-father. The yacht was constructed on the lines of a Brixham trawler and was also rigged as a gaff-ketch, but she was smaller, being 52 feet over-all and with a maximum beam of 12 feet. *Our Boy* was her name, and with one man helping as crew, my parents and I sailed to Cape Town, my mother's birthplace. The voyage out to South Africa took several months, for *Our Boy* called at many West African ports along a route that even today is seldom visited by small craft. I think this was a particularly

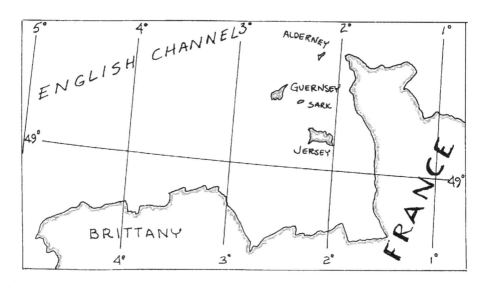

happy period in my parents' lives. A photo of my father taken at Cape Town on board the yacht shows a big robust man in his early fifties obviously content with his lot. We stayed a few months in South Africa, and my father tried snoek fishing at Walfish Bay for a few weeks, but eventually we returned to our home in Jersey. Mother and I went by steamer while father and two young men sailed the ketch from Table Bay to Penzance in 65 days, making only one stop at Dakar 34 days out.

On her return to England, *Our Boy* was reluctantly sold; she was built for deep sea sailing and was too large for us to keep around the Channel Islands. My father was not very long without a boat, though, and soon bought an 18-foot cutter named *Try Me,* which had long caught his discerning eye.

Living on a small island in close contact with boats and the sea, I naturally grew to know them both, and many of my holidays were spent sailing, sometimes in *Try Me,* and at other times with friends on an occasional cruise to French ports in their yachts. I can remember seeing square-rigged sailing ships lying in the port of St. Malo, their great yards overhanging the wharves. They were still beautiful to the eyes of a boy, though their rust-streaked hulls told sadly that their sailing days were over.

When World War II was declared in 1939, it seemed for a while that peaceful Jersey would escape the maelstrom, but soon the German Army was flooding like a tide across Holland, Belgium and France, and we realised that unless something extraordinary happened it was only a matter of time before the Channel Islands were invaded.

Many of our friends queued for hours to get aboard the small coasting vessels that were evacuating the bewildered islanders to the safety of England. In this time of crisis, holds were packed with those who had left everything behind them in an effort to escape the advancing German forces. Rather than risk the danger of being bombed or torpedoed in one of these coasters, my parents decided to reach the south coast of England, 80 miles away, in *Try Me*, so we packed what few possessions we could take and hoped the weather would allow us to make a safe crossing of the Channel. Fate decreed that it was not to be. Three times we made the attempt to leave, but the weather worsened on each occasion and we had to return to our home. On the fourth day German forces invaded the island and put an end to our hopes of escape.

The war years dragged on under the German occupation, and food became scarce, but at least we had a comfortable home to live in. Soon, though, even the comfort of that was gone, for the German Commandant of the island gave notice that certain residents of the island would be taken with their families to internment camps in Germany.

A few hours after this notice was published in the local newspaper we were en route to a prison camp at Wurzach, Werttemberg, in the south of Germany. If the time had gone slowly under German rule on the island, it went even slower behind barbed wire. For two and a half years we

Early days in Jersey

waited in the camp for Allied forces to relieve us. We were never able to discover the reason for our internment; old people in their seventies down to babes in arms were with us in the camp.

My schooling suffered as a result of our imprisonment, but my father taught me navigation which was to prove so useful years later.

With the war over we returned to Jersey and tried to pick up the threads of our former life. The island school system was in disarray and my old school which had been shut down and had only recently reopened, was reluctant to accept a student who had missed nearly three years of school. My father advised me to learn a trade, and so at the age of fifteen and a half years, soon after our return to the island, I signed apprenticeship papers with a firm of building contractors to train as a joiner. Life in the prison camp had wrecked my father's health and he died early in 1948. Jersey now held little attraction for my mother after this blow, and so we decided to return to her homeland, South Africa. We settled in the city of Pietermaritzburg, the capital of Natal, and I continued my apprenticeship there until I was qualified.

The years had slipped by quickly and I was becoming increasingly aware of a feeling of restlessness within me. I wanted to travel and see other countries, and I wanted to make my own way through life. I knew that as long as I had my box of tools and the skill in my hands I would never lack a job.

Our Boy in Cape Town, 1934

After spending two years in South Africa I decided that the time had come for me to see what lay over the horizon, so I booked a passage on a steamer to England.

Leaving home for the first time was a very sad occasion, and my poor mother was as tearful as I was when the time came for me to go. About the only thing I can remember with any humor was her serious advice that I should change my underwear and socks regularly.

My father, John Guzzwell, on *Our Boy*, Cape Town, 1933

I spent the summer of 1952 in England cycle-racing. It was a sport I had enjoyed in South Africa, but the pressure of top amateur competition during that Olympic year drained away much of the pleasure and I was not sorry when the season ended.

I visited friends in Jersey, but my two years absence had made me a stranger amongst them and I felt I did not belong there. When out sailing with one of them, my old dream of making a long voyage alone returned to me. I was confident I could do so, providing I had a suitable boat. The best idea was to build my own, and with my skills as a joiner it seemed reasonable that I could do so. I needed good lumber and materials and above all I wanted new surroundings for this venture. Like a voice from the past, I remembered the tales my father had told me of his early life in British Columbia—of the timber-clad mountains, the inlets and islands along that magnificent coastline, the logging camps, panning for gold out of the mountain streams, and fishing for salmon with the Salish Indians out of Pender Harbour. How I yearned to see it all. During the winter of 1952–1953, I decided to emigrate to Canada and call Victoria, B.C. my new home. Looking back on it all, fate was kind, and I could not have made a wiser decision.

CHAPTER *1*

Journey to a Distant Land

T OWARD THE END of February 1953 I went up to Liverpool where I embarked on the Canadian Pacific liner *Empress of Canada*, a ship of about 25,000 tons, bound across the North Atlantic to St. Johns, New Brunswick. The five day voyage was memorable in that we encountered a winter storm of such severity that the ship was hove-to for several hours. This was the first time I had seen a real gale at sea; this particular storm was logged at Force 11 on the old Beaufort scale and the sea was an incredible sight being totally white. As soon as a wave formed the wind tore the top off, turning it into blown spume so that from the height of the upper deck about fifty feet or so above the waterline, sheets of spray whipped across the surface of the sea like sand in a desert windstorm. The ship seemed to be comfortable enough just maintaining steerage way heading into the swells, but every once in a while the bow shipped a big one with a shudder and tons of solid water engulfed the foredeck. From my vantage point on one of the unprotected upper side decks it was impossible to open my eyes and look to weather, with the wind heavy with spray. I wondered at the time how a small yacht would fare in these conditions and filed the image away in my mind for future viewing.

In due course we arrived a few hours late at St. Johns, where I boarded

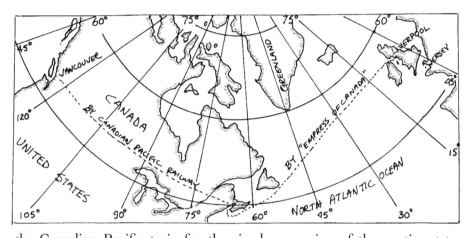

the Canadian Pacific train for the six day crossing of the continent to
Vancouver, B.C. The distance seemed enormous as hour after hour the
iron wheels beat their rhythm on the metal track, past tiny villages and
hamlets half buried under a blanket of snow. The entire land was locked
up in the frozen grip of winter and the few people about in the stations
we stopped at were wearing heavy protective clothing, resembling creatures from another distant planet. After the monotony of the prairies, the
climb up the grade leading to Kicking Horse Canyon in the Rockies came
as a welcome change and I marveled at man's ingenuity and persistence
in pushing a route through such difficult country. Over high trestle
bridges and through curved tunnels amidst the jagged snow and timber
clad peaks, the two locomotives labored with their load of Pullman car-
riages like some giant steel centipede. On the downgrade, the sky cleared
and we came through Revelstoke in bright sunshine to a different land. It
seemed as though it was already spring here in British Columbia, the timber clad mountains gave way to rolling green pastures, flowing streams
and rivers, wild flowers already in bloom. I was nearing journey's end and
my excited anticipation was tempered with the reminder that, aside from
a suitcase of clothing and a box of tools, I had less than $25.00 in my
pocket. Due to currency restrictions in Britain at the time, it was almost
impossible to convert sterling to dollars, the few I had collected had been
changed on the ship but no Canadian Bank would accept sterling. I
realised that my first priority was to get a job.

    I disembarked from the train at the Vancouver terminus; this was
obviously a big city, although it had been a tent town when my father
arrived fifty years earlier. This really was the new world.

    The Canadian Pacific Railway Company also operated a fleet of ferries
to serve the West Coast and I boarded one of these for the four hour trip

across the Gulf of Georgia through the maze of islands to Victoria, the capital city of British Columbia. I was reminded of my sick father in the German prison camp when he awoke in the bunk alongside me one morning. "I've just had a strange dream, Johnnie," he said and I could see that he was troubled. "I dreamed I got on a ferry boat to Victoria in Canada; there were very few people on board so I went on up to the bridge to have a word with the skipper. 'Not many passengers aboard today,' I said to him as he was steering past the islands, 'you won't make much money from this trip.' 'It's like this sometimes,' he replied, 'some days we're quite crowded, during the war the boat was packed every day, I think I prefer it this way.'"

As my father recounted his dream, mental pictures formed in my mind of the ferry passing many tree clad islands heading for the harbour. "We pulled into the dock," he went on, "and there were people on the wharf waiting to greet the few passengers; there was a band playing and I thought it was a nice welcome. Presently the gangway was put in place and we started to get off the ship. It seemed everyone was being met and as I stepped onto the wharf I saw my mother in the crowd waiting for me. 'Mother! what are you doing here?' I cried, not believing it could be her, she looked so well. 'Oh Jack, I've waited so long for you to come,' she said. 'Every day I come down to the docks to see if you have arrived, I knew you would be here soon.' 'But Mother, you've been dead for years,' I said, still hardly believing I was talking to her. She smiled at me, 'Yes, but now you're dead, too, Jack,' she said kindly. 'You crossed over on the ferry, we're all dead here on the island. Welcome, Son, welcome to Paradise!'"

I had the name and address of a man who was in charge of the maintenance of the ferry boats and as his office was a short walk from where we had berthed, I went immediately to see if I could get a job in the yard. Mr. McDougal was a Scot and a man of few words, he eyed me quickly and asked a few pertinent questions as to my experience and qualifications and if I had my own tools. He said I could start work the following morning. He asked me where I was staying and I told him I'd just arrived and had not yet had time to look for accommodations. "Yeel ha no trouble," he said kindly, "but dinna be late fer werk."

I decided to leave my heavy box of tools at the shipyard and go uptown to find a cheap hotel for the night. I walked past the Parliament buildings and the famous Empress Hotel along Government Street and eventually came to Yates Street where I found the Dominion Hotel which looked as though it would fit my budget. A short elderly gnome of a man was behind the desk and I asked if he had an inexpensive room to rent. "Eight dollars a night," he said pushing the register to me, "you'll have to sign in." I reached into my pocket for the few dollars I had and paid him. "Guzzwell," he said, looking at the register. "I know that name; it was a long time ago but I remember meeting a Jack Guzzwell years ago, he had a gold watch his father had given him and he lost it when we were working together in the bush. I found it for him, he was very proud of that watch." I knew that he spoke the truth because my father had told me when he gave the watch to me about how he had lost it. I had the strangest feeling that somehow this was a sign, almost like an omen, and that this old man was a messenger I was supposed to meet, who was there to let me know that somewhere my father was watching over me, that everything was going to be all right and that he was welcoming me to Victoria.

CHAPTER 2

The Building of Trekka

THE FOLLOWING DAY I went off to the shipyard and met some of my new workmates. I was probably the youngest in the group, prepared to accept all manner of teasing which can sometimes turn into hazing for a new hire, but they were a friendly lot and quickly took me into their fold, making me feel comfortable. After work that day I set about finding more permanent lodgings and was directed to a large wooden house with a rounded wing, a roofline of many angles decorated with much fretwork and filigree, all painted a bright green. It was a rather grand structure numbered 419 Belleville Street, the kind of house some retired sea captain would have had built overlooking the inner harbour so that he could observe the waterfront activity.

I pulled the bell cord at the front door and introduced myself to a portly grey-haired lady who told me her name was Mrs. Boucher. "Yes, I have a room that might suit you," she said cheerfully, "it's furnished and has cooking facilities but you will have to share the bathroom with some of the other lodgers." I followed her up the old staircase to a bright sunny room with a bow window and high ceiling. The furniture was old and well used, in one corner of the room was a double bed with headboards of brass tubing with four large brass balls at each corner. I figured it must have belonged to the captain. The cooking facilities turned out to be a small electric hotplate but there were dishes and some pots and pans, and a few pieces of silver cutlery; near the window was a well-scrubbed kitchen table with a couple of dining chairs. For my needs it was perfect. I told Mrs. Boucher that I had a job at the shipyard but would not receive my first paycheck until the following week. "That's quite all right, lad," she said kindly, "you can pay me when you get paid." I moved in that evening after collecting my suitcase from the hotel. These lodgings were to be my home for the next two years; during this time I learned to like my own cooking and followed Mum's advice by changing and washing my clothes regularly, it was good training for the years ahead.

My first paycheck seemed like a fortune to me and I realised that if I was careful it would not be long before I could afford to start building a small yacht for myself. I had read all the cruising tales of small boat voyages, of Joshua Slocum, Harry Pidgeon, Marcel Bardiaux, the men who had built their boats, then sailed them around the world. I yearned to do something similar, it was a dream that occupied my thoughts constantly and I spent a lot of time in bookstores and the public library poring over books on boatbuilding and design. I used to wander down to Thunderbird Park in the city sometimes and look at *Tillicum*, for she was proof that my dreams were possible.

Tillicum was an old Haida Indian war canoe that Captain J.C. Voss, with various companions, sailed almost but not quite round the world at the beginning of this century. Had the Panama Canal been cut then, *Tillicum* would undoubtedly have circumnavigated the globe. As it was, she made a really wonderful voyage. I tried to imagine the old canoe in her former glory and wondered if she remembered the gales she had weathered off the lonely capes of the world. She was not the type of vessel I would want to go to sea in.

The early 1950s saw some interesting trends in the boating world; new materials developed during the war years were being used by a few bold and imaginative builders and designers; waterproof adhesives that glued wood together permanently, synthetic fabrics like nylon, and a product called fiberglass that a fellow named Davidson in Vancouver was building dinghies out of. A few designers had produced a new type of yacht for offshore sailing and racing using these new materials which allowed much lighter construction than anything in the past.

One of the best known yacht designers embracing these new ideas was a British naval architect named J. Laurent Giles who had his office in Lymington. He had designed several outstanding yachts that had made long ocean passages and much of his new work was at the cutting edge of this new technology. He had a certain style to his designs that was unmistakable and I knew he was the man I wanted to design my little ocean cruiser. By now I had formed my ideas on the type of boat I wanted; she needed to be strong, yet quite light, so that in a storm she would ride to the top of the seas instead of being heavy and sluggish. She would also be quite small, for I was going to sail her alone and, of course, being smaller she would be quicker, easier and cheaper to build.

Soon after my twenty-third birthday, I wrote to Mr. Giles in England to ask him if he would be interested in designing me a small cruising boat capable of going offshore. I mentioned my woodworking skills but said that boatbuilding would be a new venture for me so the design should allow for my inexperience. The letter as I recall was quite brief. I expressed an interest in a two masted rig, light displacement, utilizing some of the wonderful woods grown in the Pacific Northwest: Douglas Fir, Western Red Cedar and Sitka Spruce. I mentioned a hazard that was a problem in these Northwest waters, the large amount of drift or floating logs that are capable of causing extensive damage to small craft. Some of these logs are lost from the great rafts or log-booms as they are being towed to the sawmills. After a period of time they become sufficiently waterlogged that they float just below the surface. Frequently, one end of the log will sink so that it floats vertically like a spar-buoy. These logs are generally named "deadheads" and many vessels have been lost by striking these submerged battering-rams. Although I did not expect him to design a boat that was immune to these dangers, it was important that the hull be constructed strongly enough to "resist" contact with floating debris.

A couple of weeks later when I collected my mail, there was a pale blue envelope from Laurent Giles and Partners Ltd. amongst the others. I tore it open with excited fingers, my eyes rapidly scanning the neatly typed two page letter. To my delight it was from Mr. Giles himself saying that they would indeed be happy to create a new design for me; however, because the office was particularly busy with other projects there would be a delay of about three months before he could start work on the drawings.

The fee for the design would be based upon a percentage of the estimated building cost in England. Would 50 Pounds Sterling be acceptable to me? I sent off a money order by return mail, and so began a correspondence that blossomed into a rather charming relationship over the years.

As the weeks went by, our letters flew back and forth across the

Atlantic and the plans gradually took shape. They showed a rather unusual looking little boat, yawl-rigged and quite streamlined in appearance. Although she was only a few inches over twenty feet in length, there was a surprising amount of room inside the hull. In the forward part of the hull were two full-sized canvas berths, immediately aft of them and separated by a structural bulkhead cut away in the middle to form a seat, was a small galley on the port side where simple meals could be prepared on a single-burner Primus kerosene stove. Opposite on the starboard side was a small chart table with storage for charts and navigational instruments. Aft of this area, which was immediately inside the companionway hatch, were two large storage lockers alongside the cockpit. The cockpit itself was really just a foot well with seating on deck which was protected somewhat by coamings attached to the small doghouse. The keel was a 3/8 inch steel plate with two big iron castings bolted to the bottom. It was fastened to the hull in such a manner that by removing a few short bolts it could be easily removed should I want to store the hull in a garage or similar building during the winter months. With this keel, the shape of the hull was such that, even if it turned completely upside down in a storm, she would automatically right herself. I was really pleased with the plans, for Jack Giles had understood exactly what I wanted.

While waiting for the arrival of the plans that summer, I decided to change jobs for the lure of more money. "Don't do it, John," my workmates advised when they heard what I intended to do, "don't you realise

Frames and longitudinals of *Trekka*

this is an old man's retirement home," one of them confided. "You'll never have it this easy outside. I'm telling you, you'll regret it and Canadian Pacific will never hire you back once you leave."

My headstrong mind was made up, however, and I joined the crew of a small building contractor framing houses. The job was a real eye-opener for me, those guys made good money but they really knew how to work. At the end of the first day I was already thinking that I had made a serious misjudgement by becoming involved with this frenzy of activity. It wasn't that I was afraid of work, it was just that these men seemed so efficient; they had the right machine tools and knew exactly what to do next, whereas for me, the whole business was a learning experience. The men were kind enough and coached me along because they could see I was willing, but I was just not able to adjust to the fast pace. My arms ached from pounding nails all day with a 20 oz. hammer and I would return to my lodgings at the end of the day exhausted. After six weeks of this, being rained on one minute and burnt by the sun the next, I came to the conclusion that these men earned every penny they made. It was a great relief when the boss called me aside one Friday and told me that because of financial difficulties I would have to be laid off work.

By this time, my savings account at the local bank had grown to a healthy amount and I was on the lookout for a suitable shed or store to start work on the boat. The drawings were still not complete but enough had arrived for me to make a start.

Beginning the planking

The search for a workshop seemed hopeless; several times I found the right kind of place but the rents were way too high for my comfort, so I kept on looking. Winter was fast approaching and it was essential to find a warm dry shop to work in. Eventually I found exactly what I was looking for, it was a store room measuring 32 feet by 16 with a wooden floor, fluorescent lighting and a large sliding access door. It was located at the rear of Johnny Bell's fish and chip shop on View Street right in the center of the city and only ten minutes' walk from my lodgings. The rent was very reasonable and soon I had moved in with lumber, tools and plans. I was getting somewhere at last.

I bought a book on boat building and learned that the first operation was lofting. This, briefly, is to draw the lines and expand the shapes shown on the plans to full size on the floor so that the various bulkheads and molds can be made and form the skeleton framework of the hull. The lofting procedure, if done accurately, guarantees that all the shapes are fair so that the hull can be built without unsightly humps and hollows. It took me several days to accomplish this task as I got confused with all the lines and made a mistake at the beginning; I ended up having to do the whole operation over again. On the second try I used colored markers to identify waterlines, buttocks, and diagonals. Boat plans are drawn in three dimensions, these being height, breadth and depth. Most of the lines are curved and in order to draw them to the correct dimensions, measurements are given at each station from a "table of offsets." These offsets are measurements from a known position, perhaps a baseline or

The planking and stem

the centerline of the hull. When these points have been marked on the floor, a long wooden batten is tacked in place to connect them together. You can now see how "fair" the batten is, sometimes it has to be adjusted slightly to do this. It is time consuming work thinking in three dimensions, but well worth the effort because it is much easier to change a pencil mark than reshape wood. With the lofting completed I was able to start work on the boat itself.

The wooden keel or backbone of the hull was made of oak, it was a curved member and had to be laminated together with waterproof glue. The instructions on the can said that the minimum temperature for the glue to set was 70 degrees F. The thermometer in the store room read 45 degrees F. I guessed that this was just one of the problems that would have to be solved before the day of launching.

Just a city block away on Blanchard Street was the Y.M.C.A. where I used to work out in the weight room occasionally. I went up to see Mr. Shoemaker who was the secretary, and asked his permission to glue up the keel of my boat in their boiler room. If he was surprised he never showed it, and after he asked me to explain again slowly he told me to go ahead. A friend helped me carry the lumber up the street to the Y.M.C.A. building and later that day, with the thermometer reading 80 degrees F, we glued and clamped the keel together. The following day the glue was set hard and we removed the clamps and carried the curved keel back to the workshop on View Street.

There was little I needed help for at this stage and I was able to set the

The planking and transom

boat up by fastening the bulkheads and molds in their positions on the keel. From the pile of lumber, she slowly took shape as first the ribbands and then the steamed frames were bent into place. Soon I commenced planking the framework after ripping the 9/16 inch strakes to shape with a handsaw; these were edge-glued together and fastened with copper nails through the bent oak frames.

Due to my European training, I had very little experience in using machine tools. Until I came to Canada I had never seen a skillsaw or router, tools that would have saved me hours of work. Even the holes I drilled for the planking fastenings were all made with an "eggbeater" hand drill. It was about this time that I got a job again working for a Mr. Maurice Green who owned a small sash and door factory which he unfortunately named the Green Lumber Company. I often wondered if business would have improved had he changed the name of the outfit. Green had the reputation of being a difficult man to please and it was fairly well known in the lumber business that he was a man of short temper who went through staff quickly. He had a long suffering foreman named Fred who was expected to keep the operation solvent while continually adjusting to new hires. No sooner would Fred train a man to use the equipment then Maurice would come along and fire him. When I came on the scene there was only one other joiner, a middle-aged laid-back character named Dave Chapman. We were soon good friends and each Friday we would quickly open our pay packets to see if there was a note inside terminating our employment. "Looks like we're spared from the axe another week," he'd chuckle, "see you Monday!"

Most of the work was familiar to me, we made wooden windows, kitchen cabinets and doors. Basically Dave and I assembled the machined parts into whatever we were making but every once in a while a special order came in that required one of us to build the item from plain lumber. This involved selecting suitable material, planing it to thickness and ripping it to size on the circular saw. Maurice Green bustled into the cabinet shop one morning and thrust a piece of paper in front of me, for a second I thought it was the "Axe" Dave talked about. "Here Johnnie," said Maurice, a little out of breath from climbing the stairs, "I want you to make a front door for a friend of mine, it's got to be nice, don't use any crappy material. Here's the size."

The door was to be quite large, three feet wide by seven feet high, mainly small panes of glass separated by thin wooden members called rails and mullions.

"It's got to be ready for tomorrow," he said "so you'd better start right away." I saw Dave looking at me from his bench with his eyebrows raised as I turned to follow the Boss downstairs.

It was a Thursday and by the end of the day I had got the door glued together. Dave and I knocked off work that afternoon and as we walked up to the street to the bus-stop he was calculating what our chances were of avoiding the "Axe" for another week. "You'd better have that door finished tomorrow," he said, ribbing me, "I think it's for his girlfriend." We both laughed at the thought. "Heck Dave, I've got it all glued together, all I have to do now is flush it off."

The following morning I began the task of leveling off all the joints with a hand plane so that the surface was smooth when suddenly who should appear but Maurice. "GODDAMMIT," he yelled, his color rising, "why are you doing that by hand? You Europeans are all the same, you waste too much time, I've got a machine that will do that in about 30 seconds flat." He shook his head irritably. "Bring it downstairs and I'll show you." He led the way grumbling about the difficulty of finding good workers as I dutifully followed with the heavy door.

We stopped before a large machine that had been hidden behind a pile of lumber. "How thick is it ?" he demanded crossly, as he stabbed a finger into a switch on the wall. "An inch and three-quarters," I said meekly as he wound a handle furiously. The machine pulsed into life, dust spurting through various apertures and filling the air. "Now watch this!" he commanded as he grabbed the door from my grasp and fed it into the machine. There was a succession of crackles and bangs and dust shot from all the openings as Maurice went to the other end of the machine to retrieve the door.

The door appeared out of the dust cloud looking considerably different from moments earlier. Only the outside frame was left, the entire center with all the little rails and mullions were gone. I held my breath waiting for the explosion. "GODDAMMIT!" he shouted, beside himself. "Just do it your own way!" When I told Dave up in the shop what had happened, I thought he was going to have a heart attack from laughing.

Eventually, we both got the "Axe" and had to look for work again. I got hired at another small cabinet shop by a tall grey-haired Norwegian named Knudsen. He was a kind man, rather nervous, and I later learned that he was a talented musician. He asked me where else I had worked and upon learning that I had been at the Green Lumber Company for six months hired me immediately. Aside from cabinet work, Knudsen also manufactured Glulam beams, the large laminated wooden beams frequently seen in supermarkets and similar wide-span buildings. This was interesting work and involved laying out all the material so that the scarfed joints were staggered, cutting the scarfs, and finally gluing all the laminations together in the press to make the complete beam. When the glue had set, the whole assembly had to be surfaced smooth, as invariably the customers had them installed bright-finished instead of painted. Some of the beams we made were over 100 feet in length and 4 feet deep.

Meanwhile, all my spare time was spent building the little boat behind the fish and chip shop. Johnny Bell told me one day that his business had picked up since I had moved in and I wondered if perhaps the flavor had improved from all the sawdust that settled on the pre-fried chips.

I feel there is something almost sacred about building a boat. It is a difficult thing to explain, but I have found that other boatbuilders have shared this feeling. It is almost like creating a living being, a boat seems to have a soul and character all her own. Some are lucky, some not. Some live short lives full of action, some seem to die of boredom, neglected in marinas. Sometimes, like humans, an old maid will acquire the love of a good man who will spend a fortune on her and take her away travelling; if he is lucky she will look after him in times of stormy weather. Is it any wonder that boats are usually thought of as being feminine?

It requires more thought to give a boat a good name than it does a child. Yachtsmen the world over have a habit of giving boats nicknames. I met a yacht named *Havfruen,* which was changed to "Half-Ruin" by Australian yachtsmen, rather unfairly I thought as she was kept in beautiful condition. A Singapore yacht named *Bintang Terang* was immediately dubbed "Orang-utang." Much thought was put into a name for my little yawl, and I finally decided to call her *Trekka* from the South African word "trek," to make a journey. I hoped she would have the same dogged spirit of the Voortrekkers who trekked up into the Transvaal and Natal in the 1860s.

When I had planked *Trekka* down to the turn of the bilge, she was ready to be turned over so that the bottom planking could be completed. After wondering how this could be accomplished, I once again made my way to the Y.M.C.A.

A friend of mine was a weightlifter there, and I told him and some of his friends about the little boat I was building just down the street. They became quite interested, and I invited them to come and have a look at her. Four unsuspecting weightlifters followed me to where the half-planked *Trekka* waited. Another little problem was solved.

When the planking was finished I had to rivet over three thousand fastenings. This was a job I could not do alone and a friend helped me for a few days at this noisy work. We were not very popular with the restaurant next door, and the staff used to hammer on the dividing wall for silence. I got the impression that they did not approve of my boat building.

My husky friends turned *Trekka* right way up again, and I fitted the laminated deck beams and then glued and screwed the 3/8 inch plywood deck down. Spring came, and work slowed as I was back at a regular job again, and could only work on the little boat at night or on weekends, but slowly and carefully I finished her. I used a new material named fiberglass to cover the deck and made myself even more unpopular with the restaurant next door, as they thought they had a gas leak and would not light the stoves in case of an explosion. The gas man soon discovered that the fumes were from my fiberglass. I heard muttered threats and decided that I'd better hurry up before they resulted in sabotage.

The planking completed

Toward the end of August 1954, just over nine months since I started, the blue-painted hull was ready to be launched. On a Saturday morning we skidded her out of the store and took her down to the inner harbour where there was a crane to lift her. The fin keel was bolted on, and then she was lowered gently into the water. She leaked badly at first as the oak garboard planks had shrunk during the hot summer months, but after a few hours they swelled sufficiently to make the hull tight.

There was still quite a lot to do aboard, and as the summer was well advanced I did not try to get *Trekka* sailing that year. I took things easy, fitted out the interior, and made the hollow masts out of silver spruce. I knew that there would be all the sailing I wanted the following year.

In January and February I saw snow on the deck and wondered where we would be when winter returned the following year, somewhere in the tropics I hoped. The wet cold days of winter passed slowly, but the sun gradually crept north day by day and suddenly it was spring. The shoots were bursting out of the tree by my window and there was much activity along the waterfront as the skippers of the salmon boats prepared for the coming season. I stepped *Trekka*'s masts and spliced up the stainless-steel rigging.

Then came the long-awaited day when I bent on the new suit of sails, let go the mooring lines, and felt life in the tiller for the first time. It was a very satisfying moment.

I realised that I had a fine little yacht, she was quite fast and stood up to her sail well in fresh conditions. I found that she would steer herself to windward quite easily and just as well as I could do.

During the next few weeks I got to know her better as I sailed about the harbour, sometimes with friends, sometimes alone. I was a very contented young man. There is something very exciting about preparing for a long voyage alone, especially when you have never done it before. It seems that the various jobs and necessary items will never be ticked off the list you have made, instead it just grows longer. My room on Belleville Street now had an enormous amount of gear in it. Every week, when I bought my groceries, I got a few extra cans of food, and now there were three hundred stacked away in the cupboards. Scattered about the rest of the room on chairs, on the table, or under the bed was all the rest of the gear I was going to need. Sails, rope, paint and charts, the sextant I had bought at a junk yard, blocks, and the patent log. The room looked and smelt like a ship chandlery. I wondered how it was all going to fit inside a twenty-footer.

A few close friends knew that I was preparing to leave on a cruise to

Hawaii. I asked them to keep it a secret as I did not want the press to send me away in a blaze of publicity. If I came back after a few days and decided that ocean cruising was for the birds, only my friends would know about it instead of the whole city.

In August I moved aboard and began getting used to living in the somewhat confined space. All the gear had miraculously been stowed away in the lockers or beneath the bunks, and *Trekka* was sitting much lower in the water. As I had no water tanks, I bought a dozen two gallon plastic chemical bottles to keep my fresh water in. I found them ideal, they stowed away easily and it was useful to be able to see at once how much water had been used.

I had *Trekka* out of the water for a few hours and painted her bottom with anti-fouling. I hoped the next coat would go on in Honolulu. She was looking very pretty; though she was very small, I felt fairly confident that she had the best of gear.

One morning as I walked into town, I saw a fine-looking ketch moored in the inner harbour. She looked more of a little ship than the usual run of yachts, and I was not surprised to hear that she had been sailed out from England in 1951. Her name was *Tzu Hang* and she was about to leave for Australia. I did not know it then, but I was to take part in a great adventure aboard her before I returned to Victoria, B.C. four years later.

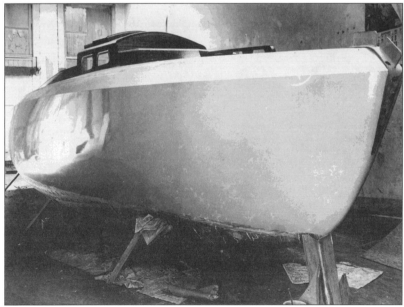

Trekka nearing completion

Trekka ready for launching

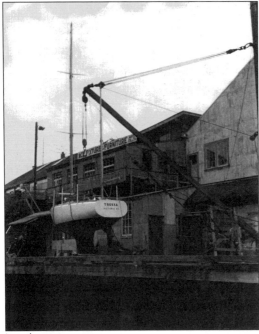

Into the water

On Saturday, 10 September 1955, I was all ready to leave. My few close friends came to see me off from the dock close to Fisherman's Wharf. As they let go the lines and *Trekka* slowly gathered way, their voices carried clearly across the water. "Good luck, *Trekka!* Don't forget to write, John." It was a strangely sad moment and I wondered when I would see them all again. I remembered the happy sailing we'd had together and how we'd gone over the charts planning the route for *Trekka's* voyage. Now here I was actually starting. As if understanding my feelings, *Trekka* quickly drew away from the little group and headed out toward the breakwater and the open sea beyond.

# CHAPTER 3

Victoria to San Francisco

I T WAS ALREADY late in the year to be going down the North American coast. July would have been the best time but I was not ready then. I had one last look at the familiar landmarks, then *Trekka* and I shot through Race Rocks Passage with the tide under us, altered course, and headed out along the Strait of Juan de Fuca toward the open ocean.

We passed Sooke, then the wind dropped and left us becalmed on the still water. A couple of salmon trollers motored by toward Victoria, their crews looking forward to Saturday night ashore. I watched them go by with a slight feeling of envy, there was an awful lot of water between *Trekka* and Hawaii—2,800 miles of it.

The sails were just hanging limp so I lowered them and went below to light the stove for my first meal of the voyage. With the daylight gone, there was quite a nip in the air. The little cabin felt very snug, and the Primus hissed away while the tempting smell of stew floated gently out of the hatchway. I switched on the radio for some music; it was a short wave portable set, made in the U.S.A., and worked off a dry battery. It proved to be a very good companion at sea. That night I hung a lantern in the rigging before climbing into the warmth of my sleeping bag and falling asleep.

I had all sail up next morning in an effort to get out of the Strait and into the open sea. The wind was very light and there were patches of fog about, so I kept close to the Canadian shore and slowly drifted out toward the Swiftsure light vessel.

I had a 4-horsepower outboard motor stowed away in the rear locker. It could only be used in calm weather, but as I only had four gallons of gasoline aboard I felt it was rather early in the voyage to use it. I spent another day drifting along with just a whisper of wind, then it freshened and I streamed the log as we passed Cape Flattery. Before *Trekka* came back to her home port again, she had registered more than 30,000 miles.

We were now out in the open sea and bouncing along in grand style.

The wind was slowly increasing, but *Trekka* was putting the miles away steadily. As if for a final farewell, a big fishboat appeared from the south and headed over toward us. She came close alongside and a voice with a Norwegian accent hailed across the water, "Vere de hell you tink you are going in dat ploody little pisspot?" I sang out, laughing, "Honolulu!" and the voice roared back, "Vell you're ploody crazee, put goot luck!" I caught a glimpse of her stern as she rolled away and read her home port, Victoria, B.C.

With the wind freshening all the while, I had to roll a reef in the mainsail, but soon there was too much wind for even the reduced sail area and I had to take in what sail was set and wait for the weather to moderate. The sea was starting to build up, and I realised that I was about to have my first gale. The barometer was tumbling down and ragged clouds were driving low across the sky from the southeast. I now had to learn how *Trekka* would lie most comfortably in a gale, so I started to experiment with the sea anchor out over the bow and the little mizzen-sail set. The idea was to make the boat lie head to the seas, but this she would not do. She lay about 75 degrees off the wind, and had a most violent motion. This was obviously not the answer for *Trekka* was complaining bitterly about this treatment. Finally she decided to do something about it and broke away from the sea anchor. We immediately lay beam-on to the seas, and though it may sound dangerous, she was far more comfortable. I went on deck and lowered the little mizzen-sail, then pulled the anchor warp aboard and saw that the shackle-pin at the end had come unscrewed.

With the helm lashed down to leeward and everything on deck secure I went below out of the weather. It was not so much the motion as the sounds I noticed below. The halyards were beating a tattoo against the mast and the wind was accompanied by moaning through the rigging. Somewhere in a locker a can was rolling backward and forward monotonously. I listened to the hiss of a big sea as it approached. There was a bang as it hit the hull and water cascaded over the deck, but *Trekka* was so light and buoyant that it was only the top of the seas that were hitting her. It is when you are riding out your first gale in a boat you have built

Sailing direct downwind toward San Francisco

yourself that you wonder about some of the doubtful workmanship that went into her. I thought about some of the bent nails I had knocked in, and remembered one of the splices in the rigging that was not as good as it could have been. But even gales end eventually, and a few hours later the wind had veered to the southwest and dropped enough for us to get moving again southwards. The gale had done me some good, though. I now had confidence in my boat, and a little more in myself, too.

During the next couple of days, *Trekka* slowly beat her way south beneath grey drizzling skies. Even my enthusiasm for sailing was damped, though I had found my sea-legs and was no longer feeling sick. I felt very cold, for my so-called "waterproof suit" was something of a disappointment. Fortunately I had one garment that kept my body warm; this was a hand knitted Cowichan Indian sweater made from hand-spun raw greasy wool and virtually waterproof in itself. I became very fond of it and invariably wore it at sea and ashore whenever I felt cold.

I had been edging offshore ever since leaving Cape Flattery for I wanted to be away from the shipping tracks and have plenty of sea-room in case another gale came along. When we were down to the latitude of the Columbia River, the wind went round to the north. This was my chance to try the twin-staysail self-steering rig I hoped to use once we reached the Trade Winds. Two identical sails were set forward of the mainmast, each boomed out, wing and wing, with the sheets led back through quarter-blocks to the tiller. It was strange to see the tiller correcting the course as the wind filled one sail more than the other. The sky cleared and I was able to get sights with the sextant and plot our position on the chart. As *Trekka* sailed herself along, I made the most of the sunny weather to dry out my wet clothes and clean up a little.

Later on I decided to take some photographs, and as my camera could be set to take pictures by itself, I clamped it to the end of the mizzen-boom and raced up forward to get in the picture myself.

The pleasant weather lasted for two and a half days, then the wind came in stronger and I had to lower the twins and set the little storm-jib. I noticed that the two twin poles had almost wrenched off the sliding ring on the mast. Soon the wind was moaning away in the rigging again and the sea was running high. I pulled the storm-jib down and lay ahull waiting for the wind to ease. After a few hours it had eased enough to hoist the twins again after I had made temporary repairs to the ring on the mast. *Trekka* fled to the south, going down the seas like a surfboard. It was wildly exciting, but when the wind began to blow hard again I realised that it was time to slow down. I got the twins down and bundled them into the rear locker, then set the storm-jib. This little sail was strongly made and only measured 24 square feet. We continued to roll along to the south at about four knots.

The wind continued to build until it was blowing a full gale. I joined all the warps I had together and streamed them over the stern to help keep us running dead before the wind, and I sheeted the storm-jib flat amidships. It was impossible for me to judge the wind strength, and it is so easy to exaggerate, but I think it was touching 70 m.p.h. at times. The sea was an awful sight. *Trekka* plunged to the bottom of a valley one moment and shot to the top of a crest the next. I estimated the seas to reach a height of thirty feet and watched the top four feet break and roll right down the face of them. This was the worst gale *Trekka* encountered during her entire voyage around the world.

I dared not leave the tiller, and as the night wore on there was a nightmarish quality about the scene. I would catch myself nodding off to sleep, then be suddenly awakened by a sea bursting over the quarter and half-filling the cockpit. My weary eyes, stung with spray, would focus on the compass and I'd realise that I was off course.

So it went on, hour after hour, and I wondered dully what had possessed me to leave the friendly earth for this madness. At daybreak the wind faltered a little and I realised thankfully that it was easing. By noon I could stay awake no longer, my eyes felt like two hot coals, and I decided that *Trekka* would have to look after herself for a while. I crawled up to the foredeck and pulled the storm-jib down and then lashed the tiller to leeward. I stood in the hatchway for a few moments watching—she seemed to be quite happy—before I turned to the warm promise of my bunk; I was asleep as soon as my head touched the pillow.

The light was fading when I awoke a few hours later. The wind had eased but the sea was still running high, so I decided to go back to sleep and wait for the morning to bring us some better weather.

With all the miserable conditions I'd had since leaving Cape Flattery, I figured that it would be a good idea to go into San Francisco for a rest. I could fix the mast ring there, and a rest would be worth the slight delay. I had no detailed chart of that section of the coast, but it would be difficult to miss the Golden Gate if I ran down the coast.

In the morning I was able to get a sun-sight which worked out quite close to my dead reckoning position. We were south of Cape Mendocino and about fifty miles offshore. I decided to make a landfall on Arena Point and altered course to close the shore.

On the thirteenth day out from Victoria, I was looking for land and sighted the Point in the early afternoon. I ran along the shore until dusk, and then set the twins and let *Trekka* steer herself for the night. With less than eighty miles to go I was looking forward to a good wash and a steak ashore.

When I awoke, I was conscious of a change. It was a couple of moments before I realised what it was. Fog. It did not appear to be too thick, but looking toward the horizon I noticed that visibility was down to about two hundred yards. According to the distance run on the log, we should have been quite close to San Francisco, but when I closed the shore, nothing was visible but sheer cliffs. Had I passed the Golden Gate or was it still south of us? It was impossible to get sights and the only thing to do was to wait for the fog to lift. I sailed offshore again for the night and the fog was as thick as ever. I heard a couple of ships go past, their foghorns blaring mournfully, and I knew that I must be near a shipping track. At daylight I got sail up and we ghosted along over a very calm sea toward the land. Then the fog lifted a little and I was able to see the entrance to what appeared to be a small bay. I guessed correctly that it was Tomales Bay, about 20 miles north of San Francisco.

There was very little wind so I decided to motor into the bay and anchor for the night. The outboard was clamped over the stern and roared into life when I pulled the starter cord. As I approached the entrance I saw a couple of black buoys, and thinking that the channel was marked with the international system, I left them to starboard. Suddenly we were hard aground, and I saw that the tide was ebbing quickly. My efforts to push us off using one of the spinnaker poles only resulted in me dropping a pole into the water which the tide quickly carried out to sea. It was too late, we were stranded.

Trekka lay right over on her side that night and I was lucky that the sea was so calm. In the morning I jumped overboard and waded out into deeper water with the anchor so that I could kedge *Trekka* off when the tide rose. I got back on board and was waiting for the tide to flood a little more when a stout-looking ketch appeared from inside the bay and came over toward me. One of her crew members jumped into their dinghy and rowed over. "We'll tow you off if you like," he offered, and as I thanked him, he pulled up my anchor and rowed back to the ketch. In a couple of minutes I was back in deeper water alongside the ketch.

I told them about mistaking the black buoys and said that the chart I had of this section of the coast was too small to show any details. I suspect that when they left me a few minutes later they were convinced that people who put to sea in such tiny boats and approach a strange coast without adequate charts would come to a watery end. I silently agreed with them and resolved never to approach a coast again unless I had a chart of the area.

I watched the ketch motor off toward San Francisco and followed in her wake with the outboard purring contentedly. A gentle breeze came in from the north and I got sail up and stowed the motor away in the rear locker. We passed the lighthouse on Point Reyes and I got the spinnaker out and set it without too much difficulty.

Fishboats were making their way toward San Francisco and as the light faded, I followed their stern navigation lights as long as I could see them, but eventually they were lost amongst the thousands of lights on shore and those that marked the approaches to the Golden Gate.

Then the lights on the Golden Gate suspension bridge came into view. Altogether it was one of the most spectacular sights I have ever seen. Though the wind was very light now, it would have been almost sacrilege to have started the motor. I was content to drift in toward the magnificent scene. At five o'clock in the morning, as the fishing fleet was heading out to sea, we ghosted in beneath the great bridge and steered for a yacht basin close by the Coast Guard Station. I fastened the motor over the stern, lowered the damp sails, and motored in through the entrance to the marina where I moored to a vacant float. Sixteen and a half days from Victoria, I climbed into my bunk and fell asleep.

The Golden Gate

CHAPTER 4

I Meet Friends

I WAS AWAKENED by two Customs and Immigration officials knocking on the hull. Climbing out of the small hatchway I noticed their badges glinting in the weak sunshine as I struggled to wake up and gather my thoughts. This was my first encounter with the entry or clearing procedure that all skippers who visit another country must complete.

"What is your name and where are you from?" one of them asked, very businesslike. I answered their questions and passed them the Customs Clearance form and *Trekka's* documentation papers. The two men in their uniforms looked somewhat intimidating standing there on the dock looking briefly at what I had given them.

"Your clearance is for Hilo, Hawaii, not San Francisco," one of them said, a note of censure in his voice. I explained that my visit was due to bad weather circumstances.

"Where do you live, and where do you work?" was the next question, one that I was unsure how to answer. Having left Victoria, perhaps for ever, I did not want to lie. My explanation that I was on a kind of holiday did not sound very convincing even to my ears.

"What nationality are you?" the other suddenly asked, noticing my accent. "British," I replied, handing him my passport. "This is a Jersey passport, " he said, examining it curiously. "How long do you think your

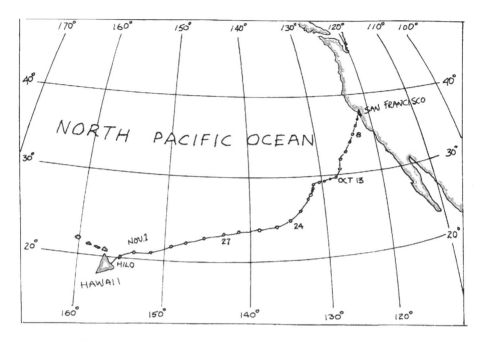

repairs will take before you can leave?" he demanded. My reply that a few days would be sufficient seemed to satisfy both of them and the one with my passport opened his briefcase, handed me some forms to complete, and told me to return them later in the day at his office where I could collect my passport. It was not much of a welcome to the United States, but as if to make up for it, a few minutes later I had a very interesting visitor aboard. He was Myron Spaulding, the well-known San Francisco yachtsman. "Come along to the Club," he invited, "you can get a shower there and meet some of the boys."

It was in this manner that I first came across the warm friendship and open-hearted hospitality that is extended to blue-water yachtsmen and which made my voyage so enjoyable. Beautiful scenery and strange places are not enough in themselves to make a visit memorable, it's the wonderful people one meets in different countries that make ocean cruising so worthwhile

As we walked along toward the St. Francis Yacht Club, he pointed across the basin and said, " There's another boat that arrived a few days ago from Victoria, B.C. She's got a Chinese name. You could moor *Trekka* just ahead of her." I looked to where he was pointing and saw the masts with the baggy wrinkle in the rigging and the sweet white hull of *Tzu Hang*.

Later that morning I moved *Trekka* over to the other side of the basin and a young couple from aboard *Tzu Hang* helped me with the mooring lines. They were Raith and Vivian Sykes from Duncan, B.C. "Come and have some tea," invited Vivian. "The Smeetons have gone into town but they will be back shortly."

Soon we were chatting below in *Tzu Hang's* cosy saloon while the Primus roared away in the galley. I learned that they were going as far as Honolulu with the owners, Miles and Beryl Smeeton, and their young daughter, Clio. The voyage down from Victoria had been a rough one and had taken them fourteen days. A backstay splice had pulled at sea and the skipper had had to go aloft to fix it.

Goodbye to San Francisco   Lou Yates

About half an hour later, when I was about to leave, Vivian said, "Wait a minute, here they come now, I can hear B.'s voice." We jumped down on to the dock and I was introduced to Miles Smeeton. He was middle-aged, very tall and slim, and carried himself like a military man. I learned later that he had retired with the rank of Brigadier from the Indian Army. Two very friendly eyes twinkled from his craggy features as he gripped my hand. "This is my wife, B.," he said, and I thought I caught a note of pride in his voice.

I turned and looked into two of the merriest blue eyes I have ever seen. They were eyes that had looked at great distances. Her long fair hair was tied in a bun behind her head, and she was dressed in a brown suit with a divided skirt. Her right foot was in plaster and she tapped it with the walking-stick she was using. "Don't take any notice of this," she said in a clear English voice, "I trod on the bucket in the cockpit on the way down here and broke my big toe. Do come aboard and have some tea, we're dying to hear all about you and your little boat. We had a simply ghastly trip down. Oh, this is Clio."

Clio was fourteen years old and tall like her father. She seemed to be all arms and legs. "May I go and have a look at *Trekka*?" she asked, and a few moments later she called out of *Trekka*'s hatchway, "Mummy, you should see his Primus stove—its polished!" I knew I was going to like these people.

When we compared notes, I found that on the way from Victoria, *Tzu Hang* had experienced the same sort of weather as I had in *Trekka*. I was pleased to know that the Smeetons had considered the passage tough going, for although they had only taken up sailing when they bought *Tzu Hang* in England in 1951, they had gained a great deal of experience when just the three of them had sailed her all the way from England through the Panama Canal to their home on Saltspring Island near Victoria, B.C.

"If you are going to Hawaii, we should rendezvous there," said Miles. "It's much more fun cruising together than by yourself." So we arranged to meet at Hilo on the island of Hawaii. The first boat to arrive would wait for the other.

There were a couple of jobs I had to do before I could leave; I needed to make a new spinnaker-pole to replace the one I'd lost at Tomales Bay, and the ring on the mast needed to be fastened on more securely.

I bought the fittings for the spinnaker-pole in the city and when I got back to *Trekka*, Myron Spaulding was there. "If I were you, I'd get out of here and go over to Sausalito on the other side of the bay," he said. "It's much warmer there and quieter too, you'll be able to work in peace." It was good advice, and later that day I motored across the bay to the lovely little yacht harbour of Sausalito.

I had only just finished mooring *Trekka* when a tall man approached me and held out his hand. "My name is Bob Frick, I live over here and have a workshop and tools available, if you can use them you're welcome to go right ahead." Through Bob I met more friends, and soon the unpleasant memories of the voyage down the coast were forgotten. Two of these friends had just returned from Hawaii, having taken part in the Trans-Pacific Yacht Race from Los Angeles to Honolulu, and they proceeded to mark on my charts of the islands all the places I should go and see.

Tzu Hang arrived a couple of days later and moored just a short distance away. I made the new spinnaker-pole and Bob got the mast ring brazed for me. It was much stronger now and I doubted it would give me any more trouble.

On Wednesday, 5 October, just eight days after I had arrived, I was all ready to go. The water bottles were all topped up and I had fresh fruit and vegetables aboard.

I waved goodbye to my friends and Raith Sykes shouted, "We'll see you in Hilo, John." A launch gave three toots on her horn in salute, then

Next stop Hawaii

Trekka was away and heading for the open sea in company with an aircraft carrier which was also bound for the Hawaiian Islands. "She'll be there in about five days' time," I thought. "I guess it will take me at least a month."

I soon found that because of my stay in port I had lost my sea-legs. Whenever I stayed ashore longer than a week I usually felt seasick for the first three days at sea. Later in the voyage I tried taking seasick pills to avoid this unpleasantness but the results were mixed. Generally, I had to accept the discomforture and purge my system of the land before settling in to the sea routine. By the third day my appetite returned and thoughts of food occupied my mind continually. Aside from nibbling on dry crackers and perhaps sipping some beef broth, the first real meal I prepared when returning to sea was a stew cooked in a pressure cooker.

The great advantage of a pressure cooker in a small boat is that the lid of the pot clamps on securely without the danger of spilling the contents over yourself in the topsy-turvy conditions. Cooking under pressure substantially reduces the cooking time which also saves fuel. For me, with a one-burner stove, it was a great convenience to be able to prepare a meal in just one pot. "*Trekka* Stew" was a meal I never tired of and though the recipe varied somewhat depending on the availability of certain ingredients, it generally comprised of three main vegetables: potatoes, carrots and onions which all keep well at sea without refrigeration. After cooking these under pressure for about half an hour I would add a can of meat and a can of baked beans. A spoon of Marmite and a little flour would thicken the gravy and some salt and pepper to flavor and Presto! another meal was ready. If I still had bread it would be spread with New Zealand canned butter or peanut butter. As an alternative, I usually had a large can of "pilot bread," the semi-hard biscuits that will keep indefinitely.

With the fine westerly breeze to send us along and lovely sunny skies, it was easy to forget the gales and cold that had been our lot farther north. By noon the first day out of San Francisco, *Trekka* had run 95 miles to the southwest and already the weather seemed warmer. I kept studying the weather chart and figuring how far we had to go before I could expect to reach the Trade Wind.

Situated almost directly between San Francisco and Hawaii is the North Pacific "High." It is an area of high pressure which has a great influence on the weather in this part of the ocean. Though it is marked on the weather maps in one position, that is only its average location and it can move very quickly or split into two separate systems. Winds near the center of the "High" are usually very light and variable so it is best to try and avoid going anywhere near the center if your means of power depends on the wind. The fastest course to Hilo for *Trekka* was not the shortest one but the one that would give the best winds. Looking at the weather chart I saw that I would have to take a curving course to the south before I could steer directly for the islands.

The next few days saw us edging farther south with the weather holding fine. "This is more like it," I thought. "You can keep that other weather farther north."

At noon on 11 October we were nearly 400 miles out. There had been a little rain in the morning, and the wind went round to the east of north. I lost no time in getting the twin-staysails set and *Trekka* rolled along steering herself.

I could make *Trekka* sail herself on most courses, but except for being close-hauled or running free with the twins, it was with a loss of speed that she did so. I usually steered after I had finished breakfast and continued all through the day until sunset when I made her sail herself, perhaps under reduced sail, while I got my main meal of the day ready. Unless there was a change in the weather during the hours of darkness, I did not go on watch again until after breakfast next morning. I would usually wake up a couple of times during the night and have a look out of the hatch to see if all was well; I got quite used to these breaks in my sleep and could return to my bunk a few minutes later and resume sleeping.

It is quite amazing how one can be in "tune" with a boat. I could be in my bunk and know almost instinctively when *Trekka* was not happy. Perhaps she had too much sail up or the main-sheet wanted easing a bit more. I think this feeling comes more easily with a smaller boat than it does with a larger one.

The wind was slowly backing to the northwest so I had to change sail and get the mainsail up again. We were really putting the miles away now, and by noon had run 103 miles during the past 24 hours. This was the first time *Trekka* had run a hundred miles in a day.

Navigation those days was pretty simple. I would go below and switch the radio on, tuned to the American station WWV on 15 megacycles which broadcasts time signals every five minutes of the 24 hours. With my wrist-watch corrected, I'd take the sextant on deck and get a sight. There was no waiting for a glimpse of the sun these days.

On 15 October we were seven hundred miles from San Francisco and well within the zone of the Northeast Trades as shown on the weather chart, but the wind had been northwesterly for the past three days and I was beginning to wonder what had become of the Trade Wind.

That afternoon there was not a breath of air to fill the slatting sails so I pulled them down to stop them from chafing on the rigging. We seemed to have arrived in a different world; the sea flattened out until it looked like glass and *Trekka* rolled slowly to the remains of the swell. I could see the log spinner hanging fifty feet below and I hauled it aboard so that it would not get tangled up with the rudder. The sky was beautiful to look at, great columns of cloud towered above and reached up into the stratosphere, and yet overhead it was clear and the sun shone down, chasing the shadows of the rigging across *Trekka's* deck.

When I left Canada a friend had given me a box of paperbacks and said, "Here's some reading material for you. When you've got nothing to do, or you are becalmed, they will pass the time away." I decided to have a look through that box, the last three had all been Western stories. I went below, got the box out, and found that the other forty-two books were also Westerns. I returned to the cockpit and was soon sharing the troubles of some rancher who'd had all his cattle rustled, lost his girlfriend to the villain, and was being attacked by a party of Indians. I concluded that life at sea was less hectic.

With the sea so calm and no wind about, I thought it would be an idea to have a swim and scrub off some of the scum just above *Trekka's* waterline. The water was quite warm and I soon cleaned off the topsides with some powder cleanser. I swam a few yards from *Trekka* to see what she looked like and was surprised to see how she was moving and rolling about; on board all seemed quite still. The water was very clear. I looked down into the depths below, a blue world that fell away to infinity. Twenty feet below me a jellyfish slowly moved along and I wondered what else was down there. I was suddenly conscious of a horrible feeling that eyes were watching me and instantly became aware how vulnerable I was out there. With a feeling akin to panic I hurriedly swam back to *Trekka* and climbed aboard thankfully. No more swimming for me I decided.

The calm continued. Sometimes a faint breeze would come along and I would quickly get up sail and steer south. We appeared to be right in the middle of the North Pacific High and the farther south we went, the better the chance of picking up the Trade Wind. By noon on the 20th we had covered only 120 miles during the past five days, but that afternoon a gentle breeze came along out of the northeast and I set the genoa and a staysail wing and wing. *Trekka* slipped along toward the southwest, the only sound being the liquid tinkling note of the bow wave.

That night the wind slowly increased and I set the other twin sail and coupled up the self-steering. The genoa was stowed away in its bag, and I climbed into my bunk happy with the knowledge that we had reached the Trades at last.

By daylight next morning the wind had freshened to moderate and *Trekka* was rolling along right on course for Hawaii. It was really grand sailing, small puffy white clouds were all marching in order across a wonderfully blue sky, while down on the sea about us the waves flashed in the sunlight. Every once in a while *Trekka* caught a wave and surfed down the face of it, sometimes she slewed a little off course and I'd watch the tiller automatically correct her and bring her back again. So it went on hour after hour, trekking across the ocean toward the distant islands.

At noon on 23 October we had reached the halfway point between San Francisco and Hilo. I wondered where *Tzu Hang* was. She was not due to leave Sausalito until a week after *Trekka*, but she'd be eating up the miles by now.

It was time to alter my watch back an hour. I would have to do this once more before we reached Hawaii, for there is a two-hour difference between the longitude of Hawaii and San Francisco.

Every evening I tuned the radio into a Los Angeles station and listened to the soap-box serial I was following. It was on the air for fifteen minutes and anything I was doing was put aside so that I could give it my whole attention. The radio was certainly a very good companion and at nighttime I listened in to programs from Australia, New Zealand and the B.B.C. in London. I was surprised one evening to pick up Radio Lourenco Marques in Portuguese East Africa. It was quite a popular commercial station and I had listened to it many times when living in South Africa.

The days seemed to go by quickly, and the little dots which marked our daily positions gradually crept across the chart toward where it was folded. Once we reached that point, I knew that there were only 300 miles to go.

Trekka was still steering herself and doing very well, too. In a week she had covered 741 miles, with a best day's run of 134. She was getting a little help now from the ocean current which was giving us about 10 to 15 miles every day.

On 2 November, my twenty-eighth day out, we were only 120 miles from Hilo. I decided that it was about time I had a shave, and I had just completed that painful operation when the wind shifted from the northeast to the southeast and became quite light. I went on deck and pulled the twins down. They had been up for thirteen days with no attention except that I had altered the sheets on the tiller a couple of times. I set the mainsail and the genoa and steered for a few hours, then put the twins up again at nightfall.

I woke up next morning with the sunbeams dancing across the cabin. I stretched rather lazily and switched the radio on with my big toe. "Let's see," I thought, "one hundred and twenty to go at noon yesterday. From the sound of her she's doing about three knots now. Yes, if it's clear, I should be able to just see the top of the mountain." I promised myself that if the island was in sight, I'd have a can of peaches for breakfast. Sure enough it was peaches for breakfast, because when I looked out of the hatchway there, right ahead, but still low down, was the 13,825-foot peak of Mauna Kea. I viewed it with mixed emotions; I was pleased to see it, yet the passage down from San Francisco had been so enjoyable that I felt a little sorry that it was almost over.

All that day I watched the mountain grow out of the sea; it never seemed to get any closer but it kept growing bigger and bigger. By sunset we were still about twenty miles off the coast, and rather than enter Hilo at nighttime, I took all sail down and stopped for the night. I was awakened during the night by quite loud squeaking noises, and when I went on deck to see what it could be, was nearly startled out of my wits when a whale surfaced right alongside and spouted with a mighty exhalation. I quickly dived below and shut the hatch tight. "If a whale is going to get amorous with *Trekka*," I thought, "Lord knows what is likely to happen." To my relief he behaved himself and I tried to go back to sleep.

I awoke at daybreak and soon had sail up. The land was only about 12 miles distant, but Hilo was down the coast another five miles, so I decided to close the shore and sail along the coast. It was fun identifying the various points and villages with the aid of the Pilot Book and the binoculars. There seemed to be numerous sugar mills and plantations along the shore, and when we got in closer there was quite a lot of waste from the cane floating on the water. Soon the little town of Hilo itself came into view and we sailed around the Blonde Reef buoy and tacked up the harbour past a couple of freighters that were loading sugar. I sailed through the rather narrow entrance to the little basin known as Radio Bay where the U.S. Coast Guard was located, then dropped the anchor over the stern and ran up to the wharf with just the staysail set. A Hawaiian took the warp I handed up to him and slipped it over a bollard. "Where have you come from?" he enquired. I let go the staysail halyard and tried to appear casual. "San Francisco," I answered. The expression on his face was so comical that I started to grin. Soon both of us were laughing at each other

Miles and Beryl Smeeton aboard *Tzu Hang* in Hawaii

and he disappeared up the wharf slapping his thighs and chuckling away. "San Francisco," I heard him say again weakly, "San Francisco!"

Soon there was quite a little group on the wharf all firing questions at me, and it seemed only a few minutes later that the doctor and Customs and Immigration officials arrived.

The doctor reckoned I looked fit enough after a month at sea, and the other officials said that I could fill in the necessary forms when I arrived in Honolulu. I asked them if *Tzu Hang* had arrived, but apparently she was still at sea for they had not heard of her.

The officer in charge of the Coast Guard Station came along shortly afterwards and offered me the use of their shower ashore, and then he invited me to have lunch with the crew aboard the cutter. I had almost forgotten what a hot shower was like, but a few minutes later when I had washed all the salt and a good bit of my "suntan" off, I presented myself aboard the Coast Guard cutter where the men were soon filling me up with cold ham and salad followed by ice-cream. I decided that there were compensations to living ashore after all.

CHAPTER 5

Hawaiian Interlude

THE DAYS PASSED pleasantly and I was able to see something of the island. A friend arrived early one morning in his car to take me to see the National Park, an area toward the center of the island noted for its volcanic activity. I was shown the steaming Kilauea crater and the vast lava flows of previous years. We crawled through a lava tube in total darkness for some three hundred feet, then drove to Kealakekua Bay where the great navigator, Captain James Cook, was killed. It was a lovely bay and I thought it would be a good place to visit in *Trekka*.

My hair had not been cut since I left Canada and it was getting quite long, so I went into Hilo to find a barber. I was a little surprised to find that all the hairdressers were women. The one that went to work on my thatch told me about the tidal wave disaster in 1950, when many people lost their lives because there was no way to warn them of the approaching danger. Since then a siren warning system similar to that used for air raids during the war has been set up, and this should help to prevent a recurrence of the tragic loss of lives.

A couple of days later I was shopping in Hilo with a friend when I looked out to sea and saw the sails of a ketch approaching. As she got closer I saw that she was *Tzu Hang*. We quickly returned to *Trekka* and put the outboard over the stern, then motored down the harbour to welcome her in.

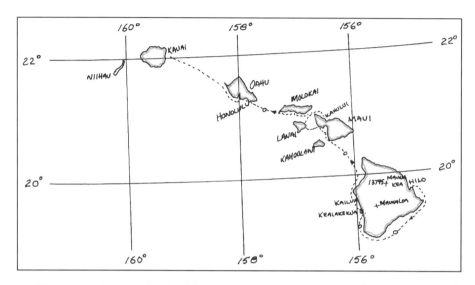

We learned that she had been twenty-five days on the crossing and had experienced light weather most of the way. The most exciting event had been when Pwe, the Siamese cat, had fallen overboard halfway between San Francisco and Hawaii and Mrs. Smeeton had immediately dived in to rescue her. Both of them had been retrieved safely without too much difficulty.

With *Tzu Hang* moored alongside *Trekka*, I got to know her crew better. Mrs. Smeeton was always called B. by her friends, and she soon had me fixing some shelves into her galley and repairing the seat in their fiberglass dinghy. One evening we held a discussion in *Tzu Hang*'s saloon as to what we should do.

"Look, John, I don't want to appear inquisitive, but where are you heading for in *Trekka*?" inquired Miles. This was something I had been asking myself the past few days. The voyage from San Francisco had been so enjoyable that I felt it would be quite easy for me to continue on, there were no ties for me in Canada—or anywhere else for that matter. Up to now my thoughts and energy had been concentrated in getting to Hawaii, now that we had arrived I was unsure where to go next.

"I was thinking that I might try to get down as far as New Zealand," I replied a little hesitantly. "I think *Trekka* can make it all right."

"Oh, she can make it all right," said Miles, with a conviction that was heartening to me. "We're on our way to Australia, we've got some friends down there and thought we'd look them up and see the Olympic Games which are being held in Melbourne next year. But there's no sense in going down that way right now, not with the hurricane season just starting. We don't want to leave the islands here until about the beginning of March. I suggest we cruise together and see as much as we can now. Then we can go on to Honolulu where we can do any maintenance and get stores for the voyage south." This sounded fine to me and soon we were bent over the chart discussing where we should go first.

"I was over at Kealakekua Bay with a friend the other day," I said, "It's a lovely bay, but it's quite a long way from here."

"We must go there," said B. firmly, "I have been reading the journal of Captain Cook's third voyage, and besides, I'm told that the other side of the island is much nicer."

Thus it was decided that we would sail around the south of the island and up the western side to Kealakekua Bay, where we would meet.

Late one November afternoon the two boats left Hilo Harbour together on the 120-mile passage to Kealakekua Bay. Outside the entrance it was blowing the usual brisk Trade Wind, and there was a very lumpy sea running. We sailed together for a few minutes, taking photographs of each other in the fading light, and then I put *Trekka* on to the other tack and *Tzu Hang* disappeared into the gathering darkness.

The 30-mile beat to Cape Kumukahi was most uncomfortable after two weeks spent in port. *Trekka* was steering herself and crashing along with the spray flying. I climbed into the windward bunk, which helped her to sail more upright, but there was no hope of getting any sleep, the motion was much too violent.

It was still dark when *Trekka* rounded the light and bore away to the southwest with the wind right astern. I waited until daylight, then set the twin-staysails and let her roll along, steering herself and surfing continuously. The enormous bulk of Mauna Loa, over 13,000 feet high, towered into the sky and I could see the courses of the lava-flows which ran down the side of the mountain and into the sea.

All that day we flew along the coast; it was sailing at its best. *Trekka* would seem to steady herself rather as an athlete does just before making a supreme effort, then the bow would dip and we'd quickly gather speed. The hull would level off, then there would be a rumble from up forward, and the white water from the bow wave would shoot up to the lifelines above the chain-plates. The whole boat would tremble as we rode the crest for a few seconds, then as she slipped off it the stern would sit down waiting for the next wave to come along. I looked at the two blue twin-staysails etched against the sky and the white wake stretching aft, and remembered the winter days at the back of the fish and chip shop when all this was only a dream.

Off Ka Lae, the southernmost point of the island, I got the twins down with a bit of a struggle as it was blowing quite hard. The working stay-sail was set and we ran up the west coast, soon coming into the lee of the land where I was able to get the mainsail up. As we went farther up the coast the breeze fell away until we were becalmed. With Mauna Loa effectively blotting out the Trade Wind, I realised that I'd have to make very good use of the land and sea breezes if I wanted to get up the coast.

It was very slow going, but gradually I worked *Trekka* up the Kona Coast. That night I dropped all sail so as to get some sleep, and then pushed on again in the morning. By late afternoon we were only four miles from Kealakekua Bay, and when darkness came I could see the light on Cook Point at the northern entrance to the bay, but I waited until the following morning before entering and anchoring close to *Tzu Hang*. She had arrived a full day before *Trekka*.

We spent a glorious week together there, doing very little apart from swimming, having picnic lunches ashore, and hiking about the bay trying to locate the sites of the villages that Captain Cook mentioned in his journal. On the southern side of the bay the ruins of the stone marae are still impressive, but on the northern side, where there is a monument to Cook, and where there was quite a large settlement at the time of his visit, all has reverted back to the bush and there is not a sign to indicate that once a whole village lived there. We found a bronze tablet set into the rock in knee-deep water which said that the great navigator had been struck down and killed near that spot on 14 February 1779.

I took B. and Clio for a sail in *Trekka* to the little harbour of Keauhou about three miles up the coast. This used to be the only safe harbour along this section of the coast during southwesterly to westerly gales until the Honokohau-excavated harbour was constructed during the 1970s. At the time of *Trekka's* visit, Keauhou was a small harbour suitable only for small craft with a maximum draft of six feet. In later years this section of the coast became the scene of much real estate development with condominiums, large luxury hotels and attendant golf courses. The changes have benefited many people who are now able to enjoy a unique part of the coastline, yet one can also mourn the passing of a naturally-beautiful wild shoreline that was accessible to only a few. This whole western coast is in the lee of either Mauna Loa or Mauna Kea, so the normal Trade Wind is non-existent, being replaced by local winds which are generated by the land mass heating up during the hot tropical day and cooling at night. You have to be within about three miles of the shoreline to experience these land and sea breezes. The three of us enjoyed a brief afternoon visit to Keauhou after mooring *Trekka* just inside the small confines of the harbour. We were hot and thirsty but after several limeades and a refreshing swim off the black lava rocks, caught the last of the afternoon breeze and drifted back to *Tzu Hang* just after sunset.

A couple of days later I sailed up the coast to the little township of Kailua which is the main settlement on the western side of Hawaii. The famous Kona Inn is now located here in company with several other large hotel complexes, for this has become a very popular tourist center. At the time of *Trekka's* visit, Kailua was a rather sleepy relaxed little town somewhat off the beaten track, appreciated by those visitors who sought the slower pace or were perhaps attracted to the sport fishing. The deep ocean water off the Kona Coast is a fisherman's dream, home to such species as mahimahi, also known as dorado, tuna and the giant marlin billfish.

Tzu Hang motored in to the anchorage one afternoon and was joined by a small ketch named *Nani* from Honolulu with owner Jack Randall, his wife Helen, and two young men who were crew. Jack was a marine biologist and was on his way to Tahiti where he would conduct research on several fish species common to those waters.

The lads on *Nani* introduced us to the fascinating sport of skin-diving and snorkeling, and for the first time I knew the thrill of descending into a new world, a world of blue where the living coral grew into the most fantastic shapes and beautiful colors. All about me, quite unafraid, swam dozens of multi-colored fish. Some, quite curious, examined the monster that had invaded their kingdom and would only move when I reached out to touch them. Others scurried about the pillars and holes in the coral, very much like people bustling about a city shopping from store to store. With my lungs bursting for air I shot to the surface, but again and again I dived down wishing that I had a breathing apparatus so that I could examine this new world more closely. I made a mental promise to equip myself with swim-fins and face-mask at the earliest opportunity, as this was an activity that I knew would occupy much of my time in the future.

A month had gone by since *Trekka* had arrived in Hawaii, and though there was still much more to be seen, the time had come to start moving up the island chain toward Honolulu. I arranged to meet *Tzu Hang* in the little port of Lahaina on the island of Maui a few days later, and then sailed out of Kailua one afternoon bound for that destination.

Separating Hawaii and Maui, the two largest islands in the Hawaiian group, is the Alenuihaha Channel, thirty miles wide. This channel has the reputation for boisterous conditions, for with the towering mountain of Mauna Kea nearly 14,000 feet high on Hawaii, and the 10,000-foot crater of Haleakala on Maui, the Trade Wind frequently funnels through the slot at nearly gale strength.

I had purposely left Kailua in the afternoon so that I would be ready to cross the channel early next morning. That night *Trekka* sailed quietly up the coast and by dawn had almost reached the channel. I could see the wind on the water a couple of hundred yards ahead, so I went forward and roller-reefed about six feet of the mainsail.

As *Trekka* came out of the lee of the land, it was as though someone had opened a giant door; there was a sudden gust of wind that knocked us down, and I heard pots and pans clanking away merrily from the vicinity of the galley. Then *Trekka* picked herself up and started to go. It was wonderful sailing as we bounced along over the crests with spray flying. I had just a swimsuit on, which was just as well, for I was soaked in a matter of minutes.

After five exhilarating but strenuous hours, we came into the lee of Maui and rapidly lost the wind. The occasional puff came along, sometimes from astern but more often from ahead, and we gradually worked along the shore off Ahihi Bay where I anchored for the night. Except for four tall radio towers for station WWVH which broadcasts time signals for navigators, the coast seemed quite uninhabited. A few years later this section of the coast became a choice tourist area with multi-story hotels, condominiums, shopping centers, golf courses, and major highways, all the result of commercial development.

Next morning I left for Lahaina, but because of experiencing light flukey winds due to being in the lee of Haleakala for most of the day, did not arrive off Lahaina until midnight. I anchored in the roads and entered the newly-made harbour after breakfast the following morning.

I immediately liked Lahaina. It has quite an interesting history and was at one time the capital of the Hawaiian Islands. In the days of sail, the whalers used it as their headquarters, and there were some lively times between them and the missionaries. The missionaries became very powerful in the early days and soon had control of large areas of land. That there is still some bitterness felt by the islanders is apparent in what a Hawaiian told me. "When missionary first come to Hawaii, he see Hawaiian all time happy, fishing, eating and laying on the sand. He say, 'This is no good, you cannot enjoy yourself all time, you must work. We will teach you how to work.' Now you come to Hawaii in your little boat, what you see? Hawaiians all working, and missionary laying on the sand."

Tzu Hang joined *Trekka* in Lahaina and we lay alongside each other.

The Smeetons were very keen mountaineers and wanted to walk across the crater of Haleakala, a distance of about twenty-five miles. They invited me to accompany them, but about three days before we were due to go, my left leg was bitten by a small insect and started to swell in a remarkable manner, until it was twice the size of my right one. I went along to the hospital where they pumped some penicillin into me, but it had little effect. B. reckoned that she could do better than that, and after rummaging about in her medical locker, produced a jar of what she called "anti-phlo" which she proceeded to boil in a saucepan for an hour or so. I realised that there was a certain ceremony to this, so willingly obeyed her when she told me to put my leg up so that she could examine the small puncture of the insect bite. She muttered something about it having to go on hot, then scooped out a large glob from the jar, smeared it on a piece of gauze, then slapped it on my leg. Wow!! I gave vent to my feelings and was halfway out of the companion-way hatch when she caught me. "Call yourself a single-hander," she admonished scornfully, "making a fuss like that over a little bit of anti-phlo!" Dear B., her methods of first aid were surely kill-or-cure and, if in doubt, just leave it. "The tendency in nature is toward a cure," she assured me on several occasions. My leg showed signs of responding to this painful treatment but it seemed unwise to go off hiking on it until it had fully recovered, so instead of going off to the crater with them I offered to scrape down *Tzu Hang*'s mainmast and varnish it while they were away.

The following morning I began working on the mast and had not progressed very far before discovering that it had some serious problems. It was a hollow spruce spar that had been laminated together with whatever glue had been available in 1939 at the builders yard in Hong Kong. Several feet of these glued seams had opened up, allowing rain-water to enter the interior. With this ready supply of moisture, fungal dry rot had attacked a large area below the upper spreaders. I ceased my scraping for it was obvious to me that the mast would need to be totally rebuilt or replaced.

When Miles got back from the hike across the crater, I told him the bad news and sent him up the mast in a bosun's chair.

"I can't understand how we didn't lose it off the Oregon coast when the backstay went," he said a few minutes later. "We can't go to sea with it like that now, just the mere thought of it is enough to scare me."

"I know what you mean," I said. "It looks as though moisture has been getting behind the spreader fitting and lodging there."

When I returned to *Trekka* from shopping the following day, B. called to me to come aboard *Tzu Hang*. "We have found a friend who has solved our problem. Come aboard and meet him, his name is Stew Milligan."

I was soon shaking hands with Stew and listening to his pleasant deep voice. "I'm working in the public relations department of a big sugar company on the other side of the island, John, and I know we've got everything over there in the way of equipment and materials."

"Well, that's wonderful," I said, "and have you got someone to make the mast, too?"

"Oh, yes," said B. with an amused smile, "You!"

"Me?" I said quite startled.

"Yes, you!" she said, and then quickly carried on before I could protest, "You made *Trekka*'s masts, didn't you? And you said last night that masts are not very difficult to make, so you can make our new mainmast." I suddenly thought of all kinds of reasons why I couldn't make a 58-foot hollow mast, but when I looked at B. I knew that as far as she was concerned the mast was as good as made.

Stew seemed to sense my hesitation, "It won't be too bad, John, there is a young fella called Bobo in the factory, he'll be able to help you."

I looked at Miles a little helplessly and he said,"We don't want to bulldoze you into it, John. But you can earn yourself some pocket money and help us out of a difficult spot at the same time."

Fiberglassing *Tzu Hang*'s new mainmast

"OK," I said, trying to get used to the idea, "but how are we going to work it?"

Miles began to explain. "I thought we could go to Lanai Island first and have a look at it while we are here, then afterwards we can sail around to Kahului, which is the main port on the other side of Maui where the company's workshops are. We can go alongside the wharf and one of their crane trucks can lift the old mast out so that you can get all the sizes for the new one." It sounded all right to me, and the trip over to Lanai would give me more time to think about the project. "When we get over to Kahului, you'd better eat with us," said B. "It will save you cooking and you'll be able to work longer hours on the mast." I realised that B. was way ahead of me.

The two boats left Lahaina for nearby Lanai, where we anchored in Manele Bay at the eastern end of the island. Lanai is noted for its pineapple plantations, and is known in the Hawaiian group as the Pineapple Island.

We visited the Hawaiian Pineapple Co. which had 15,000 acres under cultivation in what remains of a huge crater. It was most interesting to see the techniques used to get the most out of the soil and to reduce labor as much as possible. The pineapples were spray-irrigated and big combine machines were used to harvest the fruit, the pickers walking along behind a horizontal boom equipped with a conveyor belt that carried the fruit into big pens in which they were shipped to Honolulu for canning.

From Lanai, *Trekka* sailed to Kahului through the Pailolo Channel. I left in the late afternoon as the Trade Wind usually eases off at night-time and beating to windward in the channels is a rough business. *Trekka* arrived off Kahului in the early hours of the morning, and due to being tired I read the chart incorrectly and almost ended my voyage right there. The leading lights into the harbour were marked as being red and fixed. Being tired and possibly careless, I read the lights to be flashing and was sailing free on the correct bearing when I noticed I was almost in the breakers. I came up into the wind immediately and beat out of there quickly. On the way out I noticed the correct lights about a quarter of a mile to the east, they had been obscured by the rock breakwater. By this time I was fully awake and put the outboard over the stern and motored into the harbour.

When daylight came, I saw that the lights I had mistaken were on a radio-mast and were provided to warn low-flying aircraft. I was also able to see where I had been heading and watched the huge rollers breaking on the rocky foreshore.

Trekka and *Tzu Hang* at Kahului, Maui

Tzu Hang arrived later that morning and anchored near *Trekka*. Clio came over in the dinghy to collect me and I was relating my narrow escape to Miles and Raith when a man and two children swam out from the shore. When he got close alongside he called out, "My name is Guy Hayward, I'm the doctor here. When you're ready, come ashore and have a drink, my house is on the beach there."

So once again we had made a new friend. Guy and his charming wife, Anita, had five children; they took the invasion of six ocean travellers as though it were an everyday occurence and made us feel so welcome that we used their house as a kind of battle headquarters.

With their telephone we learned that the crane would arrive at the wharf the following morning and that two gallons of waterproof resorcinol glue had already been ordered from the mainland to be dispatched via air freight.

In the morning, after laying *Tzu Hang* alongside the wharf, one of the sugar company's crane trucks lifted the mainmast out of the boat and set it down on the wharf.

Until now there had been a faint hope that the damage could be repaired by scarfing in new material, but it was now obvious to all that the mast was beyond repair.

The first day I started work on the new mast at the factory, a short Hawaiian approached me and said, " You are big man, where you come from?"

I grinned at the stocky figure and replied, "Well, I was born in England, but I've been living in Canada for a while now."

He digested this information and then shot at me, "How high you are?"

"Six feet," I answered.

"Six feet!" he repeated almost reverently, and then he confided, "You know, Hawaiian all small people, all dwarf. Big sideways but not high."

He went off muttering, "Hawaiian all dwarf."

The following morning, Raith Sykes came along to see how I was getting on with the project and the little Hawaiian rushed up to him, eyes popping with excitement. "How high you are? how high you are?" he asked, barely able to contain himself. Raith looked a little startled but replied good naturedly, "Six feet three."

"Six feet three," echoed the awed Hawaiian, "and where you come from?"

"I was born in England," said Raith, "but my home is in Canada now."

"Hawaiian all dwarf," whispered the other, not able to take his eyes off Raith.

"What was all that about?" inquired Raith, after the Hawaiian had left us.

"Search me," I shrugged. "Maybe he's never seen a tall person before."

I went back to making the mast which was progressing quite well. The material had been planed and I was working on the scarfed joints.

Next day Miles brought the glue along and he had no sooner arrived when the little Hawaiian rushed up and was beside himself with excitement. "How high you are, how high?" he gasped, looking up at the towering figure above him.

Miles shot an inquiring look at me, and then, when he saw my grinning face, answered, "Six feet six."

"Big man, six feet six," gasped the Hawaiian, and I waited for his next question. His eyes never left Miles, and then he said with conviction, "Yes, and I bet you were born in England, too, and now live in Canada!"

Clio arrived later; she was the same height as I was and only fourteen years of age. The Hawaiian was now certain that English Canadians were a race of giants, so we wouldn't let B. come anywhere near the factory as she was only five feet seven.

Bobo, the young Japanese-Hawaiian who was helping me, was a good craftsman and between the two of us we soon had the mast ready for gluing together. Mast-making was something new in the factory, and we seemed to have a never-ending group of spectators. We made over sixty clamps out of scrap lumber and borrowed bolts from the stores. When it came time to glue the mast together we had just about one man to a clamp, and I doubt if any mast was ever clamped together so quickly.

Although the spar was now in one piece, there was quite a lot of work left to shape it up to match the old fittings and install the masthead sheave for the main halyard before final sanding. Instead of varnishing the new mast, it was decided to fiberglass it, and though I was against doing this at the time, it proved to be very successful and looked almost as good as new varnish and certainly much better than weathered varnish.

We stepped the mast about two weeks after removing the old one, and all agreed that it was a fine-looking spar. Clio's little dog, Poopah, immediately christened it and we felt it was accepted by him at least. Later a visitor admired the new spar and rubbed his hands on it appreciatively. He smelt them carefully and then inquired of me what type of oil we were using on it to keep the mast in such fine condition. Before I could answer, Poopah appeared on the scene and lifted a hind leg. I saw understanding dawn in the visitor's eyes and watched him carefully remove a handkerchief from his pocket.

Trekka caused me some excitement one night by vanishing. I had noticed that the wind had changed from the normal Northeast Trade and was blowing quite briskly from the south.

I had been having an evening meal aboard *Tzu Hang* with Miles and B. and left later in their dinghy to return to *Trekka* for the night. I rowed off in the correct direction and was not unduly alarmed when at first she did not appear out of the blackness, but with a rising sense of panic I realised that she really had gone and there was only one direction she could go, downwind toward the rock breakwater. I hurried back to *Tzu Hang* and told Miles who immediately jumped into the dinghy with me. I began rowing downwind as fast as possible, my heart pounding and my thoughts in turmoil wondering if I would find her smashed up against the rocks. We saw a whitish patch ahead and I knew it was *Trekka*, but she was drifting downwind quite quickly with the rocks only a short distance away. I scrambled aboard knowing what the trouble was. The anchor warp had wrapped itself around the top fluke of the Northill anchor and pulled it out of the sand when the wind had changed direction. I quickly untangled the fluke and anchored again. *Trekka*'s bow now faced the wind with the stern only a few feet from the breakwater, but we had reached her in the nick of time and I was able to fasten the outboard motor to the transom and start it. Soon we were back alongside *Tzu Hang* again and re-anchored, but that was not the end of the evening's entertainment, for soon *Trekka* was dragging again. The wind was building all the while and was now a steady 35 m.p.h. I decided that this was enough nonsense for one evening and motored *Trekka* right into the inner harbour under the lee of a large warehouse on the dock. It blew very hard for the rest of the night and most of the following day, too. I found out later that this was one of the Kona storms which sweep through the Hawaiian Islands during the winter months, and that on this occasion the wind reached a velocity of over 70 m.p.h.

When the storm had passed, I returned to the anchorage close to *Tzu Hang*. She had ridden it out to a 65-pound C.Q.R. anchor with a lot of her half-inch chain out. This anchor had bitten into the bottom so well that I

Our hike took us over this vertical terrain into Iao Valley

had to give Miles a hand to break it out when the time came for our departure.

During our stay in Kahului I went along with the Smeetons on what was to be an attempt at finding the old Hawaiian trail over the ridge of mountains separating Olowalu Valley and the Iao Valley. The hike had last been done some twenty-three years before by a party with two Hawaiian guides. Luckily someone gave us a machete just before we started, for we had to hack our way through dense tropical undergrowth. The distance was about twelve miles but much of this was vertical and it took us three days before we came down a stream bed into the Iao Valley. The trip did wonders to my waistline. The tight blue jeans I had started out with were a sloppy fit at the end of the hike; however B.'s cooking soon had me filled out again.

One evening, when just Miles, B. and I were aboard *Tzu Hang*, we got to talking about our future plans and I asked them both what they were going to do after they arrived in Australia.

"Well, Clio has got to go to school again," said B. "These correspondence courses are all very well, but Miles and I feel she ought to go to a school in England for a while."

"So will you sail her back to England?" I asked.

"No, I think she'll have to go by ship or fly," replied Miles.

"She'll fly," said B. with considerable emphasis. "No daughter of mine will make a long sea voyage alone at her age, not with some of the ghastly types I've seen aboard ships. Believe me, I know."

"If Clio flies to England that will leave just the two of you on the boat, won't it?" I said. "Vivian and Raith are going back home from Honolulu."

"Well, we sailed *Tzu Hang* out from England to Canada with just the two of us," said Miles. "Clio was only eleven then and couldn't help us much with the boat."

"Yes, but which way will you sail *Tzu Hang* back to England?" I asked. "If you're going down to Melbourne, it will be a devil of a long way to go right up the coast to Torres Straits and twelve hundred miles of tricky sailing inside the Great Barrier Reef, too."

"I suppose we could try to get across the Great Australian Bight," Miles went on. "The winds are not too unfavourable during the summer months."

"Of course, I would like to go by Cape Horn," said B. simply.

"What!" exclaimed Miles and I together, both of us quite startled.

"Well, *Waltzing Matilda* went that way, and so did Connor O'Brien's *Saoirse*," said B. "Both boats were about the same size as *Tzu Hang*, but of course they had good crews." Then she added a little sadly, "I don't think we could make the trip alone though, and I can't think of anyone who'd want to come with us."

"I'd come tomorrow," I said, quite surprised at myself.

"Would you really?" asked B. with quickening interest.

"Man, I've always wanted to do that passage," I replied. "I'll never get a chance to do it in a square-rigger, and that's the way I would like to go. But I'd jump at going with you on *Tzu Hang*."

"Now, wait a minute," said Miles cautiously, "We've not even arrived in Australia yet, and you two are already talking about leaving the place."

"What would you do with *Trekka*, John?" asked B., taking little notice of Miles.

"Well, I could leave her in New Zealand and come across with you to Australia," I suggested. "By that time you'd know if you wanted to take me or not. Single-handers are all supposed to be a bit weird," I added mischievously.

"Well, you can say that again," said Miles. "But we don't intend going to New Zealand, anyway. It's too far off to think about that yet, anything might happen in the meantime."

Just before I rowed back to *Trekka* for the night, B. got me aside and whispered, "Don't worry, it will be all right, I'll get around Miles eventually and he'll be just as keen as we are. But you've got to help me, and for Heaven's sake don't breathe a word to a soul or they'll talk him out of it."

I rowed back to *Trekka* thinking, "Miles, you don't stand a hope."

After being in Kahului for nearly a month, it was time to move on again. We had made so many good friends that it was quite sad saying goodbye to them all; some of them wanted to come on with us to the next island, and *Tzu Hang* had a full crew when she left one afternoon in 1956 for Kaunakakai on the island of Molokai. Even *Trekka* had a passenger for the forty-odd-mile run. We left early in the morning hoping to get a good start, but there was very little wind until about noon when the usual northeaster came in. *Trekka* went along very well with the main and spinnaker up and was doing a steady six knots, but once we came under the lee of Molokai the wind fell light and we arrived at Kaunakakai just after dark.

Our friends flew back to Maui that night, and when we returned to the harbour from the local airport we found that a small freighter had arrived to load pineapples. We had to move *Tzu Hang* along the wharf to make enough room before we all retired for the night.

Molokai Island is also a great pineapple-growing center, and though the plantations did not seem quite as spectacular as on Lanai, it was apparent that an enormous amount of fruit was grown there. A friend drove us to the northern side of the island where we looked down from the pali, a mountainous ridge above the leper settlement at Kalawao, one of the three main stations in the Pacific.

There is a very strong updraft near the edge of the pali, for the Trade Wind blows directly against it and sweeps up the face and over the top. A trick of the locals is to throw someone's hat over and then watch the wind blow it back again.

We were only a couple of days on Molokai before leaving for Honolulu some fifty miles away. I left at night so as to arrive in daylight at the other end and made good progress until early in the morning when the wind fell away to nothing in the middle of Kaiwi Channel. This is unusual, for the channel is noted for being very windy.

The U.S. Navy was holding manoeuvers, dozens of flying boats buzzed about *Trekka*, and it was difficult to know if I was in the way or not. However, we couldn't move as there was no wind, and presently the submarines, destroyers and carriers moved away over the horizon. When the wind returned, it was from the south. It steadily increased and from the look of the sky I knew that there was bad weather on the way. By the time we reached Diamond Head, it was blowing quite hard and I had to roll a deep reef into the mainsail. I picked out the leading marks of the Ala Wai Yacht Basin and was running in along the channel through the coral reef when a motor launch came out to escort me in. *Tzu Hang* was moored against the gas dock close to the Ala Wai Bridge so I ran alongside her and lay there for the night. The wind blew quite hard for the next few hours and this Kona storm did a lot of damage to the neighbouring island of Kauai where 42 inches of rain fell in 48 hours.

Next morning I remembered to call Customs and Immigration as I had been instructed to do in Hilo, and in an hour or so I had a visit from a uniformed officer who took care of both departments and provided me with the necessary forms to complete.

"What did you do in San Francisco?" he asked a little guardedly, as he examined my passport.

"Nothing much," I replied, "I went in there to do some minor repairs for a few days, why do you ask?"

"They put a D2 stamp in your passport" he said "that's usually only for undesireable aliens who are not welcome and have no visible means of support. What did you tell them?"

"They asked me where I lived and worked," I answered, "so as I had left Canada I didn't quite know what to say."

"Well, they certainly shouldn't have used a D2 on you," he said sympathetically. "Lucky you came to Hawaii, have a pleasant stay, Aloha!" Perhaps because Hawaii welcomes so many visitors from different countries and cultures its people know how to project the "Aloha" spirit. In those days they still had the Royal Hawaiian Band playing on the dock when a passenger ship arrived and a grass-skirted beauty to give you a kiss as you came ashore. The officials in San Francisco needed a trip to Hawaii, badly.

Harbormaster Chick Allen looked after us very well, and soon both boats had temporary moorings in the marina, while we had the use of hot showers and washrooms nearby.

We all went out to the airport to see Vivian and Raith off and understood how they felt about returning to their home in Canada in mid-winter after spending the past two and a half months cruising in the tropics.

There were some very interesting yachts and people in Honolulu which is known as the "Crossroads of the Pacific;" it is said that sooner or later everyone passes through here.

We met Bill and Phyllis Crowe who had sailed their Block Island schooner *Lang Syne* round the world, and W.A. Robinson of *Svaap* fame invited us aboard his lovely schooner *Varua*. There were many other interesting boats that had made long voyages. I also saw Dwight Long's *Idle Hour* in which he circumnavigated before World War Two.

One of the keen local yachtsmen we met was Ernie Simmerer who owned the schooner *Kitone*. He told us of a lovely walk he had made on the island of Kauai, and showed us photographs taken during the hike into the valley of Kalalau on the northern side of the island. It sounded so interesting that Miles and B. were determined to go. They asked me to join them, and as it was a good hundred miles to Nawiliwili, the only safe port on Kauai, I decided to leave *Trekka* in Honolulu and sail aboard *Tzu Hang* for the trip over. At the last minute Guy and Anita Hayward from Maui turned up and said they would like to come across to Kauai with us, and then fly back to their home on Maui. Unfortunately for them, there was very little wind and we ended up motoring the whole way there. I can remember being quite seasick from *Tzu Hang*'s unusual motion which was quite different from *Trekka*'s.

We moored off the wharf in Nawiliwili, not far from the Coast Guard cutter that was stationed there, and when the four of us were ready to leave on our walk, Miles asked the officer in charge to keep an eye on *Tzu*

Hang while we were away. There was still a lot of damage apparent from the Kona storm, which had blown away roofs and brought prodigious quantities of rain, which in turn had washed away bridges and caused extensive flooding.

We were able to get a ride out to Hanalei Bay on the north coast from where we would start our walk. The trail into the valley wound round the coast, sometimes high above a cliff, sometimes along a beach. It was very narrow and we had to walk in single file; the views were magnificent, and each bend in the trail would bring some new vista.

The distance into the valley was supposed to be seventeen miles, and by that night we thought we were about three miles from our objective. We camped by the side of the trail and pushed on again the following morning, reaching the valley about two hours later. Except for the trail around the cliffs, or by landing through the breakers on a beach by boat, the valley was quite inaccessible. Great volcanic walls of rock shot up a thousand feet into the air, their jagged skyline looking like the crest of some huge dinosaur. The thing that impressed me most was the silence of the place; it was quite deserted, yet with those towering cliffs frowning down upon us I kept feeling that someone or something was watching

A view from the trail along Kauai's north coast

and waiting for us to go away. There was a strange impressive grandeur about the place that was a little unsettling, as though we had intruded into some forbidden garden, and I, for one, felt easier that afternoon when we began retracing our tracks along the cliff trail. The weather looked threatening and all four of us pushed on purposefully. We camped in a battered old hut, the roof of which had collapsed on one side. None of us could get much sleep and we lay awake listening to rain falling steadily and trying to dodge drips that chased us around the floor.

With first light we were off again and around midday arrived at Hanalei. Some Hawaiians kindly offered to drive us to Nawiliwili and soon afterwards we were back aboard *Tzu Hang* and changing into dry clothes. The hike had been well worthwhile, but I for one was pleased to be back aboard the comfort of the ketch.

We left for Honolulu the following morning, a stiff beat against the Northeast Trade Wind. The motion was considerable at times, but my stomach was much happier now that *Tzu Hang* was sailing instead of indulging in the wild corkscrew motion I felt when she was motoring. This was the first real sail I had enjoyed aboard her, and I wondered how long it would take me to get used to her if Miles decided to do the Cape Horn passage in her. There was still some doubt that he would, but B. had evidently been working on him to good effect as he had decided that it might be a good idea to visit New Zealand.

Miles was hesitant about calling there for we had heard some extraordinary story that pets arriving aboard visiting yachts from overseas were destroyed by the authorities who were concerned that the New Zealand sheep could become infected with some tropical disease. *Tzu Hang* had a dog and a cat aboard and this story sounded quite horrible. Of course it was all nonsense, and when we eventually arrived in New Zealand, officials there were the most friendly and easygoing I encountered during *Trekka*'s entire voyage. There are regulations governing domestic animals, and sometimes a bond is required to guarantee that they remain aboard, but the pets aboard *Tzu Hang* were never threatened.

When we got back from our Kauai trip I immediately went to work on *Trekka*. There was quite a bit I wanted to do, and the next two weeks saw me putting in long hours painting and varnishing and doing all the thousand and one jobs necessary to prepare a boat for an ocean voyage. When it came to varnishing the masts, I moored *Trekka* just below the Ala Wai Bridge and was able to lift them out of the boat from the sidewalk above. It was much easier work to refinish them ashore on a couple of old barrels than to attempt sanding and varnishing hanging from a bosun's chair.

Trekka was on the slipway for five days while I painted the topsides with two coats of light blue and then the bottom with anti-fouling paint. When someone asked me what shade of blue the paint was, I told them "*Trekka* Blue." They seemed quite satisfied.

B. was amused watching me work on *Trekka* because she said that whenever someone started to ask me questions I would go below and start knocking with a hammer or just answer in monosyllabic grunts. This was quite unintentional on my part, but had I stopped to answer every question that came my way, nothing would have ever been done. And the questions: What do you do at night, do you anchor? Don't you get lonely? Why don't you take a parrot with you? What's that white stuff on the wires for? I'm sure most yachtsmen have been asked similar fool questions at some time or another.

When *Trekka* slid back into the water she looked almost like a new boat again. Someone asked me what kind of varnish I used as the masts were looking so good. I replied, "Oh, it's some stuff I got in Canada."

"Well, you won't get any varnish like that here," confided my visitor. When I arrived in New Zealand I was asked the same question and replied that it was some stuff I got in Honolulu. "You won't find that quality of varnish here," I was assured. And so it went on at each place I visited. The Australians admired the New Zealand varnish and the South Africans the Australian.

I was very pleased to meet "Woody" Brown one day while I was busy working. Woody, Rudy Choy and Al Kumulai had designed and built a large sailing catamaran which they named *Manu Kai*. She was so successful and swift that it sparked a world-wide interest in this type of craft.

Multi-hulls, which had been built before that were also successful, but somehow they just had not caught the imagination of yachtsmen. It took *Manu Kai* to do this. She was what could be termed a "breakthrough" boat, one that has had enormous influence on sailing design. The three men had designed and built *Manu Kai* using glue-laminated plywood and fiberglass and had engineered the structure so that it was lightweight yet very strong. She sailed like a witch and in the fresh conditions off Diamond Head had clocked speeds close to 30 knots. With this first design Woody had almost attained perfection, for none of her offspring had been able to overshadow her. He had just designed a small 20-foot catamaran which he hoped would become popular in the islands and be raced as a class. The name he had given this class was *Tropic Bird*. He kindly invited me to go for a sail and I willingly laid aside my varnish brush for the opportunity.

I have sailed in catamarans since but have never captured the thrill of my first ride with Woody. With a fresh Trade Wind to power us along she was touching speeds of up to 20 knots at times. After a top speed of six and a half knots in *Trekka,* it was most exciting.

Woody had built close sisters to *Manu Kai* and was sailing them off the beach at Waikiki, taking tourists for trips. It was, in fact, the beginning of a business that has flourished in Hawaii over the years, where thousands of people have, for the first time, enjoyed sailing the aqua-blue water off Diamond Head in one of *Manu Kai's* direct descendants.

Tzu Hang carried two dinghies, one the light fiberglass pram which would carry three persons in calm water, the other a heavier lapstrake planked model that would carry more but which leaked badly. B. asked me if I would make them a new dinghy out of plywood if they bought the necessary materials and arranged for a good place for me to work. With all the work completed on *Trekka*, I had some time on my hands and agreed to do this, finally going to work on the project in Ernie Simmerer's basement. A week and heaps of shavings later, it was ready for painting, and B. looked after that end of it. It was made so that it would fit over the fiberglass dinghy and still stow between the two side skylights; as it was going to stow upside down, it had been made to fit the deck. This had the effect of giving it almost straight sheer, and though it looked very well stowed, it did look a bit odd by itself. There was no time to try it in Honolulu as the paint was still wet but I hoped to see it in the water at Fanning Island, which was to be our next port of call. The new dinghy was just over nine feet in length and was built of quarter-inch plywood with the keel and chines and removable seats all of spruce so as to reduce weight as much as possible. For its size it was remarkably light.

I went with B. one day to a little Japanese ship chandler. We had decided to order plenty of supplies, for once we left Honolulu there would be few good stores available until New Zealand. B. was ordering supplies by the case, and I became infected with her enthusiasm. I also began ordering a case of this and a case of that. At one point she turned to me and said, "You don't surely think you are going to eat a case of bully beef between here and New Zealand, do you, John?"

"Man, I believe in having plenty aboard, nobody will ever hear of *Trekka* running out of food like some of the voyagers you read about," I answered.

A few days later, when a large truck pulled up alongside the dock and the driver began unloading case after case of canned food, I wondered if I hadn't perhaps overdone it.

"You don't think you are going to stow all that away inside your boat, do you?" asked a passer-by.

"It will go in all right," I answered confidentially, "she's got a hollow mast."

After several hours and much sweat and effort I did manage to get it all stowed away, but in truth there was far too much really. When I finally arrived in New Zealand there was still enough food aboard to take me back to Honolulu had I wanted to go.

Our stay in the Hawaiian Islands was rapidly drawing to a close. Though we had thought Honolulu would be just another seaport, we had enjoyed it very much. The other islands had been quite different, not commercialised, and the people lived at a slower pace which suited my temperament better. It had all been enjoyable though, and someday I hoped to return.

Stepping *Tzu Hang's* new mainmast

CHAPTER 6

Off to the *South Seas*

M ILES AND I had looked at the charts together and decided to call at Fanning Island (now Tabuaeran), a coral atoll about 12 miles in diameter situated 1,100 miles south of Honolulu. The island was British, one of the Line Islands situated between Christmas Island (now Kiritimati) and Palmyra Island. It offered a good safe anchorage, and what we had read up about the island indicated that although it was remote, it was an attractive place to visit.

On Sunday, 4 March 1956, *Trekka* and *Tzu Hang* left the Ala Wai Yacht Basin for the distant little atoll. After spending the past four months cruising from port to port, it seemed strange to be setting out on an ocean passage again.

By that night, *Tzu Hang* had disappeared over the horizon ahead and I was left alone looking at the diminishing lights astern. My stomach was acting up as usual, and I soon had *Trekka* steering herself while I went below for some sleep. The weather was grand; with the wind just aft of the beam, *Trekka* was going along in her best stride and the first four days out saw us 390 miles on our way. On the evening of the fourth day, though, the wind fell away and we were left slatting about becalmed. Next morning the sky had clouded over and rain squalls descended on us at times. It was doldrum weather, but as we were only down to latitude 14 degrees

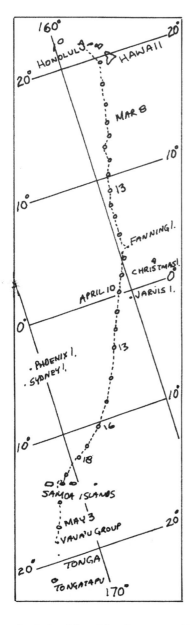

north I couldn't believe that I'd reached the Intertropical Front so soon.

The weather cleared next day and we started to make better progress, but as we got farther south, squalls became increasingly frequent. They would only last for five or ten minutes, but the rain would knock the sea flat. Instead of taking down sail, I ran *Trekka* off downwind, which was usually to the west.

I had not been able to get a latitude noon sight for days, but on the 13th we were about 9 degrees north latitude. During the afternoon the wind increased until it was blowing with gale force from the east. I pulled all sail down and lay ahull for a few hours waiting for the weather to moderate.

When the wind eased a little I set the staysail and mizzen and left *Trekka* to work herself south. She sailed herself very well under this rig when it was blowing hard.

Twelve days out, Fanning Island was only 95 miles away, but I noticed that we had lost 30 miles off the day's run owing to the Counter-Equatorial Current. The following day, too, the current had robbed us of another 30 miles, but we were getting quite close to the island now and I hoped to see it next morning. The wind left us for a few hours but returned just after midnight, a steady breeze from the east. At daylight, a succession of squalls and driving rain reduced visibility to a quarter of a mile and I wondered how I was going to find the island in these conditions. The highest point of land on Fanning is twelve feet above sea-level and the tops of the coconut palms can only be seen about six to seven miles off from the deck of a small yacht. I was wondering if I had missed the island altogether, for navigation these past few days had been difficult with the sun obscured most of the time.

For a fleeting moment I thought I saw a light ahead, but when I looked again there was nothing there. I knew that eyes play tricks when you expect to see something or when you are tired, so I did not take too much notice. Then a few minutes later I saw a dark ragged line which extended right across the horizon. I blinked a couple of times, and then I was sure I was looking at the tops of the coconut palms on the northern side of Fanning.

Soon the land itself came into view and I ran along the lee of the island, sailing in strangely calm water. The buildings of the Cable Station peeped out amongst the palms on the western side of the atoll and presently the entrance to English Harbour came into view and I saw the familiar masts of *Tzu Hang* just behind the point.

A glance at the Tide Book showed that the tide was ebbing and I wondered if the outboard would have enough power to push us into the lagoon. I fastened it over the stern and as usual it started first pull on the cord, but the current was too strong for us, and I was about to give up the attempt when a small but powerful diesel launch appeared from inside the lagoon and soon arrived alongside. The two men aboard shouted that they had been expecting me the day before. From their accents I guessed they were Australians, and a few minutes later, when we had anchored *Trekka* near *Tzu Hang*, my guess proved correct. The elder of the two introduced himself and his companion. "I'm Phil Palmer, and this is my assistant, Bill Frew," he said in an intriguing drawl. "We're running the copra plantation here," he explained. "When you have time, come ashore and meet my wife and daughters, and I'm sure Bill here will have all sorts of questions to ask you."

Bill was a tall, slim young man with brown eyes; he was very deeply tanned and had a hungry look about him. "What kind of a trip did you have down?" he inquired in a soft, almost lazy voice. "The weather's been a bit crook the past three days here. Miles was fair dinkum when he said *Trekka* was small."

I chatted a few minutes with them, then Phil Palmer suggested that we move both yachts over behind Cartwright Point where we would be out of the tide and in better holding ground. "We'll take you over at high water this afternoon," he promised.

Soon afterwards I was aboard *Tzu Hang* and comparing notes about the passage. Miles said they had experienced the same sort of conditions as I had but had got down in 11 days instead of nearly 14 in *Trekka*.

"I can't get over how much weight you've lost," said B. laughing.

"Well, what do you expect?" I replied. "Two weeks on my own cooking after two months of your enormous meals!"

"Did you see the new dinghy?" asked Clio.

"Yes," I replied. "I hope it rows better than it looks. It's the ugliest dinghy I've ever seen."

"We're very pleased with it," said Miles. "It rows very easily and will carry a very heavy load. We thought that now you have arrived we could try your outboard on it when the four of us go across the lagoon."

Later that day Phil Palmer showed us the way through the coral heads to the anchorage behind Cartwright Point. There was a wooden shed with an iron roof just above the beach, and Phil said he would bring us some guttering which we could put up to collect rain water for our fresh water needs. I put my outboard on to *Tzu Hang's* new dinghy, and Clio and I went off to the Cable Station to find the doctor so that I could clear with him and officially be allowed ashore. We threaded our way between the coral heads for about three miles. The lagoon was quite shallow as we approached the Station and we eventually found him in a rather grubby little office.

He seemed to resent the fact that I had not waited aboard *Trekka* even though he had not been aware of my arrival. He pronounced me fit, rather grudgingly I thought, and said to let him know in good time when I was leaving so he could have the bill ready.

I soon forgot his unpleasantness, the scene outside was too interesting for petty thoughts. As far as the eye could see, the pale green waters of the lagoon stretched out to the horizon. The dark green of the palm trees contrasted sharply with the blue sky, and in the distance I saw a rain squall darkening the surface of the water. Clio and I made our way back toward *Trekka* and *Tzu Hang*, the motor trying to drown our speech.

"The skin-diving will be good here," shouted Clio.

"I was told that some of the fish are poisonous," I bellowed. "The Americans dumped a lot of ammunition into the lagoon when the war finished and it contaminated some of the reef fish."

"I bet they'll be the easiest ones to catch," returned Clio. We came up close to *Tzu Hang*, I slowed the motor, and then cut it as we came along side. "Goodness, what a row you two make," said B. from below. "I heard you shouting at one another a mile away. I've got lunch all ready and thought we could go ashore and eat in the Grange. Pwe and Poopah can come ashore too, they would like a run around."

The Grange was our name for the somewhat battered shed on the beach, and it became the center of our activity during our stay on Fanning. We brought some sails ashore and made a few repairs, stitching away in the welcome shade, and Miles decided that such an establishment ought to serve morning and afternoon teas, so a spare Primus was brought ashore, too.

We had several visits from some of the staff at the Cable Station who would drive the five miles over a very bumpy road between the coconut palms in an old, rusty, and dilapidated flatbed truck that must have been shipped to the island when the Cable Company first set up operations.

It was a kind of torture sitting behind the cab bouncing from one pot-hole to the next as the wheels squashed hundreds of land crabs that were feeding on the remains of their relatives who had suffered a similar fate when the truck had come to collect us. The scene had all the ingredients of a horror movie.

The Fanning Island Station was a kind of "booster" for the under-sea cable which connected North America with Australia. Before the advent of communications satellites and advances in radio technology, these sub-marine telegraph cables provided the means of transmitting data around the world. Gradually they were phased out of existence, and the idyllic lifestyles of the personnel who manned these stations in various exotic locations on the planet also vanished. Their duty time at some of these remote islands was usually about eighteen months at a stretch. I got to meet several families in the course of my voyage who lived and loved this somewhat solitary existence, raising and teaching children on correspon-dence courses and integrating month after month with only a couple of dozen of their fellow company employees.

The occasional yacht crew who visited these lonely outposts were sometimes a little overwhelmed at the hospitality that was shown them. It was not that we were wonderful company as much as our having new faces and new stories to tell; we represented the dynamic outside world while many of them felt stagnated and counted the days left of their duty time.

The Fanning Station itself was a collection of buildings and bungalow cottages that were showing signs of disrepair, set amongst the ubiquitous coconut palms. The more energetic of the staff passed their leisure hours on the tennis court or shell-collecting in the lagoon. One of the buildings was a library which was well patronized.

Perhaps if our anchorage had been closer to the Station we would have spent more time there, but we were content to work a little in the mornings preparing for the next stage of our voyage, then having lunch ashore and swimming and skin-diving in the afternoons. It was a com-plete contrast to the bustle of Honolulu.

The four of us, together with Clio's little dog Poopah, motored across

the lagoon entrance in the new dinghy to Weston Point, where Phil
Palmer's house was, and I met Mrs. Palmer and her two young daughters, one the same age as Clio and the other a couple of years older. The
girls were soon showing us their pet fish which they kept in rockpools at
the edge of the lagoon. I was most intrigued to see them feed live land
crabs to the waiting mouths of the large fish which swallowed them in one
crunching gulp.

We also got to meet Mr. Hugh Grieg who was on the island during
the First World War when the German raider *Nurenberg* arrived and sent
a party ashore to put the Cable Station out of action. Grieg must have
been in his late seventies or early eighties, but he gave us a lively account
of the excitement and I believe it was he who eventually dived and
recovered the cut cable after the Germans had left so that contact with
the outside world was re-established and the Royal Navy warned of the
raider's position.

B. decided that we ought to walk round the atoll. According to the
chart the distance was about 33 miles, and though there were a couple of
other entrances to the lagoon besides the one at English Harbour, they
were all shallow enough to be waded across at low water. We got Bill
Frew to collect us in the launch when he was on our side of English
Harbour so that we could walk from the Palmer's house at Weston Point
in a counter-clockwise direction and end, without further, assistance at
Cartwright Point where the two yachts were anchored.

B. and I decided that we would travel light and live off the land. I carried a big knife with which I hoped to open coconuts to drink the milk.
Miles and Clio thought it would be better to take a few supplies with
them and they had two cans of peaches and a few cookies.

The trail led off from the Palmer's house winding through the groves
of coconut palms. The first few miles were quite pleasant, much of the
walking being done in the shade, but as we went farther the trail became
more difficult to find and eventually it petered out altogether. There was
no chance of becoming lost, however, as the width of the land around the
atoll was seldom more than a couple of hundred yards. It was necessary
to wade across stretches of water which were shallow channels leading
into the lagoon from the sea. One of them had the inviting name "Shark
Passage." I remember wondering what the scene would look like to a
shark: four pairs of legs, one behind the other like some large caterpillar
groping its way along a little uncertainly, sometimes the front legs stopping as if to test the bottom, while the back legs (mine!) fidgeted.

There was an unpleasant stage when we had to cross large expanses of glaring coral sand. It was terribly painful to the eyes which suffered what I imagine must have been a mild form of snow-blindness.

We eventually arrived at a Gilbertese village—the men and their families were brought from the Gilbert Islands (now named Kiribati) to work the plantation. It must have been an unusual sight for them to see four white people walking through the palms and we gratefully accepted the drinking nuts they brought us.

Soon afterwards we pushed on again and had done about a mile and a half when Miles remembered that he had left his camera near the village. The three of us watched him walk back to find it, grateful for the rest but feeling sympathetic for the tall figure in the burning sun.

About an hour later he returned, looking tired but undaunted with the camera hanging from his shoulder. My efforts at gathering drinking nuts could hardly be described as successful. Even when I managed to get a nut, the vast expenditure of energy required to open it offset the nourishment within. I concluded that there must be an easier way of doing this. Miles and Clio opened their peaches, and though B. and I protested that we were quite all right, we couldn't resist the portions Miles offered us. We reached the northwest passage and had to wait for low water to get across; by this time the sun had gone down and we were relieved from the energy-sapping heat. With a bright tropical moon to light the way, we crossed the final passage and set about the last few miles. The Cable Station lights came into view, and we went into the office where one of the young men was on night duty. He wanted to get some tea for us, but we realised that if we stopped we'd never get going again, so we just had a drink of water then set off on the last five miles. When we at last came out of the trees and saw the two boats anchored so peacefully in the moonlight, I promised myself I would sleep a week.

Clio's dog, Poopah, was the hero of the trip having made the entire distance on his short little legs but for the water passages where we had carried him across. At the finish he still had a wag in his tail.

My stay at Fanning was almost over and one day I went over to the Cable Station to get a clearance for Apia, Samoa, and found a large bill waiting for me. This was apparently the "Port" dues and the doctor's fee for giving me *pratique*. Had this amount been charged to a freighter or commercial vessel it probably would not have been out of order, but it represented a couple of day's wages to me and I was somewhat disgusted at the administration that would make such a demand for a slip of paper. I paid, but this was to be the only "port" that *Trekka* visited during her entire circumnavigation where charges of this nature were levied.

Tzu Hang was going to Pago-Pago in American Samoa, so we planned to meet again in Auckland, New Zealand, where I would see about laying up *Trekka* so that I could join *Tzu Hang* for the voyage to Australia and then back to England.

The two yachts left Fanning together late on the afternoon of 7 April. The Palmers, Bill Frew, and some of the Cable Station staff came out a little way in the launch, but soon they had turned back and *Trekka* and *Tzu Hang* were left alone sailing quietly away from the sheltered lagoon.

At nightfall we separated and I left *Trekka* to steer herself toward the southwest where, 1,200 miles over the horizon, lay Samoa.

The passage to Apia was a most pleasant one, for the weather kept fine for most of the two weeks it took me to get there. It was obvious that all the squalls and rain I'd had on the way to Fanning had been the doldrums, that area of frustrating weather between the Northeast and Southeast Trade Winds.

On 10 April *Trekka* crossed the Equator and slipped along over a very calm sea at three and a half knots. According to the weather charts, I could not expect to pick up the Southeast Trade Wind until 7 degrees south, but on Friday the 13th, which has somehow always been a lucky day for me, the wind increased until it was blowing a fine steady breeze. The sky put on its best expression, and I realised that we had indeed reached the Southeast Trade Wind. *Trekka* went along with the wind abeam, putting the miles away steadily and comfortably; it was sailing at its easiest and best.

Eleven days from Fanning we were only 300 miles away from Apia, but then the sky changed and we were enveloped in a terrific electrical storm. Great jagged forks of lightning flashed across the sky and the thunder cracked deafeningly. Rain fell in solid sheets knocking the sea flat and bouncing a foot off the deck. I never like lightning at sea knowing that there is only one thing sticking up in the air for miles around, the mast. When I built *Trekka*, I fitted extra long chain-plates so that if lightning struck the rigging it could run down the plates into the sea.

The electric storm knocked the Trade Wind for a loop and for a few hours the wind went round to the northwest. The sky remained cloudy, and though the southeaster returned, I still did not like the look of things. That night the electric conditions returned and I downed sail and waited for the disturbance to move on.

Daylight brought clear weather but only a light breeze. *Trekka* kept moving along steadily so that by nightfall we had only 45 miles to go. I left her to look after herself during the night and woke just before dawn to see a light dead ahead. Daylight revealed the cloud-enshrouded slopes of Upolu Island with Apia nestling at the foot of them.

As we approached land, the wind became very light and *Trekka* ghosted along over the calm water. It was a Sunday morning and all seemed quiet ashore except for a cock crowing, then church bells began to peal, the peaceful sound hanging in the morning stillness. I shackled the anchor and chain to the warp as *Trekka* self-steered into the harbour. When the lead-line showed four fathoms, I brought her up into the wind and dropped the anchor into the clear water. I stowed the sails and put up the little yellow quarantine flag under the starboard spreaders. *Trekka* had completed another ocean hop — 1,200 miles in 14 days.

The doctor and port officials came to clear me a couple of hours later, after they had been out to a freighter which had just arrived from Suva. It seemed a little strange to arrive in port and find no *Tzu Hang* waiting for me, and this raised another problem. How was I going to get ashore?

There was no wharf I could moor against, and *Tzu Hang*'s fiberglass dinghy was not available. I was wondering what to do when a young Samoan paddled past in an outrigger canoe. I called to him and soon we were discussing the problem. We came to terms and I arranged to hire the canoe for the few days of my visit.

The weather was very hot and humid, my shirt stuck to my back like a wet rag, but I went into the quaint little town of Apia and bought a few fresh supplies and some bread. Canned food was very expensive and I was pleased that I had bought so much in Honolulu.

A friend offered me accommodation ashore and rather than try to live aboard *Trekka* in the heat, I gladly accepted. Everyone warned me about leaving *Trekka* at night, saying that everything would be stolen, but although I had no means of locking the hatchway, nothing was ever taken during the whole voyage.

Just after daybreak one morning, my friend and I walked to the top of the mount overlooking Apia to visit the grave of Robert Louis Stevenson. The trail was quite steep, and though we had started early, it was already hot. A drenching shower when we reached the summit revived us somewhat and we were able to admire the lovely view. It is a peaceful spot where the great writer was laid to rest.

I went with friends to a beach party a few miles from Apia. We passed through many Samoan villages along the route, and I was intrigued at the way the native houses were built of plaited coconut fronds with stout poles for framing. The houses were set on a level stone platform, and the walls were plaited matting which could be raised or lowered according to the weather. They were ideal homes for the climate. I would have liked to have seen more of this beautiful island, and stayed longer too, but winter was fast approaching New Zealand and I wanted to be there before the bad weather began.

Knowing that it would seem pretty cold as we got farther south, I bought a few items of clothing and an extra blanket.

Five days after arriving from Fanning Island, I was back at sea again, running along the northern shore of Upolu Island toward Apolima Strait which separates the island from Savai'i, the largest island in the group. As I approached the strait, a heavy rain squall overtook us, and visibility was down to a few yards for nearly half an hour. When it cleared, we were through the strait and into open water again. I checked the course on the chart and noticed that there was a reef we would be passing that night, so I altered course more to the eastward to make sure that we stayed well away from it. As we were now bound for New Zealand, I had the chart of the North Island out and was looking at all the interesting places and natural harbours along the eastern coastline. In the Bay of Islands, some eighty-odd miles south of North Cape, I saw a small township named Russell. The name rang a bell in my memory, and then I remembered that this was the place my father had spoken of when I was just a boy in the Channel Islands.

He had lived in Russell at some stage of his life and was always talking of returning there with my mother and me. The war had put paid to that dream, but I thought I would like to see the place that he had remembered with such longing.

The weather became unsettled and a squall came along which seemed to alter the normal wind for a few hours. It blew from all points of the compass for a few minutes at a stretch, and finally I became so exasperated at changing sail for the progress of only a few yards that I lowered everything and waited for the wind to settle. The sea gradually flattened out and a faint breeze came in from the southeast. With the masthead genoa drawing well, we ghosted along under a clearing sky while I read a book as I was steering. The calm weather continued; sometimes a slight breeze would move us along for a few hours, but there were long periods without any wind at all and I passed the time away repairing sails or reading.

We were only about 150 miles from Vava'u, the northern group of the Tongan Islands, and I decided that as they were so close, and the winds so light, this might be a good time to have a look at them. I altered course and began reading the Pilot Book about Vava'u. There was a lot of sail changing. For a few hours the wind would be easterly, then we'd be becalmed and it would blow westerly; but slowly and surely *Trekka* kept moving along.

At daybreak on 3 May the northeastern end of Vava'u Island was only eight miles off, and a breeze came in which soon had us sailing along close to the shore toward the entrance to the sound between Vava'u and Hunga islands. *Trekka* rounded a point and there before me lay a most beautiful scene, dozens of little palm-clad islands set in the sheltered water of the lagoon like so many jewels. Small motor launches filled to capacity were ferrying happy, laughing Tongans to their homes on various islands.

I had to tack up toward Neiafu, the main settlement on Vava'u. Although I knew that the village was hidden by a point, I thought I must have come the wrong way, but at the last moment buildings came into view and soon *Trekka* had come in close to the wharf where I anchored. A crowd of islanders quickly collected, and presently the port officials arrived. The doctor was a huge man and rather than trust his weight to *Trekka,* he asked me to come ashore. This apparently disappointed the crowd who evidently wanted to see how the doctor was going to get down *Trekka*'s hatchway. I was shown a very nice little landing where I could

Close encounter with the S.S. *Crofter*

moor *Trekka* and just step ashore without having to use a dinghy. A Tongan lad who spoke quite good English came and introduced himself. His name was Lino and he had been one of the crew on a large American schooner cruising through the Pacific islands. He had been to Honolulu and Tahiti, and said that he had enjoyed his cruising very much and would now try to make me enjoy my stay on Vava'u by showing me around.

CHAPTER 7

An Underwater Cave

ONE OF THE places I wanted to visit in the area was Mariner's Cave. This cave is located on the island of Nuapapu about ten miles from Vava'u, and Lino was able to arrange with one of the launchmen who was carrying some freight to the settlement there to take us along.

Lino explained that the entrance to the cave was underwater and therefore was difficult to find unless you knew the exact place on the cliff to look for. The man we wanted as a guide was a fisherman named Benny who lived on Nuapapu.

When we arrived, Lino found that all the village elders were engaged in some conference and we were asked to join them. None could speak English, but Lino was able to act as interpreter and the men were most interested in my voyage. One of the old men called to a young girl and spoke to her and presently she brought a large wooden bowl into which she poured some rather muddy-looking water, then crushed up in her hands some stringy-looking stuff which she put into the water. She mixed the lot up with her hands and then poured a coconut cup of the liquid and handed it to me. Lino whispered that it was kava and that I should drink it. I cannot honestly say that I enjoyed the national beverage of Tonga; to me the preparations were the most enjoyable part, but soon we were all

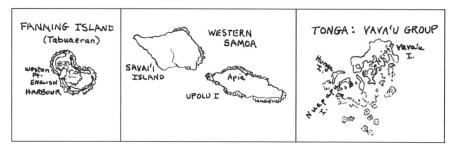

drinking out of the little coconut cups and chatting away. The proposed visit to the cave was discussed and someone was dispatched to find Benny. When he appeared I saw that he had only one arm. I learned that he had lost this while fishing—by holding on to the dynamite charge too long.

As the launch had left for another island to deliver freight, we decided to walk across the island to the place where the cave was. The trail was very muddy, and as we went farther it petered out until we were just walking through dense bush. There were about fifty islanders accompanying us and the whole affair had a school holiday spirit about it. Some were singing, others skylarking around, and many of the younger ones eyeing my swim-fins with curious expressions on their faces. Finally we came to the edge of the cliff which was about forty feet above the sea. Some of the boys were pointing excitedly into the water and when I looked I saw a fair-sized shark swimming lazily away. This seemed to be the signal for everyone to dive or jump into the water. Soon I was the only one left standing on the cliff. I looked down at all the figures in the water beckoning me to jump. I threw the fins and face mask to them and jumped. A world of blue exploded about me and as I rose to the surface I could see the brown bodies swimming and splashing about. I retrieved my fins and face mask, the fins causing quite a stir amongst the men as I put them on my feet. It was obvious they had never seen them used before. Benny beckoned me to follow him, and when he dived, I followed. There is something a little frightening when you dive for the first time into a cave like this, not knowing how far you have to swim before you can breathe again, and wondering if you have already passed your point of no return.

Down he went into a large black hole and, as I followed, he disappeared for a moment into the shadow of the rock; then I, too, was in shadow and conscious of rock above me and the need to go deeper down into the unknown. My ears began to hurt a little with the pressure, then I saw Benny turning toward me and pointing to the surface. With my arms outstretched I shot upwards and broke the surface at the same moment as Benny. We gasped air into our lungs and laughed at each other.

"Is good?" he inquired as I looked about me at the great dome of the cavern.

"Is very good," I replied.

We climbed up on to a rock ledge at the back of the cave and, as my eyes grew accustomed to the darkness, I was able to see how large it was inside. It was huge; the roof appeared to be a good thirty feet above us and, from the entrance to the back of the cavern, extended easily sixty feet. The only light was from the tunnel entrance; as I watched, it dimmed for a moment and I saw the brown figure of an islander swimming strongly toward us through the entrance. As he came into the shadow, his body seemed to change to dark blue and then he broke the surface and shook his head, clearing his eyes. Drops of water splashed from his hair like diamonds and sapphires in the dim light.

Soon everyone was in the cave and we climbed farther up at the back to make room for the others. One of the young men asked to try my fins, and there was much good-natured banter and laughter as he put them on, but when they saw how well he swam with them, everyone wanted to try and the cave rang with their happy laughter.

I noticed that my sight was distorted every few moments, and it was a little while before I realised why this was so. When the ocean swell surged against the cliff outside, the water level in the cave rose several inches and, as there was no other entrance, the air pressure suddenly increased causing blurred vision. Even though the cave was completely sealed except for the underwater entrance, the air inside was quite pure.

One by one the islanders began leaving and I realised that someone had taken my fins with them. However, knowing the distance I had to go now and swimming toward the light, it was not too far and I managed to reach the outside without any help and with a little reserve left.

We climbed up the rock cliff and I had nearly reached the top when I heard one of the men calling excitedly. Thinking that it was another shark, I looked down into the water below, but then one of them pointed, and I saw the familiar sails of *Tzu Hang* just entering the sound between Vava'u and Hunga Island.

It was a tired and hungry group that made their way back to the village, and when we arrived the delightful smell of broiled chicken assailed our nostrils. We had only time for a quick snack as the launch arrived shortly afterwards.

The old chief stood tall on the dock, looking me square in the eyes and gripping my hand as he spoke gently in Tongan while Lino translated. "He says he is happy that he met you, and he wants you to know that he is very pleased that you came such a long way over the ocean to see the cave on his island."

On the way back to Neiafu, the launch stopped at Swallow's Cave. This cave can be entered in a boat and we went right inside. Though certainly worth seeing, it did not have the excitement of Mariner's Cave and I realised that I should have seen this one first.

When we came round the point, I saw *Tzu Hang* alongside the wharf. Soon afterwards we were exchanging news and comparing notes. I was delighted to find that *Trekka* had made the drift down from Samoa a day quicker than *Tzu Hang* but, as Miles said, "We weren't trying very hard."

I told them about the cave and the long way they would have to swim underwater. "Might as well make it sound good," I thought, "then when they make that first dive into the cave, they'll be wondering, as I did, just how much farther to go."

Tzu Hang moved from the wharf and moored to a large black buoy that was used for the freighter that called once a month.

"Come on, Clio," I called, "let's see how long you can stay underwater. I'll time you with the stopwatch."

"All right," she said, "I'll go and change, you do the same and I'll time you, too."

Clio dived a couple of times. But each time I said, "You'll have to stay down longer than that if you're going to get in the cave."

"Very well, let's see how good you are," she said, just a trifle worried. I dived deep and swam along underwater until I came to the large buoy and slowly surfaced on the far side so she could not see me. I waited for a few seconds, catching my breath before swimming back the way I had come, and surfaced just beneath her.

"Gosh, that's not bad!" she exclaimed. "Two minutes and forty-three seconds."

"Well, it doesn't take that long to get in," I comforted her, "but you'll have to practise a bit first."

I had intended to sail for New Zealand the day after my visit to the cave, but when I saw *Tzu Hang* again I thought that another couple of days would not hurt.

On the day that the Smeetons went to visit the cave, I left Vava'u in *Trekka*. As there was no wind, I got the launch to give me a tow as far as the cave. Once there, I couldn't resist another visit and left Lino to look after *Trekka* while I swam again into the blue cavern. It took a little persuasion to get Clio in, but after a while she dived deep and went right through the hole to surface inside. We splashed around inside and swam in and out several times. Then it was time to go. I climbed back aboard *Trekka* and said my goodbyes to everyone. It was a sad moment for Lino and me, we had shared each other's company for several days and I knew I would miss the stocky Tongan. Ten years later, on another boat and island, we were to renew our friendship, but that is another story.

"See you in Russell!" I called out to the Smeetons on the motor launch, then the two boats parted company and I was left alone, sailing past more islands toward the open sea.

Russell, Bay of Islands

CHAPTER 8

To New Zealand

BY DARK *TREKKA* had almost put Vava'u out of sight below the horizon, and with a fine northerly breeze to drive us along I decided to keep awake while still close to the islands. In the morning we passed the almost perfect cone of Koa Island which rises to a height of 3,380 feet. Just after noon the active volcano on Tofua Island was abeam, and I watched the smoke from it curling up into the clear sky.

At daybreak the next day we passed over the position where Falcon Island used to be. This island was some 500 feet high in the 1930s and has undergone many changes due to its volcanic nature. It consisted of ash which was easily washed away by the sea after an eruption, so that it frequently disappeared altogether. According to my recent American chart, there were nine fathoms of water over it when we sailed over the spot. Years later when sailing in Fiji waters, I encountered large areas of floating pumice from one of these Tongan volcanoes which are a part of the Pacific "rim of fire" and continue to remain very active.

In the afternoon, the island of Hunga Ha'apai was abeam and we were now in open water, and there was no danger of running into an island while I caught up on sleep. I was not feeling very well and had a sore throat as though coming down with flu. The island of Nukualofa was about a day's sail away and I did briefly consider calling there just to be

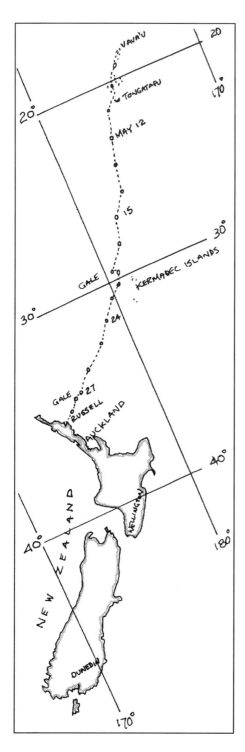

safe, but after a good rest I felt once again my healthy self. This was the only occasion during *Trekka's* voyage that I ever felt ill at sea. Providing you leave port healthy, you are almost certain to arrive in similar condition at your destination, as there are no germs to be collected at sea. Normally it is a healthy life away from the smog of cities and contact with people; the only other danger apart from injuring yourself is from eating contaminated food and I was always careful to examine canned foods, particularly meats, to avoid food poisoning.

As we got farther south it began getting colder. At first I just had to wear a shirt, but soon I was wearing my old Cowichan sweater. The nights were cool and I wished that I had bought another blanket at Apia.

When about fifty miles northwest of Sunday Island in the Kermadec Islands, the wind increased from the west until it was blowing a gale. It was quite a long time since *Trekka* had ridden out a gale, and I realised that as we got farther south I could expect more of this sort of weather. The wind moaned through the rigging all that day, and the sea built up to quite an impressive height. After darkness I listened to the radio for a while, but there was quite a bit of static and I eventually turned it off. At midnight I swabbed the bilges out with the sponge and was emptying the half-bucket of water over the side when I saw a strange sight. The moon was out and low clouds were racing across the sky, but it was something else that caught my attention. It was a great silver bow across the sky, like a rainbow, but this was night-time and I felt a shiver go down my spine and the hair behind my neck bristle as I looked at the eerie sight. I concluded that it must be a moonbow, though I had never seen one before.

When the wind shifted to the southwest it rapidly eased off, and I was able to get sights the following day that showed we had drifted 23 miles during the blow. Sailing again over the remains of the gale swell was pretty lively but *Trekka* was going well, right on course for New Zealand. The weather-cycle hereabouts seemed to be that the wind continually changed direction anti-clockwise; in the northern hemisphere we call this "backing" and the opposite clockwise direction "veering." However, in the southern hemisphere these rules are reversed which caused a certain amount of confusion in my mind. The following day *Trekka* crossed the International Date Line and we went straight from Sunday to Tuesday. Gradually I was able to accept that instead of being twelve hours slow of Greenwich time, we were now twelve hours fast. I hoped that I had got it all figured out correctly.

One weather cycle after another passed, and then when we were about 280 miles from Cape Brett at the southern entrance to the Bay of Islands, a fine breeze from the southeast had us going along very well. It gradually went round to the northeast so the twins were set and I turned in for some sleep. The motion was pretty violent, and when the wind began increasing I decided to slow down and took the twins down. We ran under bare poles for a while, but soon I had set the staysail again so as not to waste this fair wind. By noon the following day we had run 120 miles on the log in the past 24 hours. We were still going well a couple of hours later, then suddenly the wind stopped. From a fine, steady breeze one moment it just stopped dead, and the sails came aback as *Trekka* slowly came to a halt. I dropped all sail and we rolled about drunkenly waiting for the wind to return.

A gusty westerly sprang up the next day, and we went along close-hauled toward Cape Brett, now only eighty miles away, but soon the wind had increased until it was again blowing a gale. I was getting the mainsail down when there was a crash from aloft and the whole boat shook. I was still wondering what had happened when there was a splash alongside and I saw a large albatross shaking his head in a stunned manner. He had evidently flown into the rigging and I wondered if he had been asleep at the time on auto-pilot. He flew away rather crooked, but otherwise appeared unhurt.

Late that night the loom of the light on Cape Brett was visible. The weather forecast on the radio was for westerly winds of 35 knots which is what we were experiencing. I remained laying ahull waiting for a break in the weather.

When we got going again the wind was from the north and soon afterwards I sighted the Poor Knights Islands. I stopped for the night about ten miles off Cape Brett, and with the dawn got sail up and let *Trekka* sail herself gently toward the land while I got breakfast ready.

It was wonderful to see the the green slopes and hills of New Zealand and to know that *Trekka* had crossed the mighty Pacific.

All that day we tacked toward the land. There was very little wind, but it was so enjoyable sitting there in the sunshine looking at the coast that I was in no hurry to get in. At dusk we tacked past the lighthouse, and a couple of hours later we were becalmed. I got the outboard motor out of the rear locker and clamped it over the stern, and soon we were moving along over the calm water.

The moon came up and I could see the light on Tapeka Point blinking away to guide us in. Around the point we motored, then the red light on the end of the wharf at Russell came into view. Just a few lights were visible and I realised that it was not a very big town. I had expected that it would have grown since my father lived here years before. I ran in toward the wharf and let the anchor go over the stern, then slipped a bowline over a bollard on the wharf to complete the twenty-three-day passage from Vava'u.

The delightful smell of fresh baked bread came across the water and I looked sleepily at my watch. It was midnight. I wondered where *Tzu Hang* was and how long she would be getting down, and I thought about the next voyage coming up when I would join her for the crossing to Australia. "Ah, well. I'll think about that tomorrow," I mused, and then turned to the hatchway and the comfort of my bunk.

I was awakened by the sound of voices from the wharf, schoolchildren were boarding one of the ferry boats that operate across the bay to Paihia, and several swordfish launches were alongside the wharf, their skippers preparing for the day's fishing. Someone notified the doctor that I had arrived and he came along just after I had finished clearing away the breakfast things. I learned that there were no Customs or Immigration officials at Russell, but was advised to write to Auckland letting them know that I had arrived and would report to them when I got down there.

I got chatting with the skipper of the sport fishing launch *Alma G* near-by which was being readied for the day's fishing. "I wouldn't leave your boat alongside the wharf if I was you," he said with a soft Kiwi accent, "one of the ferry boats could damage her. You can use my mooring off the beach, it's the red buoy there with the dinghy tied to it. I'm going to be gone until this evening but you'd better come and have tea with the family when I get back. Oh, by the way, I'm Francis Arlidge."

I introduced myself to this very fit, bare-footed man wearing shorts and a singlet. He was probably in his early fifties with thinning hair, kind grey eyes set in an open face that was lined and weathered from much exposure to the elements.

Of all the people I met there in Russell, I remember Francis and his wife Mille best. They took me to their hearts and looked after me as though I was one of their six children. Francis took parties fishing for the big striped or black marlin which come to the Bay of Islands from about the beginning of January to the end of May. He had been sport fishing most of his life and had fished with many well known people, one of them Zane Grey, the Western writer, who had visited New Zealand several times and engaged Francis as his personal skipper. Francis told me about fishing with him in Tahitian waters before the war when he was a young man, how they had motored from Russell to Papeete loaded down with drums of gasoline, not daring to cook any meals for fear of igniting the fuel. How on their safe arrival in Tahiti, Zane Grey had insisted on going out every day for nearly three months looking for a big marlin without success until finally one day they hooked a huge one.

"There were not that many people involved with the sport in those days," he said to me one evening when I had got to know him a little better, "and you know how news of that sort gets about the waterfront; we reckoned that's how Hemingway got the idea for his "old man and the sea" story which came out a year or so later."

I found Russell to be a charming little place and fell in love with it immediately. Everyone I met seemed so friendly and hospitable that I felt I was among people I had known all my life. Apart from the good friends I made there, it was easy to like this little township. Like Lahaina which had once been the capital of the Hawaiian Islands, Russell had, in its early days when the whalers and early settlers arrived, also been the main settlement, but known by its Maori name, Kororareka.

The green-pastured hills about the Bay of Islands, its beautiful islands and sheltered harbours, and a mild climate make this part of the world very attractive and many overseas visitors have ended up staying to become permanent residents.

I visited the large town of Whangarei by road a couple of days later with a friend who was going down for a day's shopping and invited me along to see something of the countryside. We stopped several times to admire the scenery and I was shown some huge Kauri trees, one of the finest boat-building timbers in the world. This species is now protected to prevent it from being logged completely, with small amounts being allocated for boat-building.

Whangarei, situated about halfway between the Bay of Islands and Auckland, is situated at the head of a long inlet, about 12 miles from the open sea. It is a pleasant country town with all the amenities, and from a boating point of view, a wonderful place to prepare a boat for a long voyage as the yacht basin is right in the center of town and close to everything.

When we drove back to Russell that afternoon, *Tzu Hang* had arrived from Tonga and was anchored not far from *Trekka*. Clio saw me and came to fetch me in the dinghy.

"Hello," she said, "someone told us that you had gone away for the day."

Francis Arlidge's *Alma G*

"Yes, I went down to Whangarei with a friend," I replied. "How many days from Tonga?"

"Fourteen, I think . . . and oh, I've got lots to tell you. We had an island feast after you left Vava'u," she said excitedly.

We pulled alongside *Tzu Hang* and climbed aboard.

"Hello, Miles. Hi, B. Did you have a good trip?"

"Yes, not too bad, thanks," said Miles.

"Trust you to arrive in time for dinner," said B. "Well, come on then, you know where the plates are, what have you been doing with yourself?"

We were soon exchanging news over the evening meal and later, when I began gathering up the dishes for washing up, we discussed the voyage to Australia and beyond. "I think there are a few jobs that want to be done before we attempt the southern passage," I said.

"Yes, I know," said Miles. "The point is, can we do them here? If we go down to Auckland there'll be so many visitors we'll never get anything done."

"Well, I can manage my end of it here OK, once I've got the materials," I answered. "How about both of you?"

"I'm all for staying, too," said B. "And it will be much better for Clio here."

So it was decided we should stay at Russell and go down to Auckland by train to buy the items and materials we would need. Thus began four months intensive work preparing *Tzu Hang* for a passage round Cape Horn.

There were several jobs that would keep me busy for quite a while, and one of the first I tackled was the rebuilding of the side skylights which had always leaked and required the addition of canvas covers to keep them reasonably watertight. By making new hatch-lids out of teak and plexiglass, and fitting them carefully, the canvas covers were no longer necessary to keep them watertight. The new lids were also much stronger. There was a hatch over the forward cabin that was given the same treatment, and then I turned my attention to rebuilding the cockpit which was really just a foot well with seating on deck. In the sides of the well were locker doors which gave access under the deck on each side of the cockpit. If the cockpit filled, quite a lot of water leaked past these doors and we felt that it made more sense to seal up these openings and get to the storage from inside the boat. Miles was a little reluctant to adopt the same type of twin-staysail rig I'd had on *Trekka*, but finally agreed to try it. I made two 12-foot poles to boom the sails out, and these were painted white and stowed along the lifelines amidships.

I asked Miles if I could build a quarter berth for myself alongside the cockpit, and as some of the tanks had to be renewed and moved, he agreed. Meanwhile, he was splicing up rigging and adjusting turnbuckles. Then he pulled out the old fuel tanks which were rusty and leaking so that we could replace them with new ones.

Though B.'s jobs were not as spectacular, she was just as busy, making new seat covers with her sewing machine, cleaning up after Miles and

Francis Arlidge with the day's catch

me, seeing that Clio kept working at her correspondence course, and just feeding us, an all-time job.

It was not all work, though. At weekends we would sail down to one of the islands where a couple of our friends lived, and we also visited other parts of the lovely Bay of Islands.

With the weeks going by quickly, I had to find some place to store *Trekka* while I was away on *Tzu Hang*. Francis Arlidge came to my rescue when he said I could store *Trekka* in his big shed. And so a few days later I was getting the masts out of her and transferring a pile of canned food to *Tzu Hang*. I put *Trekka* on the hard alongside the Russell wharf and removed the bolts that held the fin-keel in position. At high water she floated clear of the fin and I towed her to the beach where I had a cradle ready. By the end of the day *Trekka* was sitting snugly inside the Arlidge shed along with the masts and sails. I knew that she was in good hands and would come to no harm while I was away. Sixteen months were to pass before I saw her again.

CHAPTER 9

A Change of Yacht

SOON AFTER LAYING up *Trekka*, we left for Tauranga in the Bay of Plenty, where we stayed for about two weeks moored at the head of a long channel, close to town. There were still quite a few jobs left to do, but by the time we left for Auckland most of them had been completed. We had quite a rough passage to Auckland during which I managed to gybe the mainsail which slammed over hard against the running backstay and smashed the main boom. We should have had a preventer on the boom to stop this from happening, but the boat had been steering easily and we had neglected to rig one. In the fresh conditions I was steering and being sick at the same time, and was somewhat crestfallen about the whole business when Miles came on deck to assess the damage. To my relief he was almost cheerful about it. "Never mind, John, the boom was in pretty bad shape. Now you can make us a new one!" he said.

We arrived in Auckland and anchored off the Akarana Yacht Club, a club that was noted for having members who were experienced sailors. Miles went ashore to pay his respects to the Commodore and returned an hour or so later to say that the Commodore had graciously allowed us the use of his personal mooring as his boat was on the slipway for a few days.

"We've got to do this right," he said earnestly to B. and me. "These

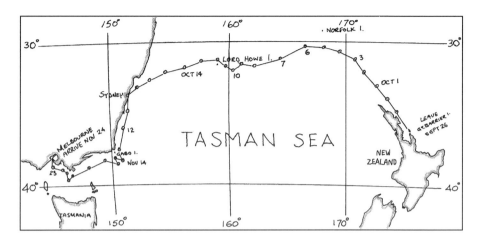

people are real sailors so we don't want to do anything stupid. Here's what I think we should do."

The Brigadier-General spread the harbour chart on the saloon table and directed his troops in the upcoming maneuver.

"The Commodore's buoy is painted white and it's down here amongst a group of moored yachts. I know which one it is so I'll go off in the dinghy and leave you two to bring *Tzu Hang* over," he explained. "This way we'll be sure of picking up the correct buoy and when you get there, I can take a line from you, John, and pass it through the ring in the buoy, then give you the end back to secure on board." B. and I nodded that we understood, and as Miles got into the dinghy I noticed that the wind had increased a little.

B. got the engine going and I went up in the bow and began cranking the anchor chain aboard with the windlass.

I saw Miles had reached the mooring, and as the anchor came aboard, he gave the signal to B. that we were all clear. She pushed the gear lever forward and *Tzu Hang* began to gather way as we turned downwind to approach Miles. Unknown to us, below the deck, the gearshift lever became disengaged from the transmission, with the engine still in gear turning the propeller.

I saw Miles cup his hands and shout, "Take her out of gear, B.," as we approached him.

From aft I heard B. ask, "What did he say?"

"He says to take her out of gear," I relayed from the bow, standing ready with the line I was to pass.

"OK, I've got her out of gear," said B., moving the now-useless lever back to the neutral position.

"Give her a touch astern," directed Miles from the dinghy looking a little anxious.

"What did he say?" B. asked me from aft.

"He wants you to give her a touch astern," I called as the distance to Miles decreased rapidly.

B. moved the lever to the astern position and revved the engine. *Tzu Hang* surged ahead and I heard Miles shouting, "No! Astern, B. Go astern!"

"What's the idiot shouting now?" asked B., a steely note to her voice. "I've got her astern," and she increased the power as *Tzu Hang* headed directly for the figure in the dinghy who was now waving his arms and yelling, "Astern, B.! You've got her ahead!"

B. was quite angry now, she did not like being shouted at when she knew perfectly well what she was doing, she had moved the gear lever to astern and done what she was told. She was not about to listen to Miles or anyone else now. *Tzu Hang* was now making 7 knots and a respectable bow wave as we bore down the last few yards on Miles and rammed him square amidships. In a split second he managed to transfer himself from the sinking dinghy to the bobstay below the bowsprit. He was still shouting, "Astern, B., go astern!"

I looked aft at B., not sure what to do.

"Did I get the bastard?" she demanded in a cold voice, "Oh, good!" she said with satisfaction as the upturned dinghy disappeared astern.

I looked ahead to see us rapidly approaching a large motor yacht that we were going to hit in the next few seconds unless we were very lucky. I quickly let go the anchor, and the chain came rattling out of the hawse pipe and whipped past Miles, still clinging to the bobstay. Closer and closer we came to the motor yacht, and there was no doubt in my mind that we were about to sink her, too. Twenty-two tons of teak, bronze and lead were not to be denied. I closed my eyes and was suddenly jerked off my feet as the anchor grabbed something and *Tzu Hang* sheered away at the last possible instant. We proceeded to go round and round in a circle, just missing the motor yacht each time. I helped Miles up over the bow and he rushed aft and cut the engine. We slowly came to a halt and I thought I saw the flash of binoculars from the balcony of the yacht club. When I went below, B. was sitting very quietly in the saloon knitting, the sounds of the needles unnaturally loud. Miles and I knew when to shut up.

Despite our inglorious arrival, we were well received at the club and Ralph Sewell, who ran the maintenance operations, kindly made space available so that I could build a new main boom. Ralph was a red-headed dynamo of a man, always dreaming up projects that seemed impractical until he finished them. He was a genius at improvisation, being capable of making wonders out of other people's scrap, a man who was a free spirit and embodied the best traits of the "hippie" movement long before the word existed.

B. organized the supplies for the Tasman crossing, not too much because rumor had it that the Australian Customs sometimes charged duty on the stores of visiting yachts.

We had completed some major projects aboard *Tzu Hang* during the southern winter months and had good reason to feel satisfied that our schedule was on target. A westward crossing of the Tasman Sea in the winter months is likely to be all to weather, and with all the expected sail changes we realised that there would be a lot of work on deck. Before we left New Zealand, we outfitted ourselves with some heavy-duty rain wear. The gear I had used on *Trekka* had been almost useless off the Oregon coast and we all felt that the normal yachtsmans "oilies" would be very inadequate in the Southern Ocean. It was B. who discovered the attire we eventually bought. Made for New Zealand farmers who spent many of their working hours outdoors in a climate that alternates continuously, the tractor suits—as they were called—were designed with a jacket that was long enough to sit on, which we felt was essential for long hours spent in the cockpit. The pants were bib and braces style, and to cap the rig, the suit came equipped with a Afrika Korps-style hat which had a neck flap that could be tied over the jacket collar to avoid drips down the neck; this flap could also be folded around the brim of the cap when not required. The suits were made of an industrial-strength material and came in only one color, a rather drab loden green. They were not yachty, but they were very serviceable. For footware, I equipped myself with a pair of farmers milking boots that were made of a white rubber, no-nonsense material.

We realised that our forthcoming voyage from Melbourne to England via Cape Horn was a very ambitious undertaking; we knew of only one yacht that had attempted the route so far south and she had been lost in the attempt. With the idea of keeping a record of the voyage, I purchased a 16mm movie camera in Auckland and several rolls of color film. I would get more in Australia before we left, but I wanted to use the camera to familiarize myself with it and see the best angles on board, and the Tasman crossing would be an excellent indoctrination in the skills of nautical cinematography.

We left Auckland on 23 September 1956 bound for Sydney, but decided to visit Great Barrier Island for a couple of days before setting off across the Tasman. The stop there gave us the opportunity to stow all our gear and try out the new Terylene sails, a mainsail and a genoa. These sails had been made in England and shipped out to New Zealand in bond. The New Zealand Customs delivered them to the yacht a few minutes before we left so there had been no chance to see if they were the correct size and shape. The sails were a great improvement, being so much lighter in weight than the old flax suit, and the boat responded beautifully by pointing several degrees higher than she had ever done before.

We left Great Barrier Island on the 26th, and as the wind was north of west, we did not close the shore of the North Island but sailed close-hauled on the port tack about thirty miles off the coast. It was wet, every few seconds the bow would dip and spray would burst over the weather rail as she worked her way to weather. The motion soon got to me, being quite different to the liveliness of *Trekka*. This was a much softer ride but the pitching soon had me feeding the fish. I'd be quite all right for a while and think I had finally found my sea-legs, then I'd be sick again. I told myself I'd be OK in a few days time.

The wind held westerly and we kept going farther north up toward Norfolk Island.

We had just finished our evening meal on the fifth day out when Miles sighted a light. It looked too small for a ship, and as we got closer we saw that it was a yacht. To our amazement it was friends of ours, Tony and Bridget Reeves, in the *White Hart* from Victoria, B.C., who were on their way to Auckland from Apia, Samoa. They launched their dinghy, leaving a crew member to look after the boat while we all had a wonderful chat together aboard *Tzu Hang*. A couple of hours later they rowed back and we each went our separate ways.

We had a lot of westerly weather on our Tasman crossing, but there was the odd day or two when the winds favoured us. We were about half-way across when we were becalmed for a few hours in the warm sunshine.

"Let's go for a swim," said B.

"Yes, come on," said Miles and Clio together.

"Not me," I said. "They have sharks off the Australian coast. There could be some out here."

"Nonsense," said B. "I'm going for a swim."

"No, seriously, B.," I pleaded. "Don't go in, it's not worth the risk, you'd never be able to get back aboard in time if you did see a shark."

"But we won't see any out here," she returned. "They stay close to land. Anyway, I'm going in."

"Miles, stop her," I begged.

"Well, I can't stop her," said Miles. "But I'll join her, I don't think there is much risk."

"I'm going, too," said Clio.

Miles could see that I was a bit uneasy about the whole thing. "I'll tell you what," he said kindly. "you stay on guard with the rifle; I'll go get it for you."

I watched the three of them swimming about enjoying themselves while I looked about for any signs of a fin in the water. To my relief they all climbed back aboard intact and I was about to hand the gun back to Miles when I saw a tin can floating in the water some distance off.

"Oh Miles, may I shoot at that tin can?" I asked.

"Sure, John," he said. "Wait a minute and I'll load the gun for you!"

When the wind returned we got going again and two days later sighted Lord Howe Island. We closed the shore and considered stopping for a brief visit, but *Tzu Hang* drew too much water to get inside the reef, and the only other anchorage at Ned's Beach on the northeastern side of the island looked too exposed. The weather at the time was looking squally and that decided us. We kept going for Sydney.

On our twenty-third day out we entered the heads at Sydney Harbour and anchored in Watson's Bay awaiting Customs. Later in the day we moved to the Cruising Yacht Club in Rushcutter's Bay where we stayed for just over two weeks. There were a few more jobs to be done, and the mizzen mast needed a new section scarfed into it near the truck. At Charlie Busch's yard, we pulled the mizzen out and I glued the new piece in. The fiberglassed mainmast had been such a success that we decided to do the mizzen, too, while we had it out. I sanded it down well with a machine sander and Clio helped me to do the fiberglassing.

Miles and Clio were invited to take part in a radio quiz program hosted by Jack Davey, a well-known celebrity whose weekly program was one of the most popular on the Australian airwaves.

As they got ready to go off to the show, Miles promised that if they won anything, part of the proceeds would go toward a suit of clothes for me and a paint job for *Tzu Hang* by the yacht yard.

Between them, Miles and Clio answered all the preliminary questions with ease, then came the "jackpot" question worth over seven hundred pounds. The organ in the background wound up the music and there was a clash of cymbals as Jack Davey asked the final question. "What famous British institution was founded upon the proceeds of a lottery?"

There was complete silence for a few seconds, then Miles said, "The British Museum?"

Tzu Hang fitting out in Melbourne
A. Campbell-Drury

"He's right! you've won the jackpot!" shouted a surprised but delighted Jack Davey.

I was not sure why Miles and B. thought I needed a suit, particularly
as we were about to set off to the Southern Ocean, but I suspect that my
"best" attire, when invited out with them to various social events, left
much to be desired. I spent an interesting morning shopping with B. as

we went the rounds of several clothing stores in the city. Our views on a suitable style were somewhat contradictory, but we eventually found a grey-blue outfit that was acceptable to both of us and would allow my presence with them at various functions to be without embarrassment to all concerned.

Miles ran up quite a bill at the local marine store buying new Terylene sheets for the boat and several other items which were something of a luxury for a cruising yacht. These purchases were based upon the expected cheque from the radio show which failed to materialize, causing Miles some concern. Just before the situation got too sensitive, the cheque finally arrived to the relief of the store and the yard that had completed the painting of *Tzu Hang*.

While the boat was hauled out on the slipway being painted, we were visited by a certain English yachtsman who had just lost his boat on a reef off the New Guinea coast. He was apparently looking for a suitable vessel in which to continue his voyage, although from his manner I thought he ought to have been in hospital for he had all the symptoms of shock after a trying ordeal. I remarked that I knew of a small boat that was for sale in New Zealand, having just been sailed out from England. "Well, what is she like?" he asked me.

"Her name is *Jellicle* and she's a folkboat about twenty-five feet over-all. . . . "

"Twenty-five feet!" he snorted, interrupting me. "What would I do in a boat of that size? I might as well go round the world in a dinghy with an outboard motor! I want to be the first Englishman to sail around the world single-handed and it's got to be in something not less than thirty-five feet."

I don't think he knew that I had *Trekka* and was also an Englishman. But his contempt for small craft stung me and I thought, "Just you wait, Mister, and I may show you what a dinghy and outboard can do someday."

The first member of *Tzu Hang*'s crew left us in Sydney. Poopah, the dog, was sent to England aboard a freighter and would arrive there a little sooner than Clio, who was going to fly from Melbourne and go to school again.

The Olympic Games were due to start in Melbourne toward the end of November, and as B. had some tickets for the opening ceremony, we wanted to arrive in Melbourne in good time. The distance from Sydney was about 600 miles and we had allowed ourselves twelve days for the passage.

The voyage down the coast was a rough one. I was soon feeling seasick again, not being able to adapt to *Tzu Hang*'s motion. I began to wonder if

I ever would and with the long passage to England ahead of us it was causing me some concern.

We got down as far as Gabo Island off the New South Wales and Victoria border, and there we stayed battling headwinds. The wind came in hard from the southwest, and there was little else we could do except wait for a wind shift and hope that it would moderate. A couple of times we got sail up but there was a big sea running and we decided to wait laying ahull. When we did get going again we went well and passed Wilson's Promontory with still three days to go for the opening of the Games. But then another westerly came along which blew hard for a few hours and forced us to lie ahull again. When we eventually arrived at the St. Kilda Yacht Club just outside Melbourne, the Games had been underway for two days. The St. Kilda Club was the headquarters for the Olympic yachting events and most of their moorings were in use, but we were offered a berth on the Yarra River just below the Spencer Street bridge and opposite the Royal Yacht *Britannia.*

Melbourne was happy with a holiday spirit. Thousands of Olympic visitors thronged the decorated streets and shops and their enthusiasm infected us. *Tzu Hang* was basically ready to leave on the long voyage except for loading stores. We decided to have a break from the weeks of work and take a few days off seeing the Games and visiting friends.

I was pleased to renew many friendships with several cycling competitors on the various national teams and got to see many of the other events, too. When at last the Games were over, we watched the Royal Yacht being towed down the river and knew that we would be travelling the same route in a few day's time.

And then the day arrived when we took Clio out to the airport and watched her climb into the waiting aircraft to be flown to school in England. The three of us felt miserable when we returned to *Tzu Hang.* With Clio gone, there was now a feeling about the ship of wanting to get started on the voyage so that we could all be reunited again.

We loaded six months supplies aboard and attended to a few last minute jobs. I'm sure *Tzu Hang* had never looked better. She may have looked newer when she was first launched, but she was now a fine example of a well-equipped ocean-cruising yacht. The months of work had not been spent polishing brass or rubbing down varnish; we had worked at replacing doubtful fittings and gear, installing perspex windows in the doghouse in place of the glass, and stopping any annoying leaks in the deck, making the boat as dry and comfortable as possible at sea. She was a good boat, and because we all loved her, she came first. We were going

down the old sailing ship route to the Horn in a small vessel, but we had
confidence in her and we knew she could do it.

We left Melbourne on 23 December 1956, bound for Port Stanley in
the Falkland Islands some 6,600 miles away. We sailed down Port Phillip
Bay, anchored for the night off Dromana, and left early in the morning as
we wanted to catch the tide at slack water while we went through Port
Phillip Heads.

There was quite a slop outside and we were tossed about a bit as there
was very little wind to steady us. Shortly afterwards we noticed that the
main gooseneck had broken; it had apparently seized up while we had
been in Melbourne. The voyage was still young for this kind of thing to
happen, so we decided to go in to Cowes, Western Port, and see if we
could have it repaired. It was Christmas Eve but we managed to find a
garage in Cowes that was open and someone to braze the fitting. The

wind was starting to
blow quite hard from
the west and was mak-
ing *Tzu Hang* surge up
against the wharf; it
was time to move even
though it was a black
and wet night. We
anchored in twelve
fathoms with a lot of
chain out but the boat
was in no danger and
we spent a quiet Christ-
mas waiting for the
weather to moderate.

On the following
day the wind had eased
and we set off after half
an hour's struggling to
get the anchor up. Now
we were off at last, off
on the voyage we had
planned in the harbour
at Kahului, Maui just a
year before.

Final days in Melbourne   A. Campbell-Drury

Chapter 10

Roaring Forties

EVER SINCE JOINING *Tzu Hang* I had been plagued with seasickness, being unable to adapt to her pitching in a seaway. Naturally this had caused me some concern as I wanted to be able to pull my weight as a crew member and I also wanted to enjoy the voyage. A friend in Melbourne had told us that in order for seasick pills to be effective you had to take them about four days before you went to sea. We had all done this and were delighted to find that this approach worked.

Tzu Hang seemed to know that we were off on a long passage, for she went along at top speed all that day, and by noon the next had run 168 miles on the log. We went through Banks Straits and then out into the Tasman Sea heading for the south of New Zealand. A strong blustery breeze drove us along over a rough sea and under grey skies. It seemed as though we were following a depression across the Tasman and moving along at about the same speed. It was wet uncomfortable sailing but the ship was going well, and nine days later we were between the Snares and the Auckland Islands, getting down to about the 50th parallel of latitude.

Then the weather changed and we were becalmed. The sea went down and the skies cleared; it was a welcome change from the grey days, and soon the deck was covered with bedding being aired while we attended to a few jobs that could be done in these pleasant conditions.

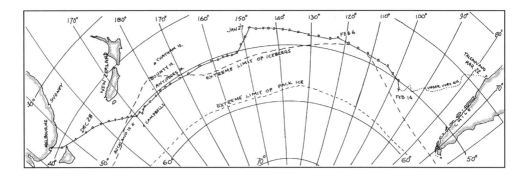

I had long decided that the two little doors in the aft end of the dog-house should be changed to washboards, so while the weather was good I made the alterations using some materials that B. had collected.

She never believed in throwing anything away and had little hiding places about the ship which, from time to time, Miles and I stumbled upon. They reminded me of secret bank accounts from which necessary withdrawals were sometimes made if the situation demanded it. On this occasion she parted with a nice piece of three-quarter-inch plywood which was just large enough to make the two washboards. The bottom one was made about 2/3 the size of the opening and had a small window in it; when installed with the hatch shut, it was possible to see the helmsman from down below without opening the hatch.

It was during this fine weather period that I had the first opportunity to get off in the dinghy and film *Tzu Hang* under sail. She looked so small, rolling along quietly under the twin staysails over that endless expanse of undulating westerly swells which were to accompany us constantly in the weeks ahead. There was something rather gallant about the way she carried herself, every line was clean and pleasing, she was a lady and a beautiful one at that. Looking through the view-finder as the camera ran gave me an intense feeling of satisfaction. I was very happy to be where I was, making a film of a unique voyage aboard a fine ship with a couple of people I had come to love dearly. What more could a young man want?

"We've got to have some scenes of big seas," I said as the dinghy pulled alongside *Tzu Hang*. "Come and see her from the dinghy, B.," I called. "She really looks great but you have to be away from her to see how much motion there is." I passed up the camera to Miles and scrambled aboard quickly as a swell lifted the dinghy almost level with the rail for an instant. B. jumped in smartly and Miles and I watched as she rowed away, sometimes disappearing out of sight behind a crest. I wondered how many other women had rowed a dinghy in those latitudes. None, I decided.

When the wind came back, it was from the northeast and we held on to the port tack, going south of east. This weather seemed unusual to us as we had been expecting steady westerlies, rather as we'd had across the Tasman Sea.

We drove on until we were down south of latitude 50 and inside the red line on the weather chart which indicated that ice extends that far north. It was a sobering thought, and rather than go farther south we decided to wait for a shift in the wind.

Slowly we made our way across the vast expanse of ocean, sometimes with fair winds, sometimes with foul. There were the constant sail changes to suit the particular conditions of the moment, being awakened from a warm bunk to put on on wet rain gear and boots, climbing out of the hatchway into the blackness of a squall, clipping on your lifeline as you went forward to let go a halyard — the scenes and sounds of our little world as the low clouds raced across a sky lit only by starlight; the hiss of an approaching sea, the movement of the deck, the automatic grabbing of familiar handholds as we made our way back aft to a figure in the cockpit crouched over the binnacle holding the course by its flickering light; the satisfaction of knowing that the rest of the world was going about its business beyond the discomforts of yours and that you wouldn't trade any of this for it.

The big seas of the Great Southern Ocean

We were on watch at the same hours every day and got used to our own personal routines. Miles and I each did three three-hour watches during the 24 hours and B. was on for two, as she did all the cooking. This meant that we each got six hours off during the hours of darkness, which was usually enough, but could be supplemented during the day if necessary.

Apart from reading during my off-watch hours, I had other interests—photography or making various little projects from some of the materials that B. guarded so zealously. I found myself thinking more and more about taking *Trekka* on round the world when this present voyage was done, and passed many pleasant hours sketching on paper the various alterations I planned to make to the little boat.

The days and weeks slipped by, and we got used to the ever-changing weather systems, the highs and the lows, the great long swells which were always with us, and the magnificent southern albatross that were our only other companions. On watch at night, I could picture the old windbags loaded full of grain, running the easting down in these latitudes half a century before; now only their ghosts, the birds, and a 46-foot ketch were going down the old route to the Horn.

We were almost halfway across the Southern Ocean to South America before the winds steadied in the westerly quarter. I had thought that the wind was always westerly in these latitudes, but it was not. It moved about as each depression came along and sometimes blew from the east, leaving us to decide which tack was the best one.

Early on the morning of 14 February I was on watch from 3 a.m. to 6 a.m. *Tzu Hang* was running fast under twin-staysails and steering herself, but the wind was increasing and I heard the tops of the sails fluttering, which they did when it was blowing quite hard.

Miles came up from down below to check on the weather and we decided to take in the twins and run along under bare poles for a while. B. came on deck and took the helm while Miles and I went forward to get the twins down. Each sail was set on its own stay and could be lowered one at a time if need be. We let both come down together, unhanked the sails and bundled them down the forehatch, then snapped the twin poles to the lifelines.

We made our way aft along the wet side decks to the cockpit where B. had already untied the sheets from the tiller. After coiling them they, too, were put below out of the way.

"How's she steering?" asked Miles, sitting down and putting an arm around her.

"She seems to steer all right," B. replied, eyes still on the compass.

"I think we'll let the stern line go anyway," he said, getting up again. "It may help some."

I gave him a hand to pay out the stiff 3-inch hawser which was made fast to the mooring bitts on the starboard quarter, then hauled in the log spinner so that it would not get all twisted up with the trailing hawser.

There was still an hour to go on my watch, but Miles was well awake by now; as he was on watch next, he decided to take over now instead of waiting until six. B. and I went below, pulling the companion way hatch shut after us, and I got undressed and climbed in to my bunk which was the quarter berth I had built on the starboard side alongside the cockpit. It was a dry comfortable bunk and I was soon asleep.

I was awakened by Miles tapping on the side of the cockpit, which was the usual way B. called me on watch to take over from her. I was reluctant to leave the warmth of the bunk and wondered if he wanted a hot drink of cocoa or something. I slid the hatch back and saw that it was light outside.

"What do you want, Miles?" I asked rather sleepily, hoping it would be something easy so that I could go back to sleep again.

"You should see some of these seas now, John. They are really quite impressive and the biggest I have seen so far. How about filming some with your movie camera?"

I thought of getting back into wet oilskins and going out into the cold

"I had never seen the sea look like this before."

and part of me rebelled. "No, Man, the sea never comes out and besides the light is not very good," I said hopefully.

But then Miles was looking aft, and he turned to me and said, "Look at this one coming along now. You've never seen a sea like that before. Get the camera, you may never have a chance to get a shot like that again."

When I looked at the scene I saw what he meant. The sea looked different from the weather we'd had the last fifty days. There was a feeling of suppressed power about it, almost as though it were awakening after a long sleep. I saw another sea a quarter of a mile away roll up astern, higher and higher; then *Tzu Hang* began to climb the slope until the crest passed beneath her and she sank into the trough behind. Miles was right, I had never seen the sea look like this before.

"Wait a bit," I said, now more awake, "I'll have to get dressed and see if I can rig the camera up."

A few minutes later, with the camera inside a plastic bag to prevent it from getting wet, and only the lens exposed, I got some shots of a worried-looking Miles steering before that dangerous-looking scene. Abreast of us the wind was blowing the crests off the big seas, flinging the spray to leeward.

"I'll shoot more later on, Miles, when B. is on watch, the light will be better then and I'd like to have some shots of her steering."

The exposed film I put in a plastic bag, and as the tins I had been using were full, I put the bag in Clio's school locker. I was pleased later that I had done so.

B. tumbled out of her bunk at seven o'clock and started making breakfast. I ate mine and then went on deck to take the helm while Miles had his breakfast. He was soon back again at the helm and said to me, "Before I called you up to film the sea, two quite large seas broke over the stern and washed me right up to the doghouse. You can see how they burst the canvas dodger."

I thought that he could not have been dead before the sea because during the few minutes I was steering, while Miles had his breakfast, I had been quite impressed at the ease with which the boat steered and rode those enormous seas.

"Goodness, just look at those seas!" exclaimed B. when she came on watch at nine o'clock. "You should be happy now, John, surely. You've been asking for big seas ever since we started for your film. I hope you're satisfied with these."

"Yes, they ought to look good on the screen, even though the sea always looks flat on film," I replied.

I went below to get the camera and noticed that Miles was in his bunk reading. Pwe was sitting on his chest purring. I went on deck again and shot more film and finished the roll with a scene of B. steering.

"I must just go and put another film in the camera, B.," I said and slid the hatch back to go below.

I got a roll of film out of the locker and went aft to my bunk to load the camera. I sat on the seat by my bunk and opened the camera. The exposed film I laid on the bunk, then I started to thread the new film into the spool.

Tzu Hang gave a violent lurch to port and I put my hand out to grab the fuel tank opposite. I had a sudden feeling that something terrible was happening. Then everything was blackness and solid water hit me. I was conscious of a roaring sound and that we were already very deep. "She's been hit by an enormous sea and is full of water. She is already sinking. I must get out." These were the thoughts that flashed through my mind. I knew I had to go forward, then up out of the doghouse hatch and I started to fight my way against solid water. Suddenly I was looking at a large blue square. "What on earth is that?" I wondered. Then I heard Miles's anguished voice, "Where's B.? Where's B.? Oh God, where's B.?" and still dazed I watched him climb into the blue square. I realised that I was laying on my back in the galley and looking at the sky through the opening in the deck where the doghouse had been.

I scrambled out on to the deck and almost immediately saw B. in the water about thirty yards away. It is a picture I will never forget. She was wearing a bright yellow oilskin, the sea was almost white with spume and overhead the sky was a hard blue. B.'s face was covered with blood and for a crazy moment I thought, "Oh, what a shot for color film."

B. raised her hand and shouted, "I'm all right, I'm all right." While she started to swim toward us I looked about me and saw that both masts were in the water and all smashed into short lengths as though they had exploded apart. The doghouse had been wiped off at deck level and I noticed that both dinghies had gone. The side skylights were both smashed and the lids were gone too. I looked up and saw another monster of a sea approaching and I thought, "What a bloody shame! No one will ever know what happened to us."

"Hang on," I shouted to no one in particular, and *Tzu Hang* lifted sluggishly to meet the crest; she had a slow hopeless feel about her and I watched more water pour down the great hole in the deck.

Miles called to me to give a hand at getting B. aboard. I looked at the ruin everywhere and thought, "I might as well jump in alongside her."

B. had something the matter with her arm, for when we hauled her aboard she thought I was kneeling on it.

"Well, this is it, Miles," I said, knowing that we had come to the end of the trail.

He nodded. "Yes, it looks like it, John."

"Hang on!" I cried as another big sea came along. *Tzu Hang* again made a tremendous effort, but she lifted and I felt a spark of hope. "We've got a chance," I cried. And just then B. said, "I know where the buckets are."

The two of us climbed down into the waist-deep water that was splashing backwards and forwards in what a few seconds before had been our comfortable little home. My main thought was to prevent more water getting below and that meant we had to cover the doghouse opening with sails or something. I climbed into the forecabin and started pulling the twin-staysails aft; they would help.

For bearers to cover the opening, I took the rods from Miles's canvas bunk and the door off his hanging locker. My tools were still intact and the box was jammed on top of the galley sink. By some extraordinary luck the galvanized nails were still in the paint locker though everything else had gone. It was difficult working on deck for there was nothing to hold on to, everything had been wiped bare except part of the aft end of the doghouse, the winches, and the mainsheet horse. Miles gave me a hand to cover up the doghouse opening and we spread the Terylene genoa over the bearers I had nailed across, but soon I was able to carry on alone and he went to help B. with the Herculean task of bailing out a few thousand gallons of water from *Tzu Hang*'s bilges.

I let go all the rigging-screws except the forestays in the hope that the wreckage of the masts and sails would act as a sea anchor and hold us head to sea. For a few seconds she came around into the wind, but then she broke free and fell back with the wind on her beam.

I transferred the warp trailing from aft to the bow and secured the jib to it in the hope it would act as a sea anchor, but there was not enough drag to it and we continued to lie with the seas on our beam.

Just inside the forehatch there were two gallons of fish oil together with the canvas bags it was supposed to be used with. I thought I'd never have a better opportunity to try oil on breaking seas, so I punctured both cans and emptied the lot over the side; there was no time to fill the bags. I felt that even a few minutes respite would help. I also emptied four gallons of engine oil over the side. There was no sign of either on the water and it did not have the slightest effect.

The one thought that gave me hope was that I knew the barometer had started to rise again just before the smash, which indicated that the center of the depression had passed. If we could keep *Tzu Hang* afloat for a few hours we stood a reasonable chance of getting out of this mess.

Miles and B. were bailing out of one of the side skylights.

I covered the other with the red storm-jib, lashing it down as best I could. I could hear B.'s steady call, "Right," as she handed another bucket of water up to Miles who emptied it over the side. I got a bucket and bailed out of the forecabin skylight, my feet spread wide on each bunk as I bailed. At first I could easily reach the water bending down with the bucket, but as we slowly made progress it was necessary to climb down to fill the bucket then step up onto the bunks to empty it out on deck.

By dark we had got most of the water out of *Tzu Hang*. But what a pitiful condition she was in! The bilge was full of wreckage—hundreds of cans of food, most of them now without labels, clothing, broken glass jars, books, coal and eggs, parts of the stove, and miles of B.'s colored wool that had somehow tied everything together in a most infuriating way. B. had been wearing a pair of my sea boots when she went overboard and had kicked them off while in the water. For hours she had stumbled about in the wreckage below with only thick socks on her feet; that night she noticed that one foot was badly sprained.

Miles and I were still vague as to what had happened but B. was able to give us a fairly good idea. She said that she had been steering *Tzu Hang* down wind and had met each of the big following seas stern on, but when she looked over her shoulder again she had a brief glimpse of an enormous wall of water bearing down on *Tzu Hang*. Water appeared to be running down the face of it and she could see no white crests. She could not see how *Tzu Hang* could possibly rise to it but knew that she was dead stern on. There was a feeling of being pressed down into the cockpit, then she was in the water and thinking she had been left behind. She looked around and saw *Tzu Hang* very low in the water and dismasted.

I managed to get one of the Primus stoves working and heated up some soup. Miles had a little, but B. did not want any.

We dozed that night only to be brought wide awake as big seas hit the boat and water trickled below through the cover over the great hole where the doghouse had been. I thought about how to make it pretty watertight if I got the chance. It was an awful night, everything was soaking wet, and now that we were not bailing or covering up the openings, we had time to realise the serious position we were in—a thousand miles from the nearest land, and that was the inhospitable coast of Patagonia, and no hope of a passing ship picking us up.

With the masts and booms gone, there was not much left to make a jury-rig from either. If we got out of this one all right it would have to be on our own efforts and with a good helping of luck. In the morning the sea had gone down quite a bit, but it was still running a good thirty feet high and the wind was about 35 knots. We bailed the rest of the water out of the bilges, then after we'd had a snack of ship's biscuits and cheese, I set about making a better job of the doghouse opening. I nailed the two-inch square bearers from Miles's bunk round the edge of the hole to form a sill so that water running along the deck did not get below quite so easily; the hanging locker door, a piece of cockpit coaming, and some plywood from B.'s secret stash made quite a strong roof. And when the Terylene genoa was folded several times and laid over, then nailed to the deck through battens, surprisingly little water came below.

Miles went below to start the awful job of cleaning out all the mess in the bilges and trying to find the parts for the cabin stove. Pwe, the cat, was in a bad way; she had been soaked and neglected during the time we were bailing and her distressing cries from somewhere way forward had grown weaker as we fought to stay afloat. We did find her later and she recovered from her ordeal. Fortunately, Miles found the missing stove parts, and although the chimney on deck was gone, he and B. were able to coax some wet wood to burn after dousing it with kerosene. Without the chimney the stove smoked badly, and as all the deck openings were now sealed up there was insufficient draft to allow it adequate air. We worked away steadily, Miles sorting out the ruin below, B. getting the galley into working order, and I doing my best to stop any water from getting below. I sealed *Tzu Hang* up tight and the smoke from the stove below swirled across the cabin making our eyes smart. Slowly we made progress. There were no worries about going ashore for a few weeks so we decided to make the boat as comfortable as possible meanwhile.

CHAPTER *11*

Jury-Rig

MILES CAME BELOW a couple of days after the smash and announced that the rudder had gone. I went up to have a look and saw that although the top of the stock was there and still moving, the rudder itself had been torn off and the 2-3/8-inch diameter bronze stock had been snapped off just where it emerged from the trunk.

Three days after the smash I began work making a jury-mast out of two broken booms, one a twin-staysail pole and the other a spare staysail club.

When these two were fished together we had a spar 15-feet 6-inches long. We stepped this spar using jib bridles for shrouds and the old mizzen shrouds for a forestay and backstay. The only sail on the boat that was small enough to use was a raffee that B. had made and which had long been regarded as useless. It now became the best sail we had.

The jury-mast bent badly when we hoisted the tiny sail so we took it down and screwed two splints alongside the mast to strengthen it. When the sail was set again, it did not bend so alarmingly and we noticed to our delight that we were slowly moving along at about two knots. *Tzu Hang* was on the wrong tack, however, she was still headed on a course for Cape Horn and we wanted to go northeast so as to make for a Chilean port. Miles and I struggled with sheets and paddled frantically with the

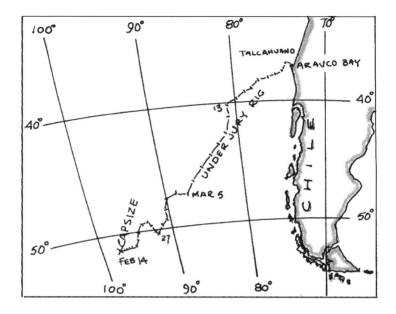

dinghy oars and finally got her round on to the other tack. We returned below feeling pleased that we were at least pointing in the right direction and moving along slowly.

Miles got some sights that day and to my amazement I found that my radio was still working. We checked the chronometer and noticed that its rate had not altered. Miles's sights put us at 51 degrees seventeen minutes south latitude and 98 degrees west longitude, just under a thousand miles due west of the entrance of the Straits of Magellan.

During the night *Tzu Hang* went about on the other tack so we dropped the sail and waited for daylight before trying to get her round again. In the morning we tried just about everything to get her on the other tack, and just got madder and madder. We paddled until our arms ached, we tried towing a drag from the quarter and juggling with the sheets, all to no avail. Miles and I went below, sick at heart, and B. cheered us up by making a cup of tea.

Miles was for trying out some new scheme and I was for making a steering oar.

"Out of what, though?" asked B.

"Well, there is a lot of material here that I could use," I said. "The bulkheads are all tongue-and-groove boards and the door frames are quite solid."

"Well, you make the steering-oar," she decided. After tea I started.

Poor *Tzu Hang*. I removed door frames and any pieces that were not vital to the boat, and after a couple of days work had the most crazy-looking oar imaginable. It was about sixteen feet long and was made up of short lengths all scarfed and screwed together. The blade was a locker door. We took this contraption on deck and screwed it together again. Then I put it over the stern with a rope grommet to hold it in position. Miles set the raffee, and once we were moving, I gradually exerted pressure on the oar. *Tzu Hang* slowly responded, and to our delight gybed over on to the other tack. We hauled the oar aboard and altered the sheets of the raffee before returning below, very smug with ourselves. The only compass we had was a small one by Miles's bunk, the main compass on deck had gone overboard with all the other gear. I saw Miles looking puzzled as he looked at the small compass and went over to have a look. Evidently during the two days I had been making the oar, the wind had changed direction and we had just put *Tzu Hang* on to the wrong tack toward Cape Horn again. We went on deck again and put her about again. Then we saw that we were now heading northeast.

B. had been below all this time, for her foot was in a bad way. Huge blood blisters were breaking out on her skin, and though I urged her to pop them she was wise to leave them alone. B. had been knocked about worse than we thought. The wound on her head had looked most spectacular, though it proved to be just a deep cut, but her shoulder was very painful and Miles and I thought she had broken a collar-bone. She sat by the stove most of the time trying to coax the scraps of teak into flame. The stove smoked horribly, and with everything battened down tight, there was no fresh air below. When Miles and I could stand it no longer, we'd go on deck for a breath of fresh air. When we looked aft, we could see smoke emerging from the rudder trunk. Nothing ever seemed to come out of the chimney.

When we returned below the smoke seemed worse than ever, and it was difficult to see from one side of the boat to the other. The figure of B. crouched by the stove, her long hair unkempt and her face soot-streaked, slowly stirring a steaming pot as the cat sat on her lap, gave the impression of a witch's cellar in a Walt Disney movie.

The days passed quickly and *Tzu Hang* slowly crept northwards out of the "Screaming Fifties" and into the "Roaring Forties." One of the nice things about this kind of sailing was that, with no rudder, no one had to steer and we all slept in at night.

I would go on deck sometimes and watch *Tzu Hang* limping along. It tore at my heart to see her reduced to such a sorry sight, no more the loftiness of her masts or the delicate upward tilt of her bowsprit, instead just a battered hull and scarred deck. But they were honorable scars, and though she was limping she was still proud. I swore that if she brought us to port safely, I'd help heal her wounds so that she'd sail the ocean swell again.

The smoky saloon and forecabin were hives of industry these days. I was making a twenty-foot box-section mast out of the stump of the old mainmast and bulkhead material. Miles was splicing up wire rope for the shrouds of the new mast, and B. was unpicking the new Terylene main-sail so that we could make a lugsail out of it. Meanwhile *Tzu Hang* kept moving along slowly but surely, gradually reducing the distance to Talcahuano, the port we hoped to make in Chile.

Miles was hoping that we might be able to sail to windward, if the need arose, with the aid of the sail that B. was altering. When it was ready and

I had completed the gaff, we took the new mast on deck and screwed it together, and then stepped it next to the small one. The little mast we set up aft as a mizzen.

We decided to try the new rig right away and hoisted the Terylene sail and its gaff. It looked as though we needed some-thing set for a mizzen, so we set a tiny jib-topsail as a mizzen with a dinghy oar as a boom. *Tzu Hang* immediately started to come up into the wind but I was watching the mast when it suddenly broke in half and collapsed.

I went below and Miles passed me the two pieces and I began repairing it. Next day it was stepped again and had two extra

Jury-rigging a main and mizzen   pieces fastened halfway up to stiffen it. We decided to leave the big sail until the wind fell lighter. Meanwhile we had quite a bit of sail up considering what we had before with the little mast. The jib I had used as a sea anchor had split across the center. This was now set upside down as a mainsail, with the raffee as a kind of balloon-jib. The tiny mizzen helped make us point a little higher.

We had done just about half the distance to Talcahuano under the tiny raffee alone and with the extra sail set we seemed to be moving along very well. *Tzu Hang* was knocking out some wonderful runs considering the rags she had up and the fact that she was steering herself without a rudder. Our best day's run on the log was 77 miles in 24 hours. There were other days when the total was over seventy, and we really felt we were coming along very well. The ocean current was giving us another 10 miles a day, too.

About two weeks after the smash, B. came on deck for the first time since she had bailed below amidst all the ruin. She had acquired quite a tan from the cabin stove, and though I had seen her looking better, it was encouraging to see her on deck and getting about again. The cockpit drains had become plugged with pieces of coke and Miles and I tried to unblock them using bits of wire. It took B.'s persistence finally to clear them and let the water drain back into the sea instead of slopping about in the cockpit.

As we crept farther north the weather became warmer, and the sea seemed almost calm after two and a half months of the Roaring Forties. The wind had swung more to the south and we realised that we were coming into the influence of the South Pacific High. All our charts had been lost in the crash except a National Geographic Magazine map of the Pacific which was printed on cloth, and a chart of the South Atlantic which showed just a little bit of the Chilean coast where we were heading. Miles was drawing a map using the little information from them and consulting the Pilot Book. From the look of it, Talcahuano was no good for a landfall as we would have to beat our way into the bay. The best place to head for was the little port of Coronel, some 40 miles south of Talcahuano. It was easy to enter and we could perhaps arrange a tow once we got there.

We had plenty of food aboard, but there were a few items that we missed. Sugar was one of them. The sugar sack had been kept in a bin which formed the seat by my quarter berth. It was quite a large bin and as the sack of sugar took only half the space, there were a few other things stowed with it. B. had a pair of climbing boots there and I kept my photographs and magazines there too.

B. gave Miles and me a surprise one day by producing some fudge she had made while the two of us were on deck.

"Why that's wonderful, B." exclaimed Miles. "May I have another piece?"

"Yes, there's plenty more. Help yourself," said B.

Now when B. gave away precious stuff like fudge generously, I became a little suspicious.

"Where did you get the sugar from, B." I asked, quite innocently.

"Oh, I found some," she answered. "Here, have another piece."

Then suddenly I knew what she'd done. I went aft and lifted the lid of the sugar bin; it was half full of thick brown treacle, and submerged in it was the sugar sack, the remains of my magazines and photos and B.'s climbing-boots.

"You surely didn't use that?" I said unnecessarily, for I knew she had. "Why, your climbing boots are floating around in it."

"So what?" she said, quite unperturbed. "They're quite clean, and you said you liked the fudge, didn't you."

There was a wonderful feeling of comradeship between the three of us. We all realised that without the other two we would never have survived; though we all wanted to get into Coronel, I think we also realised that we would never be this close again.

Thirty-four days after the smash, B. sighted the top of Mocha Island early in the morning. We began to realise that the long journey was almost over.

As we went farther up the coast, we encountered thick fog. This was nerve-racking as we knew that it took us nearly a quarter of a mile to get *Tzu Hang* from one tack on to the other. If land loomed up suddenly out of the fog we might lose the ship.

Three days later the fog was just as thick but Miles had been able to get sights farther offshore where the fog was patchy, so he was reasonably sure of his position. We went on steadily through the fog, and we took turns at the bow peering through the whiteness. Then suddenly we emerged into sunshine and left the blanket of fog behind. Miles had got us right on course and the little town of Coronel was dead ahead.

All that day we crept toward it, *Tzu Hang* still steering herself. The sun was low in the sky when we anchored near the wharf, 87 days from Melbourne, having brought our crippled ship into port by our own efforts.

Three days later *Tzu Hang* was towed to the Chilean Naval Base at

Talcahuano where she was lifted out of the water by a gigantic floating crane and set down on the ground near the sea wall where we hoped to repair her.

Of the months of hard work, the frustration, and the many friends we made, I can do no better than recommend that you read Miles Smeeton's book *Once is Enough*. He has described far better than I ever could the voyage and the repairs in Chile, as well as *Tzu Hang*'s subsequent voyage. Technically, there was not very much wrong with *Tzu Hang*. The hull was as sound as the day she was launched in Hong Kong. The new doghouse and skylights presented no difficulty to me to make. But good materials in Chile were very hard to come by. The local wood, lingue, would have been quite good had it been properly seasoned, but it was discouraging to see it opening up and twisting once it was fastened into position. The masts and spars had to be made out of material that would not have been used as scaffold boards in Canada, but we put the best we could get into her and made everything as strong as possible.

I could not leave *Trekka* in New Zealand for too long. I had been away a year already and if I stayed with *Tzu Hang* it would be at least another year before I could return to Russell. Miles and B. said they hoped to leave

for England some time in December via Panama. I hoped to be fitting *Trekka* out by then as I wanted to cross the Tasman to Australia before the southern summer ended.

The last few days I spent in Chile were active ones. Although most of the big jobs had been completed, there were endless little ones, and I tried to show Miles and B. what had to be done and explain the drawings I had made of the masts and spars and other details.

It was a wonderful experience to know them both; they were courageous people, steadfast in their friendship and with a set of

Tzu Hang's jury rudder

values that provided a fine example for a young man. They had in fact become surrogate parents, yet always treated me as an equal human being, showing understanding and accepting my quirks of character. Like good parents they taught without being overbearing or dominant and would hear the other person's point of view without being judgemental. Our paths were to cross several times in the future, and on each occasion I felt privileged to know them. Certainly the time I spent with them aboard *Tzu Hang* was largely responsible for the successful conclusion of *Trekka*'s circumnavigation.

CHAPTER *12*

Return to Trekka

FROM CHILE, I flew to South Africa to visit my mother, who was living in Pietermaritzburg, Natal. It was not an easy route by air and involved taking a small plane to Santiago, from there over the Andes to Buenos Aires in a DC3, changing there to fly up to Rio de Janeiro for the South Atlantic crossing to Dakar. Here it was discovered that I lacked an inoculation certificate to enter South Africa and had to visit a hospital for the necessary shot. When you consider the dangers of transmitting diseases through the use of contaminated needles, I was probably extremely lucky not to contact some dreadful disorder as a whole line of people were injected with the same needle, with me being the only Caucasian there.

From Dakar we flew to Brazzaville in the Belgian Congo to refuel; there we had some excitement on takeoff when an engine quit and we had to circle the jungle dumping fuel before landing for another attempt. I finally arrived in Johannesburg where the authorities insisted I stay for several days as they were upset at my recent inoculation certificate from Dakar, but finally I caught a train and arrived in Pietermaritzburg to find my rather frail, aging mother waiting for me. She had decided in my absence that she could no longer accept a life in that country under a system where the majority of the population were denied basic human rights, and she told me that she wanted to return to Jersey where she still had friends. I could see that she was not in good health, and because of her condition, it was obvious that she could not travel alone. I would have to take her there. She had already sold the house, but there was all the furniture and household effects to dispose of plus organizing the necessary paperwork, passport, income-tax clearance and all the nonsense that goes with modern travel. Two weeks later we were on a Union Castle ship bound for England, and not long after back in Jersey again.

My mother's health had deteriorated while I had been away and she needed to have constant attention. This was something I was able to arrange in Jersey, and I felt a little easier that many of her old friends were still living on the island. Toward the end of October, I boarded a ship in London bound for Sydney, for it had been impossible to obtain passage to New Zealand. I watched the daily positions marked on the chart in great 500-mile jumps and remembered the days on *Tzu Hang* when we thought we had done well doing seventy.

I disembarked the ship in Sydney and left the same day for Auckland aboard another one, the S.S. *Wanganella*. Three days later I stepped ashore in New Zealand again. It had been a long way back.

I spent a few days in Auckland shopping around for the various materials needed for *Trekka*'s refit. Over the past few months I had spent many pleasant hours dreaming of the alterations and modifications I wanted to

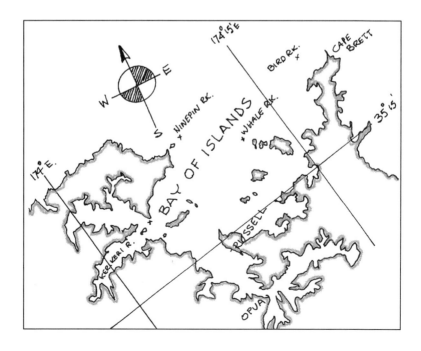

make to the boat. I knew exactly what was required so my shopping was relatively easy.

While my plans for the future had been uncertain when I left New Zealand in *Tzu Hang*, I now returned with the unshakable determination to take *Trekka* on around the world. This certainly had never been my intention when I first left Canada as my experience was so limited and the concept seemed beyond the capabilities of myself and the boat. Now, however, the idea seemed reasonable enough; although I knew it wouldn't be easy, I felt it was possible.

Loaded with gear I caught a train north to Opua in the Bay of Islands and boarded a ferry at Paihia for the ten-minute crossing to Russell. A wonderful feeling of peace swept over me when we arrived at Russell and I immediately recognized several friends on the wharf. A little farther on I saw *Trekka*'s keel lying in the sand, looking a little rusty perhaps, but still a comforting sight.

Then a few minutes later I met Francis and Mille Arlidge again, and these two really made me feel that I had come home.

"Go on, John," said Mille. "I know you won't be satisfied until you've seen *Trekka* again."

And they both laughed when they realised how true to the mark they were. I walked across the garden to the big shed and opened the door quietly. I am not ashamed to admit that my eyes were wet as I viewed the sweet little hull sitting in her cradle where she had waited patiently for my return. Sixteen months had passed since I last saw her.

Francis and Mille insisted that I should stay with them, and though I was afraid of being in the way, for they had a family of six children, I gladly accepted their kind invitation knowing that there was no one I would rather stay with than these two.

The same day I arrived back in Russell, work began on *Trekka*.

Christmas was only three weeks away, and there was much work for me to do before we could leave for Australia. Unfortunately my tools and other gear I had used on *Tzu Hang* had not arrived yet in New Zealand. This gear had been packed in a large crate and dispatched shortly after I left Chile, but it had gone astray somewhere. Francis came to my rescue, loaning me some of his tools, and other friends in Russell lent me others. Several weeks later the crate of tools arrived, apparently delayed in Valparaiso for weeks until a ship sailing to New Zealand was available.

The main job I had decided to do on *Trekka* was to make the hull completely watertight by fiberglassing it. This was something I had regretted not doing when she was being built, but now I had a splendid

Sanding the newly fiberglassed hull in Russell

opportunity to do so as she was bone-dry from being in the shed so long. Before glassing the hull though, I removed the oak garboard planks and replaced them with mahogany ones which I felt would hold the glass resin better.

These were carefully fitted, glued, and fastened into place without the use of steam. With two machine sanders, one a disc and the other an orbital one, I cut all the paint off the hull and prepared it for the fiberglass cloth. Then when all was ready, the hull was tipped up to an angle of about forty-five degrees and the glass resin and cloth applied. One side was completed before doing the opposite side. Because there was quite a waiting period for the resin to harden, I got busy with some of the other jobs, making new cockpit coamings, widening the seating on deck, painting the interior of the boat, and installing some new laminated knees in the way of the chainplates to replace the old steam-bent ones.

I then turned my attention to building a small dinghy which could be stowed upside down over the doghouse. I had always thought that *Trekka* was too small to carry a dinghy, but after taking a few measurements with the steel tape, I saw it was possible to have a very small one providing it was made so that the transom was removable, otherwise I could not possibly get down the hatchway. The voyage down from Canada had shown me how inconvenient it was without a dinghy and I knew it would be used a great deal up the Great Barrier Reef if I ever got that far.

The dinghy turned out quite well even though it was small, measuring only 5 feet 6 inches long. It was made of fiberglassed 1/8" plywood and looked like a regular yacht dinghy, yet it would carry me easily. Providing the passenger was not too heavy or the sea too rough, it would just carry two if nobody coughed.

With *Trekka* all fiberglassed, she was skidded out of the shed into the summer sunshine where I could see what I was doing. The fiberglass was sanded smooth with the orbital sander and any holes filled with resin. Then the hull was painted with undercoat before finishing off with a light blue marine enamel.

Instead of using the original rudder which was of steel and had rusted badly, I built a new one of mahogany. This had more balance to it and was a lot lighter.

I went down to the wharf one morning with a friend and dug the keel out of the sand where it had been while I was away. Although it was quite rusty, some hard work had it looking more like its former self, and it was generously painted with a rust-preventive paint.

The masts and spars were brought down from the rack in the shed and were rubbed down and varnished several times. Then, toward the end of March, 1958, *Trekka* was launched off the beach after the fin-keel had been bolted back on again.

When the masts were stepped and the rigging set up, I knew that the

Refitting *Trekka*

little boat had never looked better and the past four months work had been worth it.

While in Chile helping repair *Tzu Hang*, I had ordered a new suit of sails for *Trekka* from England. They were made of Terylene and were now being held at Customs in Auckland, together with a short-wave transistor radio from the U.S.A. which was replacing the one I had taken away on *Tzu Hang*.

I decided to collect these items just before leaving for Australia so that there would be no duty to pay on them.

Most of the work on *Trekka* had been completed, and what was left could be done more easily from a dock or at least somewhere it was sheltered. I knew just the place, Whangarei, the small town halfway to Auckland that I had visited briefly when I was here waiting for *Tzu Hang* to arrive from Tonga. The town was some sixty miles down the coast and was a popular stop for overseas visiting yachts as the moorings in the yacht basin were well protected and close to the main shopping center. Most supplies could be obtained there; if not, it was only about four hours from Auckland by either rail or road.

One afternoon toward the end of March I left Russell to sail down to Whangarei, but decided to call at Motu Arohia Island on the way. This lovely little island was owned by Colonel Bill Browne and his wife Myra, who had the place to themselves except when stray visitors like myself suddenly arrived. I had met them two years before with the Smeetons and had spent many enjoyable weekends with them, leaving *Trekka* anchored off the crescent-shaped beach in company with *Tzu Hang* and Bill's little sloop, *Truelove*, a fine little vessel that had been built in England and shipped out to New Zealand.

Bill and Myra must have met more ocean-going yachtsmen than anyone else in the country; for most yachts visiting New Zealand, the Bay of Islands is the first port of call. Motu Arohia is one of the prettiest islands in the Bay and affords good anchorage so that the two of them seldom lacked company.

I had always enjoyed being with these two interesting people who had lived in various parts of the world during Bill's military career. He was a surveyor and, for his own satisfaction, was engaged in producing a chart of the coast which showed considerably more detail than the existing Admiralty chart of the area. The chart he was making was a beautiful piece of work and his professional training was evident. He had used his boat, which was equipped with an echo-sounder, to accurately obtain soundings of the area and in the course of doing this had discovered a reef of rocks missing on the official Admiralty chart. He was obviously fascinated with the subject and had collected many early maps and charts of the country. One of the most interesting to me was a chart of New Zealand which had been compiled by Captain Cook when he surveyed the coast of the entire country in 1769. It was astonishingly accurate, and I learned from Bill that Cook had anchored the *Endeavour* off the same beach where *Trekka* and *Tzu Hang* had anchored so often.

When I rounded the point and approached the beach, I saw *Truelove* on her mooring as she had been two years before, but instead of *Tzu Hang* being there, a large blue ketch from England named *Havfruen III* was in her place. When I went ashore, I met the owners, "Batch" Carr and his wife Ann, and I learned that they were on a round-the-world voyage accompanied by a crew of two, a young New Zealander and a West Indian. *Havfruen* was a huge boat compared with *Trekka*, 70 tons against one and one-half, yet it was interesting to compare the two. I was quite awed at the size of her gear, the enormous blocks and the cordage, yet here were two yachts both doing the same job, carrying their crews safely across the seas, though so different in appearance. She was a very comfortable vessel and beautifully maintained. I was to meet her again many times during the next few months as *Trekka* followed in her wake for thousands of miles before we finally went our separate ways at Barbados in the West Indies.

The following morning *Havfruen* left for Sydney, and I got sail up for the run down to Whangarei. There was little wind, and the two yachts were in sight of each other for quite a while before *Havfruen* passed the Ninepin Rock and disappeared from view. In the middle of the afternoon *Trekka* rounded Cape Brett, passing inside Piercy Island, and I noticed the curious cave through it. There were a few swordfish boats patrolling near by and one of them came close alongside. She was Francis Arlidge's *Alma G*, one of the most successful boats at Russell and certainly the best kept. With her pink cabintop, she was very distinctive, and it was difficult to realise that she was getting on for forty years of age.

The wind fell away and the next couple of days were spent slowly drifting down the coast in brilliant sunshine and a nearly full moon at night. It was wonderful to be cruising again after the months of repairs, first on *Tzu Hang* and then *Trekka*.

I spent a day in the little natural harbour of Tutukaka, one of the loveliest anchorages *Trekka* ever visited. It was a quiet, peaceful place with just a couple of farmhouses backed by the green rolling hills on which sheep graze contentedly. I walked up over a hill to see what the scene looked like from the top. *Trekka* looked very pretty anchored in the bay, and I felt that this would be the kind of place it would be great to settle down in someday.

There was a good strong breeze when I left the following day for Whangarei and I had a few hectic minutes changing the genoa for the staysail, but finally the sail was bagged and bundled into the aft locker. Working on the foredeck seemed quite dangerous as the lifeline stanchions were not yet fastened in place; this was another job that had to be done before I could leave for Australia.

The weather deteriorated rapidly and by the time we came up to Bream Point it was blowing quite hard and pouring with rain. Williwaws swept down off the high land with surprising force, blowing sheets of water into the air. *Trekka* was knocked down with one of these before I hurriedly downed the mainsail and proceeded under staysail only. Once inside the Heads, the wind rapidly eased off and I was able to find a sheltered anchorage for the night.

By next morning the sky was clear and I followed a rather large ketch that was motoring up the dredged channel to Whangarei. Later on when I arrived there she was moored close by and I learned that her name was *Arthur Rodgers*. She was an old Brixham trawler and her owners, Tom and Diana Hepworth, had sailed her out from England just after the war. She was now engaged in carrying copra and general freight from island to island, but she clearly had seen better days.

I was becoming anxious at the way the time was slipping by. There seemed to be no end to all the work, and I knew that if we did not get away soon the Tasman Sea crossing was going to be a miserable business. The best time to leave New Zealand was February-March and here it was April. The next few days at Whangarei were very busy ones for me and I finally completed the remaining jobs. All that I had to do now was to collect the new sails and radio in Auckland and put stores aboard for the passage to Australia. On April 8th I left the yacht basin at Whangarei and sailed down the coast toward Auckland, stopping for the night at Kawau, one of the favorite haunts of Auckland "yachties." I promised myself that someday I would come back and enjoy this part of New Zealand when I was not in such a hurry. This part of the world is known as a yachtsman's paradise and it's easy to see why. There are dozens of islands and anchorages, calm water, and usually plenty of wind. Yachting is a very popular sport, and yet it is by no means a rich man's pastime. There are all kinds of boats, both power and sail, but there seem to be far more sailing craft—ranging from dinghies to ocean

Tutukaka—"... one of the loveliest anchorages *Trekka* ever visited."

racing yachts—than powercraft. It appeared to me that a very large pro-
portion of the boats here had been built by their owners; perhaps this is
the reason why people from all walks of life enjoy the activity.

When *Trekka* arrived in Auckland, there was no convenient moorage
close to the city center as with Whangarei, so I went to the marina at
Westhaven close by the newly-constructed Harbour Bridge. For the
shopping I needed to do, this was an inconvenient location as I was without wheels so I contacted the Harbourmaster who kindly allowed me to
moor *Trekka* in the lighter basin inside the Western Viaduct. Although it
was not very clean there, it was well sheltered and within easy walking
distance of the main shopping area.

Shortly after moving *Trekka* to her new berth, I began hustling about
the city collecting stores and the last of the gear I would need for the
Tasman crossing; oilskins and sea boots, plastic bottles to keep fresh water
in, and the new sails and radio from the Customs. The five days spent in
Auckland were one constant rush, and toward the finish I gave up trying
to stow the gear away tidily as each shopping trip brought more and more
packages to be stowed away somewhere when there was more time.

On the morning of 16 April, *Trekka* went down the harbour on the ebb
tide with clearance papers for Sydney aboard. I thought it would be
much easier to go somewhere quiet to stow all the gear away for going to
sea but perhaps it was only an excuse to visit Russell just once more.

With a fine blustery southwest breeze to send us along, *Trekka* reeled off the miles in grand style, and late the following day we were back in the Bay of Islands again.

A full day was spent stowing everything away carefully in the lockers and under the canvas bunks. The water bottles were topped up, and with fresh vegetables and bread aboard, everything was finally ready for an organized departure. It seemed incredible that the only thing to do now was leave; the past five months had been very busy and yet it was difficult to see where the time had gone.

I went ashore for the last time to say goodbye to all the wonderful people I had met in Russell. Hardest of all to leave were Francis and Mille Arlidge who had looked after me as one of their own sons, never complaining or asking for anything in return. I have met no finer people than these two, and we were all teary-eyed when the time came to part. I rowed the dinghy back to *Trekka* feeling very sad at leaving them and this little place which had so many happy memories for me. The anchor came up from the bottom caked with mud as though it too were reluctant to leave this spot, then *Trekka* gathered way and the figures on the beach waved a final farewell as we rounded the point and Russell disappeared from view.

CHAPTER *13*

The Tasman Crossing

T HE WIND WAS out of the northwest which meant that it would be a head wind after leaving the Bay. There was little point in starting off having to tack up the coast, so I went in to Motu Arohia Island to see if Bill and Myra Browne were at home. Their yacht *Truelove* was not on her mooring and I realised that they must be visiting friends. I anchored near the house and hoped they would return before I left.

Although I had done a lot of work on *Trekka* during the last five months, one job had eluded me. This was painting the bottom with anti-fouling paint. There was no danger of worms getting into her planking because they could not penetrate the fiberglass, but I was concerned about weeds and growth, for this will grow quickly on anything that is not painted with the poisonous paint. The weather always seemed to be wrong when the tides were right and vice versa, so it had not been possible to put her alongside the Russell wharf to apply the coating when the tide was out. The bottom was still clean though, so I hoped for a fairly quick passage to Sydney where the job could be done on the slipway at the Cruising Yacht Club.

Truelove returned that afternoon and I went ashore with the Brownes and had one of Myra's delightful teas. It seemed that only the previous weekend Miles, B. and Clio had sat about the same table discussing *Tzu*

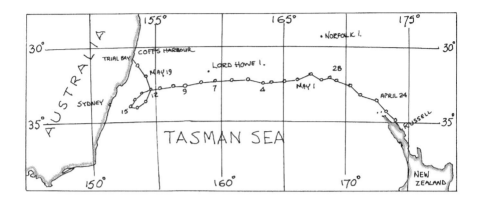

Hang's passage to Sydney. Now here I was again about to leave in *Trekka*.

In the morning the wind had swung round to the southwest, which was fine for going up the coast, so I bade Bill and Myra farewell, leaving them standing in front of the whitewashed walls of their lovely little home, bathed in the warm morning sunshine, an unforgettable picture and two unforgettable people.

Trekka slipped along over the calm water and presently the little house was obscured by the point. The Ninepin Rock at the entrance to the Bay of Islands came into view, and I altered course for it. Looking at the green hills and the timbered islands that morning, I realised how much I had come to love this country of New Zealand. In some ways it could be considered backward yet perhaps that was one of its attractions. The pace of life was slower than in any other place I had known, and people did not seem to be concerned about making a mint of money; they seemed to enjoy life more and found more time for leisure activities. I was not conscious of anyone trying to keep up with the Joneses because somehow there didn't appear to be any Joneses. No people could be more hospitable, and sometimes their generosity was almost embarrassing. The climate in the North Island above Auckland is almost tropical in the summer months, and though the winters may be wet, they are not cold.

Toward the end of the afternoon we passed inside the Cavalli Islands, and as darkness fell Stephenson Island was abeam. I went below to start peeling potatoes and to prepare something to eat. *Trekka* was steering herself perfectly with the new self-steering gear I had made for her. This was quite a simple arrangement and the idea was really stolen from model yachts. The tiller arrangement on *Trekka* was a little complicated because the rudder-stock is aft of the mizzen-mast and the tiller forward. It is linked to the rudder-stock through two short cables with the mizzen-mast in between. I had made up a fitting for the tiller, which had an arc on the aft side of it, on which it was possible to clamp a slide in a variety of positions. One end of the mainsheet fastened to this slide and it was possible to set it in a position so that the helm was perfectly balanced. This arrangement, sometimes known as the Braine self-steering system, was to prove a most useful addition and saved me many countless hours of sitting at the helm, for though it would not steer on all points of sailing it worked perfectly when the wind was forward of the beam.

I was unable to get any sleep that night as we were so close to the coast, but at least I was able to rest in one of the bunks after having a glance out on deck periodically.

By noon the next day we had passed North Cape and were approaching the Three Kings Islands—the lonely sentinels which lie some thirty miles northwest of Cape Maria van Diemen. These uninhabited islands are the scene of many shipwrecks, for they can be quite dangerous to approach owing to the strong tidal currents around them. I steered well to the east of them but passed through heavy ripplings in the water and was well pleased when we had left them astern.

Sydney was now 1,100 miles due west of us and dead to windward. Had I left New Zealand toward the end of February, I would have stood a reasonable chance of carrying a fair wind much of the way across, but now, at the end of April, I could only hope for westerly winds that were not too strong. It had taken twenty-three days to get across in *Tzu Hang* and we'd had our share of bad weather then. The Tasman Sea has quite a reputation for these conditions and I knew that I was going to be very pleased when *Trekka* reached the other side.

We carried on close-hauled on the port tack, as there was a better chance of favorable winds farther north, and even if we didn't find them, it would at least be a little warmer. With *Trekka* going to windward there was no need for me to steer, which meant I could catch up on sleep and stay warm and dry below. I spent much time reading in my bunk, the most comfortable place, for I had not yet found my sea-legs and food was still unattractive. Not for long, however, and a couple of days later I developed a ravenous appetite which threatened to empty the boat of all the stores.

A few days went by with *Trekka* still doggedly working her way to windward, then the weather worsened and I knew from the way the barometer was tumbling down that a gale was on the way. I went through the procedure of rolling a deep reef in the mainsail and then rolling down more just a half-hour later, after which it was not too long before just the staysail and mizzen were too much sail area and we were reduced to riding the swells under bare poles, with only a solitary albatross for company. I stood in the hatchway watching him soar above a crest and then glide down the lonely valleys, the perfection of flight as performed by the king of all birds. I have watched them for hours, endlessly wheeling and banking, sometimes with a wingtip just brushing the surface of the water, then doing a half-roll to disappear behind the ridge of the next swell. What do these remarkable birds feed on? I have never seen them eat anything apart from scraps thrown overboard from some passing vessel. They are big birds, with a body as large as a goose, and must require plenty of food, yet they never seem to feed off sea life as other ocean birds do. No bird except the southern albatross can make flying look so easy, such fun or such a beautiful thing, and if the Good Lord allows me to come back to earth in the guise of some animal, I shall ask to return as an albatross and let my spirit roam the reaches of the Southern Ocean.

The wind whined in the rigging, that depressing mournful note that always seems to accompany the low driving clouds that hurry their way across the grey murk as though fleeing for shelter. This is a time when you need patience and confidence in your boat, for there is little you can do except wait for a return of calmer conditions. At least this was not like a gale in the Roaring Forties, there I really would have something to worry about, for loyal as I am to *Trekka*, I don't think she could survive a real gale down there.

When the conditions had moderated enough, I got sail up again and *Trekka* continued working her way to the westward. Sometimes the wind went round to the southwest and we could just about lay the course for Sydney, but the track on the chart showed how we were being forced to the northward.

On the tenth day out, the wind freed for the first time and I had the masthead genoa up for a few hours before the wind finally backed to east and I joyously set the twin-staysails. *Trekka* surged along quietly and I stood in the hatchway watching the tiller kick over by itself every so often. With nearly a full moon overhead, I was reluctant to go to sleep now that the weather had at last given us a break. I made a cup of hot chocolate and sat reflecting that this was the kind of sailing many people dream about and knew just how lucky I was to be there.

The weather did in fact remain fine for a couple of days, although the wind became very light and the day's runs suffered badly. All too soon, though, the westerly winds were back again and *Trekka* was bucketing along over a lumpy sea. At least I was not feeling seasick as I had been over this stretch in *Tzu Hang*. The motion on a small boat at sea can be something wicked. If you were to go through the same motion in a room, you'd be rising to the height of the ceiling every few seconds and jerked back from one wall to the other as well. Yet after a time you hardly notice it. I have found myself using this motion to advantage sometimes, waiting for the right moment before climbing into a bunk or for the gimballed stove to swing over before I put the kettle on top. At the same time it was easy to be fooled, too. I'd get so used to the movement that I'd forget about it and open a locker door only to be showered with the butter, jam and condensed milk.

The big bread knife I bought in Auckland attempted to stab me a couple of times before I found a place to stow it where its humor was less likely to cause me bodily harm. This constant motion must also provide good exercise, for I never arrived in port suffering from the somewhat confined space, no matter how long the passage. The addition of the dinghy over the doghouse had provided me with another wonderful source of exercise, for whenever I climbed through the hatch I had to bring one knee up until it touched my chest, otherwise it was quite impossible to get out. When I could do this wearing oilskins and sea boots, I felt I had reached Olympic standards.

Time to read at last

The next three days saw very unsettled conditions over this central part of the Tasman. The wind blew hard for an hour or so only to fall away to nothing while the barometer shot up and down in a most confusing manner. I was kept on the move changing sail until I grew so exasperated that I pulled everything down in a sullen rage and went below to wait for the weather to make up its mind what it was going to do.

On 7 May we were only 60 miles from Ball's Pyramid and a gentle breeze from the northeast sent us along steadily right on course for Sydney. I had been noticing an odd smell below the last couple of days and decided to investigate. It was not long before the cause was found! Half-a-dozen eggs had been cracked underneath my bunk.

At nine o'clock in the morning of 9 May I was still in my warm bunk wondering if it was worthwhile getting up to face the day. *Trekka* had been going along closehauled and I had glanced at the spare compass at the side of my bunk at odd hours during the night to make sure she was still on course. Thoughts of breakfast eventually moved me and I stood up in the hatchway to have a stretch . . . there just a few yards away was the towering bow of a freighter. I scrambled out on deck and grabbed the tiller, my knees turned to water and my heart thumping madly. She slid past to leeward and I looked up at her bridge to see several pairs of binoculars examining my somewhat scanty attire. Someone raised a hand in a salute vaguely similar to the V sign Winston Churchill made so famous during the war, though I was doubtful if the gesture was meant to have the same significance. I waved rather shakily and watched as each of the binoculars waved a hand in reply. When the stern rumbled past with the blades of the propeller clearly visible, I read her name, *Kaitoa* from Wellington, probably bound for Newcastle as she was well north of the Sydney track.

The wind was slowly backing to the east, and as soon as it was possible to use them I set the twins and retired below to make pancakes which had suddenly caught my fancy. Something went wrong with the recipe, or I must have left out some vital ingredient, for it was quite impossible to flip them; indeed the only possible way to remove them from the pan was with the paint scraper. Still smarting from my failure I decided to make a chocolate cake in the pressure-cooker. Now I've made many cakes in the cooker when living ashore and they were very good, satisfying is perhaps a better word, but somehow my efforts at sea have been somewhat disappointing. They always look a bit seasick and usually have a hollow in the center; this can sometimes be filled up with custard and then the cake becomes chocolate pudding. Some of my other recipes can be altered at short notice like this, and I have found that this can be very useful especially when entertaining visitors.

13 May was the twenty-second day out and we were only ninety miles from Sydney and about sixty from the nearest land. I was quite sure that another day would see us moored snugly in Rushcutter's Bay, but then the wind fell away until we were becalmed on a strangely still sea. The following day there was still no wind, but when I worked out our position from sun-sights, I realised that we had been set south nearly sixty miles by the strong current which flows down the east coast of Australia.

When the wind came back it was very light from the northeast and we were able to steer the course for Sydney, but although we made sixty miles on the log in the next twenty-four hours, sights showed that we had in fact been set even farther south. I was in a quandary what to do. If we went on like this we might get set a long way south, even as far as Gabo Island, and I knew that the current was likely to be strong all the way in to the coast. One Australian yachtsman took his boat outside Sydney Heads for an afternoon's sailing when the current was running hard, and it took him thirteen days to get back inside again. He was a hungry man by the time he returned, for the boat only had the usual weekend supplies aboard.

All my charts of the Australian coastline were north of Sydney, and it

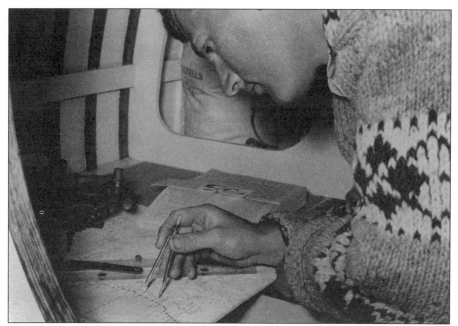

Planning the route along the east coast of Australia

was this that decided me to sail off to the eastward back the way we had come before going north and having another attempt at approaching Sydney from the northeast.

It took a couple of hard days sailing to get north again, but on the 18th we were in just about the same position as we had been on the 12th. Then, to cap the lot, the wind went round to the southwest, a dead muzzler. It seemed that I was not meant to go to Sydney. I went below to look at the charts. "To hell with it," I decided, "I'll go north to Coff's Harbour." So I went up on deck and altered course. With the wind now on the quarter, *Trekka* began putting away the miles and I felt happier to be heading for a definite destination rather than beating about all over the place. Just after noon on 20 May I sighted land which turned out to be Smoky Cape about thirty-five miles south of Coff's Harbour. But the wind became light and we were still bucking a strong current, so it was not until the following afternoon that we came up to the cape and I put the outboard motor over the stern and motored into Trial Bay where I anchored near a rock breakwater. There were some rather grim-looking stone buildings behind a breakwater, and I later learned that these had been a prison in years gone by.

The next morning, after a wonderful night's sleep, I hove the anchor up and set the spinnaker for the run up the coast to Coff's Harbour, but we had no sooner left the bay when the spinnaker collapsed through lack of wind. The morning sun climbed into a cloudless hazy sky, the beach shimmering with heat. There was not a breath of air and the only sound to break the silence was the drone of a fly that was listlessly examining my right knee. It was the start of a typical Australian summer's day. I was surprised at the heat for the time of the year and had to go below and rummage through one of the lockers to find the sun awning without which it was quite uncomfortable on deck. There was only a gallon of fuel left for the outboard, which would do about ten miles, so I anchored instead in fifteen fathoms to wait for a breeze.

It was during this calm period that I put a face mask on and looked over the stern to examine *Trekka's* bottom. For the past few days she had seemed somewhat sluggish and now I saw why, for the entire bottom had become a marine garden. Long streamers of weed and barnacles covered the fiberglass sheathing and steel fin and I knew that this was one job I'd have to see about once we got in to port.

It seems ridiculous but it took five days to sail and drift the thirty miles to Coff's Harbour, hours went by without a breath of wind. Then a few puffs would goad me into hanging every available stitch of sail up and another couple of hundred yards would be won before the anchor was put to use again the prevent the current from robbing us of our hard-won gains.

On the morning of 26 May, thirty-five days after we had left the Bay of Islands, a breeze came along which finally allowed us to cover the remaining miles and *Trekka* entered the harbour at Coff's where I secured to a mooring buoy and launched the dinghy to go ashore and see the Harbourmaster.

A short time later I was speaking to Captain Merritt, a stocky jovial man who was the Harbourmaster, Customs and Immigration Officer, as well as being the Pilot of the port. He went around to various cabinets and cupboards in his office collecting a whole sheaf of forms for me to fill in. "I don't know what the hell you need to be filling all these in for," he remarked goodnaturedly, "but I have to treat you the same as a big ship. I guess it will keep someone in Sydney busy." Between the two of us we completed the forms, and as he stamped them he told me that the stamp had the British Coat of Arms on it and was the oldest one in use by the Australian Customs.

I mentioned the marine growth on *Trekka*'s bottom and asked if there was a slipway which could handle her here instead of waiting until I got to Brisbane.

"We can pull her out with one of the cranes on the wharf," he assured me. "We've got wire slings so you need not worry, we won't drop her. All the fishing boats here are done the same way whenever their skippers want to paint them. The charge is the same for everyone. To be hauled out and put back in again will cost you eighteen shillings and sixpence. You'd better go have a word with the crane driver and tell him when you want to haul out."

I walked back down the wharf and met the crane operator who showed me the wire slings lying beside a fishboat out for an overhaul. I arranged with him to haul out on the Friday afternoon so that *Trekka* could remain in the slings over the weekend without me having to block her up. So that the wire slings would not scar *Trekka*'s paintwork, I wrapped some sacks around them which were seized on with marline. On the Friday afternoon, when *Trekka* was lifted gently out of the water and set down on the wharf, the paint on her topsides was intact.

It was easy to see why progress had been so slow the last couple of weeks, for the whole bottom was completely covered with goose barnacles, long grey, watery stalks with a small grey-and-yellow shell at the end. Some of these stalks were over four inches long and they caused much interest amongst the local fishermen who said they had never seen the likes of them before. However, I was in no mood to exhibit them on *Trekka*'s hull and in an hour or so had scraped the lot off and washed the bottom down with fresh water.

Over the weekend I painted the bottom, first with zinc chromate and then with anti-fouling paint, so that by Monday morning when the crane driver returned to work he found *Trekka* all ready to go back into the water. This operation was completed without incident, and I went along to the Harbourmaster's office where I paid the eighteen shillings and sixpence fee, sure that it was a very long time since I'd had such good value for my money.

I bought a Sydney paper one morning and read with astonishment that on my arrival at Coff's Harbour I had been "mobbed" by teenage girls. I was described as a "blond Viking" and I could not believe my eyes as I read the rest of it. Australia is such a wonderful country and there are so many really fine people there that I cannot understand how the press, with a few exceptions, can be so incredibly bad. For straight accurate news reporting, the New Zealand papers are exceptionally good, but on the weather side of the Tasman are examples of the other extreme.

CHAPTER 14

Cyclone!

A COUPLE OF DAYS LATER the English ketch *Havfruen III*, which I had met in the Bay of Islands, arrived at Coff's Harbour and I was very pleased to meet up again with Batch and Ann Carr. That evening I had a meal with them in *Havfruen's* spacious saloon and we passed away a couple of very pleasant hours comparing notes on our progress and planning the future routes.

In the morning they motored off toward Brisbane, leaving me to wait for a breeze so that I, too, could get started on my way again. I was feeling a little impatient at these calm conditions and regretting that *Trekka* did not have a diesel engine to make use of this long calm spell. I cursed the weather and lack of wind but did not know then that in the next few days I would bitterly regret my impatience.

Over a thousand miles away in the center of the Coral Sea, trouble was brewing for me. A mass of air heated by the intense tropical sun was rising and creating a great hole in the atmosphere. Cooler winds moved into this hole, but they, too, were soon heated up and rose. An intense depression was being formed, and with each passing hour it was becoming stronger and stronger. While it waited for its strength to grow, for it was still just an infant, it remained stationary and quite undetected, but when its awesome power had reached maturity, it began to move deliberately toward the southwest to wreak its havoc on the eastern seaboard of Australia. This berserk giant, which began to move so slowly, was now no longer a mere depression, it was severe enough to attain the title of Cyclone.

Meanwhile, quite unaware of what was heading toward me, I was pleasantly surprised to find a steady southeasterly breeze blowing when I awoke on the morning of 5 June. I quickly got sail up and let go the mooring buoy. With her bottom clean, *Trekka* soon passed between the breakwaters and began to knock off the miles. Brisbane was only 260 miles away, and with a breeze like this to send us along, I knew that three or four days sailing would see us moored snugly in the Brisbane River. I was to be proved quite wrong.

Throughout the day *Trekka* slipped along close to the shore to avoid the unfavorable current, but as darkness fell I edged offshore so that we would not run ashore during the night. By daybreak the following day we had covered some more useful miles, but I edged inshore again as the day progressed and in the late afternoon passed the entrance to the Clarence River.

The steady breeze had increased and was blowing at about twenty knots from the southeast, which had *Trekka* really boiling along, but with the sun gone the wind increased instead of easing and some sixth sense warned me that all was not well. The weather report on the radio gave no indication of bad weather and the barometer was still high, yet something about the sea looked wrong. At first I did not take much notice, but as the hours went by I saw that there was a long swell rolling down from the northeast. There was no shelter along this section of the coast, and with growing apprehension I realised that if this wind was to shift a little we'd be on a lee shore. I sheeted in the main and staysail and furled the mizzen. Then I proceeded to gain as much sea room as possible by driving hard offshore.

What had been exhilarating sailing had now become a desperate bid to gain as many miles as possible before we were forced to heave to. *Trekka* was being driven as she had never been before. Sheets of spray stung my eyes and trickled down the collar of my oilskins; drops ran down my back to be temporarily halted by my belt, which acted as a dam, before flooding over into the seat of my pants. Then one big sea broke over the beam and completely soaked me; after this there was no point in trying to keep dry.

As the wind increased we were slowly forced to head more north than east, and at last I knew that the time had long gone when I ought to have reefed the mainsail. I waited for what seemed to be a lull, then quickly eased the halyard and cranked the reefing-gear, rolling the wet sail around the boom.

Although this was a big reduction in sail area, it did not appear to make a great deal of difference, and half an hour later I stowed the sail, realizing that if I left it up any longer it would either blow out or carry away some of the rigging.

The sky which had looked so innocent at midday was completely

Courtesy *Yachting Magazine*

clouded over, and occasional squalls drove the rain horizontally so that it
was impossible to look to weather. *Trekka* staggered on with just the staysail and mizzen up, heading into the long swell that rolled down from the
northeast. At times it was like a ride on a roller-coaster as we climbed the
face of a swell to plunge down the other side. The queasy feeling in my
stomach erupted and my breakfast and lunch were blown off to leeward
to mingle with the elements. Leaving *Trekka* to look after herself, I stiffly
climbed down the hatch and removed my sodden garments before easing
my weary frame into the lee bunk.

Sleep was quite impossible, but at least the bunk was warm and dry
and the flickering cabin lamp gave a brave attempt at cheerfulness.
Throughout the long night *Trekka* clawed herself offshore until, at daybreak on Saturday morning, the only sail set was the tiny storm-jib. Our

Anchored in the lee of Cape Moreton

speed through the water was no more than two knots, but it was better than laying ahull and drifting off toward the coast.

My worst fears were realised when late on Saturday the wind backed round to east. I crawled out on to the foredeck and pulled the tiny storm-jib down; then I lashed the helm to leeward and let the little boat ride the seas beam on.

According to my reckoning, we were about 35 miles offshore. I usually figured that, in a gale, *Trekka* drifted off downwind at a rate of about one knot, so we had only 35 hours left before the surf on the beach got us. It was a grim prospect.

Through the night at odd intervals I looked anxiously toward the mainland, expecting to see the light on Cape Byron which has a range of 26 miles, but daylight revealed no land in sight, though a haze about the horizon kept visibility down to about three miles. The wind eased a little about midday, and I set the storm-jib for three hours which won us a few miles before conditions worsened again and the sail had to be taken in.

Another anxious night passed, a night of listening to the shrill note of the wind in the rigging, the halyards rattling against the masts, and the sudden hiss of a breaking sea before it burst against the side of the hull. Again I peered off to the west straining my eyes for the loom of the light from the shore, but Monday morning arrived without any sign of land.

I turned the radio on to get the weather report and for the first time learned that this was no ordinary gale but a tropical cyclone. The storm center was five hundred miles away to the northeast and moving toward us at the rate of 10 knots. The news broadcast told of the damage already inflicted on shore, and how the beach and sea wall had been washed away along sections of the coast by huge breakers. My morale was very low now.

Our position was east of Danger Point, not a very cheerful name in the circumstances, but I had no means of knowing how far we were offshore. The correct thing to do was to save as much of that sea-room as possible with the aid of a sea anchor, but not having one I did the best with what I had. I secured the two manila anchor warps to cleats, one forward and one aft, then I attached the free ends to an eight-foot length of 2" x 2" spare lumber, which had the effect of keeping open a fair-sized bight in the water without it sinking. I could quickly tell from *Trekka*'s changed motion that the fifty fathoms of warp were checking her drift downwind, although she was not as comfortable as before.

Through Tuesday the wind was as strong as ever, and knowing that there was no more I could do, I climbed into my bunk and attempted to get interested in a book. Tuesday night was one of the most nerve-racking I can remember; the insane violence of the conditions outside was bad enough, but the thought of being driven ashore in these seas in complete darkness was worse. I had the feeling that this was a nightmare from which I would soon awake, but it went on hour after hour with no change and little hope.

Wednesday dawned at last, and a searching look to the west relieved my fears for there was still no land in sight. Greatly cheered by this I had some breakfast, the first real meal I had eaten since the storm began. The weather report on the radio placed the storm center 500 miles due east of Brisbane and heading more south than it had been. It looked as though the storm was starting to recurve away out to sea. By noon I was fairly sure this was happening as the sky was starting to break up and one or two patches of blue large enough to darn a Dutchman's pants appeared. For a few minutes the sun peeped through one of these holes and I was able to take a sight with the sextant though the sea was still very rough.

The sight placed us on the same latitude as Cape Byron, but I was still unable to determine how far offshore we were. The wind was veering at last from east round to southeast, and there were periods when its strength fell quite noticeably. I set the storm-jib for nearly four hours in the afternoon before another succession of squalls forced me to take it in.

The radio reported *Trekka* as missing and said that aircraft flying along the coast had been instructed to keep a look out for me. I was somewhat concerned about this latest piece of news, for the last thing I wanted was a costly air and sea search for me which might end up in some of the searchers losing their lives. It was my fault in being out in this cyclone, and there was no reason for anyone to risk their lives in attempting to rescue me.

With the wind now in the southeasterly quarter, the danger of being driven ashore had greatly diminished and I dropped off to sleep that night in a much easier frame of mind than I had been for the last five nights. At daybreak the light revealed the same scene of breaking seas and flying spray, but the appearance of the sky had improved, and when the sun appeared above the horizon it was visible for long periods through the clouds.

After a quick breakfast of porridge, toast and coffee, I went on deck to see if we could proceed on toward Brisbane. The wind was still blowing in excess of thirty knots and the sea was quite high, but after being hove-to for so long, I was eager to get moving again. With the wind in the south now I needed to run dead before it, so I decided to tow our makeshift sea anchor astern and set the little storm jib. A few moments later, when we were moving along at about three knots, I saw a large sea approaching; as it came closer it carried the warps before it until there was a lot of slack in them, then the crest reached *Trekka* and she immediately began to surf down the face of it. I held her running true with the tiller but then she slipped off the back of the crest and sat down in a hollow. Shortly afterwards a similar sea came along, but this one broke over the stern, soaking me completely, and would have taken me overboard but for the lifelines. I was still spitting out salt water when another sea did the same thing. Before it could happen again I got the sail down and lashed the tiller to leeward. It was too dangerous to let *Trekka* run in these conditions and I decided to wait until the sea had gone down more.

On the radio that evening was a report that the American schooner *Venturer*, sailed by her owners Jack and Peggy Burke, was also reported missing. She had left Port Stephens going north about the same time I left Coff's Harbour and had probably met much the same kind of weather I had been encountering.

On Friday 13 June, my usual lucky day, the wind and sea had moderated to such an extent that *Trekka* was able to carry her full mainsail with the staysail boomed out. I hauled in the warps over the stern and we flew along to the northwest looking out for land. Later in the day I was able to get sun-sights which showed that we were in fact much farther offshore than I had imagined, nearly eighty miles in fact. This was something of a surprise, and the only explanation I could think of was that the East Australian current, which normally flows strongly down the coast, had temporarily altered its course during the cyclone when opposed by strong southeast-to-east winds and flowed offshore at Cape Byron, the most easterly point of the Australian Continent. It had been lucky for me to be in the right place when caught in the storm.

I put *Trekka* on course for Cape Moreton, feeling very relieved to be moving again, and stayed on deck steering long after the sun had gone down.

Saturday was a good day and saw us making good progress with a blustery southwesterly wind. The only sign of the cyclone now was the swell that rolled in from the east, but the storm was moving off into the central Tasman Sea where it eventually blew itself out.

The radio news in the evening reported that the *Venturer* had been wrecked on the reef at Lady Musgrave Island, some 300 miles to the north of our position. Jack and Peggy Burke survived being washed across the coral reef and then swam and drifted nearly three miles across the lagoon to the tiny islet of Lady Musgrave, an incredible escape in those conditions. The news continued that *Trekka* was presumed to have foundered in the storm and that wreckage from her had been washed ashore north of Coff's Harbour. I could well imagine how the Sydney newspapers would lap this lot up—if there was one thing they were quite nutty over, it was yachts getting into difficulties at sea. It never seemed to make any difference that usually the vessel turned up safe and sound a few hours later.

At midnight, the light on Cape Moreton came into view, and as dawn was breaking we passed the lighthouse and carried on along the shore of Moreton Island.

In the early afternoon we arrived at Cape Moreton, where I anchored in the lee of the high cliffs in company with some fishing launches. One of these was a very able-looking vessel with a flying bridge and a long pulpit on her bow, and the name *Tennessee II* on her transom. She came over to inspect the new arrival. I was hailed and asked if we were the yacht that was reported missing in the cyclone, and on my replying that this was so, the skipper on her bridge told me he would report my safe arrival on his radio.

I learned that some of the buoys marking the channel through the sandbanks of Moreton Bay had been washed away in the cyclone, but that if I wanted to go on he would tow me as he knew the channel and also had an echo-sounder on board. Now that I was anchored and in calm water, I was in no hurry to leave again and decided to wait until the following day before going on to Brisbane.

An hour or so later a light plane appeared on the scene and I could see a photographer taking pictures of us. It looked as though this time we might even make the front page.

Later in the afternoon the *Tennessee II* came alongside and the skipper invited me to have a meal aboard, which I gladly accepted. I learned that he was Bob Dyer, an American who had a weekly radio show on one of the Australian networks. He and his wife, Dolly, were very well-known anglers and were looking for a really big shark to break the world record. Two days later they found the one they were looking for, and they got their record with a shark that weighed just over a ton.

Feeling greatly refreshed in the morning after a sound night's sleep I went on deck to find a warm, sunny day. I tidied up the cockpit and made new staysail sheets as the old ones had chafed badly. This was the only gear failure the cyclone had inflicted on us.

Later in the morning the *Tennessee II* came alongside and I secured her nylon tow line. Shortly afterwards, *Trekka* was towing astern like a yacht dinghy.

Brisbane, which lies 11 miles up the river of the same name, is forty miles from Cape Moreton. To get there it is necessary to navigate extensive shoals at the entrance to Moreton Bay. As usual, their positions are constantly changing but the channels through them are normally marked with buoys. In a little over an hour we were clear of the sandbanks and I signalled to the *Tennessee II* that I was casting off the tow line. She circled around slowly while I got sail up. With a final wave from all aboard, she set off back toward Cape Moreton to resume her shark fishing.

Trekka could just lay the course for the Pile Light at the entrance to the Brisbane River, and a gentle southeasterly breeze sent us along over the water at a steady four knots as I sat in the cockpit enjoying the warm morning sunshine.

Later in the day, a Brisbane yacht named *Alvis* escorted *Trekka* up the river and that evening, after anchoring for the night, I met Fred Markwell, her skipper. At the Markwell home the press finally caught up with me and the following day I read colorful accounts in the newspapers, one entitled "The Man who came back from the Dead."

I motored *Trekka* up the river to Bulimba the next day where I berthed alongside a small private jetty owned by Norman and Helen Wright. Many cruising yachtsmen have been fortunate in meeting these two wonderful people. Their house beside the river became the home of many yachtsmen visiting Brisbane. Norman and Helen were both keen sailors and they ran a profitable little business of tending to the mooring-lines of freighters docking along the river waterfront. They owned several high-powered launches in which they towed the lines from the ships to the wharfs. Many freighter skippers visiting Brisbane for the first time must have been somewhat surprised to hear Helen's voice call up, "Ready for your starboard spring!" Norman, an excellent dinghy helmsman, was an expert in the class of dinghy known in Australia as an unrestricted eighteen-footer. You have to be something of an acrobat to sail these dinghies, for with their enormous sail area and as many as six crew sometimes out on trapezes, they are not the most stable of craft, to put it mildly. These eighteen-footers are sailed mainly in Australia and New Zealand, but their popularity has spread and they are also sailed in other countries including the U.S.A. Each year there was a championship series of the best boats from each country, and Norman had won the competition the previous year in his *Jenny VI*.

Also at the Wright's jetty was a fine little blue-painted cutter from Auckland named *Revel.* I had met her owner, John Smith, briefly in Auckland, and now I got to know him and his wee wife, Marlene, better. They were both in their early twenties and were cruising to the Great Barrier Reef in place of the honeymoon they missed when they were married a few months before. I really enjoyed meeting these two, for although I met quite a few couples around the world who were cruising in their own yachts, I never met any as young as John and Marlene. He was no stranger to the sea, for like so many Kiwis he had grown up and around boats and had done several long passages in small craft. This, however, was Marlene's first long voyage but she had adapted to the life quite easily. I was much amused at her remark that the morning after her wedding night, John had taken her down to the harbour and given her a

I'M AWFULLY SORRY, SAYS MAN WHO BEAT CYCLONE

JOHN GUZWELL, the man who beat a cyclone, apologised last night: "Look, I'm awfully sorry about all this bother I caused."

The 27-year-old globe-trotter reached Brisbane last night in his 20-ft. yawl Trekka after having been posted missing, believed drowned in last week's cyclone.

An air, sea, and land search for the home-made Trekka was called off last Friday night after Guzwell had been missing for eight days on a voyage from Coffs Harbour to Brisbane.

Last night he told how he had "sweated out" the cyclone for four days off Cape Byron, the most easterly point of Australia.

The blond, six-foot Englishman ("I was born among boats in the Channel Islands") relaxed ashore for the first time in 11 days and said:

"I know that people who get into trouble at sea—or think they do—can be an awful trouble and expense.

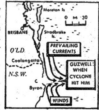

CHART shows effects of winds and currents which saved the Trekka from being wrecked on the coast.

"No radio"

"That's really why I don't carry two-way radio. I have rather strong views on it. There are too many cases where people holler for help when they don't really need it.

"In America it has got quite out of hand with one launch calling for help because it didn't have a can opener.

"If I had had a radio I might have hollered, too, but, as you see, here I am without help. I did not know there would be a search started for me automatically."

But Guzwell believes only chance saved his tiny craft being smashed to pieces on the coast.

When the cyclone struck him a prevailing current was coming from the north-west, and the cyclonic winds from the south-east, causing a current from the same direction.

"The two currents must have met just off Cape Byron, having the effect of pushing me seawards. That was just what I wanted.

"I had headed for sea, while I could still make way and threw out a long one-inch rope to act as a sea anchor—one end tied to the bow and one to the stern."

"I was never really worried about sinking or overturning — only of being dashed on a lee shore.

"The Trekka was specially designed for me by British naval architect Laurent Giles, and his yawls simply do not sink in gales."

Article that appeared in Brisbane newspaper, June, 1956

brush to scrub the weed off *Revel*'s bottom. They were young and in love, and I enjoyed much of my time in their company.

Trekka was still very much in the news, and sometimes I would return from some shopping expedition to find quite a crowd of people gathered on the jetty. There would usually be someone shooting questions at John, and I would creep up behind to listen.

"Is that the little boat that was out in the cyclone, mate?"

"Yes, that's her," replied John with a stony look on his face.

"That joker must be crazy sailing about in a little thing like that. When are you leaving, mate?"

John would stifle a sigh and reply, "Oh, in a couple of weeks."

I would work my way through the crowd and suddenly ask, "Eh, mate! Is that the little boat that was out in the cyclone?" John's expression would never alter, and he'd give the same reply, "Yes, that's her."

Sometimes he got his own back when I was alone on *Trekka* and he returned from the city to find me answering the inevitable questions. One day I received a surprise when an elderly lady suddenly shot a question at me: "Which Guzzwell are you? The son of John or James?"

I was quite taken aback, but stammered that I was the son of John.

"Well, young John, I used to work for your grandfather in Grimsby, forty years ago."

This was an extraordinary link with the past. I had never known my grandfather, he had died long before I was born, so I was most interested to hear about him and her life in the home where she looked after the two sons. I remembered an old family story about how Grandfather was in disgrace because he had been caught in bed with the maid by Grandmother; the old man was taking it rather badly until son James got him aside and whispered, "You've really buggered up the situation haven't you? What are John and me going to do now that Mother's fired Elsie?" Grandfather looked at his grinning son and gasped, "You and John, too?" then he howled with laughter. Had I been older and a little more sensitive, it is possible that I could have learned more family secrets but the subject was a little too risqué for me to pursue even though I was extremely curious.

I also got to meet Mrs. Palmer and her two daughters whom I had last met on lonely Fanning Island two years previously. The girls, now blossoming young women, missed the atoll very much and wondered if their pet fish were still there.

I received a telephone call one day from a young lady who told me her name was Trekka and that she would like to see the little boat. My imagination began working overtime, so that I was somewhat disappointed when she eventually arrived with her father to find she was only twelve years old. The Kiwis on *Revel* pulled my leg for days afterwards.

I was able to visit by road the section of the Queensland coastline known as the Gold Coast, an area famous for its miles of beautiful beaches and the small settlements with many hotels which cater for tourists from Sydney and Melbourne. It is no wonder to me that in many fields of sport Australia leads the rest of the world. With the wonderful climate, people spend more time outdoors than in, and the children are the healthiest I have seen anywhere. Everyone goes to the beaches and all the youngsters threaten to become champion Olympic swimmers. If ever there was a nation of sun-worshippers, it's these Australians.

Queensland hospitality can be quite overwhelming and it was seldom that I ate aboard *Trekka*, so it was not surprising that the days were rapidly going by. I met many friends at the Royal Queensland Yacht Club who kindly presented me with a silver plaque to commemorate *Trekka*'s visit. The name "Cyclone" was bestowed upon me, and for many months afterwards I received mail addressed to "Cyclone" Guzzwell.

Norman Wright's father, also Norman, slipped *Trekka* free of charge in his small shipyard nearby where I gave the bottom two coats of anti-fouling paint, as I had no idea when there would be another opportunity, perhaps not before we reached South Africa.

Trekka and *Revel* were joined by *Havfruen III* for a few days until eventually the big blue ketch departed for parts farther north. It was rather curious that all three yachts were from overseas and all painted blue. But there the similarity ended, for each was as different from the other as could be: *Trekka* with her reverse sheer and light displacement, *Revel*, the normal full keel type of small cruising boat, and *Havfruen*, a 70-ton ketch designed by the great Colin Archer. All three of them were doing the same kind of ocean sailing, which only went to prove that size has little to do with seaworthiness.

Meanwhile I was preparing to leave and was delighted when John Smith said he would sail *Revel* north in company with me. I went through the familiar routine of putting stores aboard and filling up water bottles, fuel for the stove and outboard motor, and saw to all the little items that needed attention before I could leave.

Friendly yachtsmen warned me of the dangers along the Great Barrier Reef, in particular the tourist resorts where the beautiful sun-tanned

Australian girls far outnumbered the men. I was told of other yachts that had been bound farther north, but had not been able to resist the siren calls. I promised to lash myself to the mainmast and let *Trekka* steer herself clear of these islands.

On the morning of 12 July, nearly a month after arriving in Brisbane, *Trekka* and *Revel* went down the river on the ebb tide bound for the Barrier Reef. The two boats sailed alongside each other across Moreton Bay and by dusk had negotiated the shoals at the entrance without incident. It was now that we parted company, for although *Revel* could stay close inshore and avoid the strong coastal current, I could not expect to stay awake constantly when close to the shore so I started to edge out to sea. Before darkness swallowed them up, I called to John and Marlene, promising to meet them at Lady Musgrave Island in a few days' time, but this in fact was the last I was to see of them on this voyage. Weeks later I learned that we missed each other at the island by just eight hours.

I set the twin-staysails which just filled to a gentle southerly breeze. The sea was quite calm and I sat in the cockpit feeling very happy to be going north to the tropics at last. The light on Caloundra Head flashed its message every ten seconds against a background of dark blue hills and a few twinkling lights from homes along the shore appeared. Then suddenly it was night and once again I was alone at sea.

CHAPTER *15*

To the Great Barrier Reef

THE NEXT THREE DAYS were spent running before a gentle southerly breeze, and though we made good progress during the day when I came in close to the shore, we sometimes lost quite a few miles in the hours of darkness when I went offshore to avoid the danger of running aground.

The weather was quite perfect, and though this was the middle of winter, it was more like summer to me after the tough going we had encountered farther south. Owing to the settled weather I was not concerned about staying close to shore except at night-time, and it certainly was far more interesting and profitable to sail well in to the coast.

The wind swung round to the north on the fourth day out and the combination of wind and current against us resulted in extremely slow progress. On a couple of occasions I anchored off the beach when we seemed to be losing instead of gaining ground.

I spent one night becalmed just south of Sandy Cape and anchored for a few hours while I caught up on sleep. When the wind returned it was still from the north, and the following day was spent beating up past Breaksea Spit, a dangerous coral reef which extends northward from Sandy Cape for a distance of nearly twenty miles. This reef is really the southernmost extremity of the Great Barrier Reef, that wonderful coral

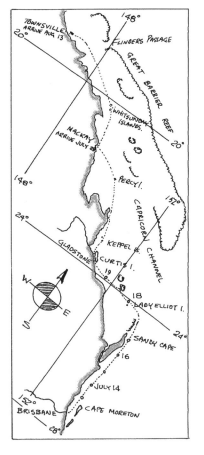

bastion which protects the Queensland coast for the next twelve hundred miles.

Early in the morning of 18 July, I passed the Breaksea Spit light vessel and bore away to the northwest with the wind now abeam and *Trekka* moving really fast. At noon we passed close to Lady Elliot Island which is very tiny and stands only a few feet above the sea. Much shipping passes close to it and there is a prominent lighthouse built on the southwestern side of the island and three tin-roofed houses, the homes of the keepers. I passed close enough to get a cheery wave from two figures ashore, then a few moments later the island was astern and appeared to sink beneath the sea.

In the late afternoon the palm trees on Lady Musgrave Island came into view, but as the wind rapidly eased off it was not until dusk that I came close to the island. There is an extensive lagoon inside the reef and an entrance on the northern side, but as the light was fading I decided to anchor on a three-fathom patch to the west of the island. I fastened the outboard motor over the stern in an effort to arrive before dark and was motoring along quite quickly over the calm water when suddenly, without any warning, there was a dreadful clunk! *Trekka* had hit the bottom hard. My knees all turned to water, I cut the engine and went forward to look the situation over. The bow was about four inches out of the water but I realised thankfully that she was not seriously aground, and after a couple of minutes of rocking the boat from side to side, she slid off the coral into deeper water where I gratefully anchored for the night. Thanks to the steel fin-keel there was no damage except to my shattered nerves.

In the morning I motored along the northern edge of the reef to see if *Revel* was behind the island, but unknown to me she had left the previous morning. When I saw no sign of her, I decided to continue on to Gladstone and see if she was there.

The sea was like a sheet of glass and just as clear. Beneath the hull I could see a couple of fish swimming along lazily in the shade, occasionally darting out into the sunlight to inspect some morsel but always returning to their position by the rudder. The outboard purred away steadily, and every two hours I filled the tank hoping that a breeze would appear and put an end to all this motoring. But toward sunset there was still no wind, and so I decided to anchor off the entrance to Port Curtis for the night. The calm continued throughout the night, and in the morning I started the motor again and proceeded on the flood tide up the South Channel to the small town of Gladstone where I moored *Trekka* among some small craft in a little creek to the west of the town.

I went ashore and reported to Customs, for although I had cleared at Coff's Harbour, it was still necessary to report to them and have clearance papers from the last port visited. I now handed in my Brisbane papers and arranged to collect a clearance for Townsville in a couple of days' time.

Gladstone itself was quite small and had the rather sleepy air of a frontier town. It lies beside the magnificent natural harbour of Port Curtis, an extensive area of sheltered water which is navigable to large freighters. Because of this it was quite a prosperous little town and much produce from the surrounding districts was shipped out from there. One of the chief items of produce was meat, and the Swift Company had a packing plant in Gladstone that was quite a fair-sized operation, being capable of handling five hundred head of cattle a day. A couple of days later I was given a tour of the meat works which was interesting, but since that day I have never been able to look a can of bully beef square in the eye. A visit to a meat packing plant would make most people vegetarians; perhaps it is as well that we are ignorant about much that we eat and take for granted.

The townsfolk of Gladstone had become quite yacht-minded as a result of the annual yacht race from Brisbane which finished here. Brisbane sailors had given me glowing accounts of the hospitality they had received here and it was not long before I began to receive similar treatment. There was a very fine little ketch moored just ahead of *Trekka* which had won the Sydney-Hobart race one year; her name was *Moonbie* and I was most interested in meeting her American owner, Hal Evans. He told me that he was about to go north to the Whitsunday Islands, but what really interested me was that he planned to take the short cut inside Curtis Island, a route called the Narrows, instead of the outside course which was many miles longer. The mere description of the Narrows in the Pilot book was enough to frighten me off, but I knew that if *Moonbie,* who drew a foot more water, could get through, then *Trekka* could too.

I told Hal that I was also going north to the Whitsunday Islands and asked him if he would mind me tagging along behind through the Narrows.

"Sure, you come along," he said. "I've never been through myself but I was shown the first bit yesterday aboard a fishboat, and I don't think it will be too bad, providing we catch the tide right."

We set off in the morning, motoring across the still water to the entrance to the channel. As we went along we kept careful note of the beacons and markers, constantly referring to the Pilot Book. As much of the route wound through mangrove swamps, it was often difficult to determine where the true channel lay but usually, at the last moment, a marker would become visible and our doubts would vanish for another mile or so.

The channel became narrower as we went along until we at last reached the Narrows where the description in the Pilot Book became quite frightening. At low water the channel is two feet out of the water at this point. Taking great care now not to let the beacons come out of line, as there are rocks on both sides of the channel, we slowly edged past the worst bit, bucking against the tide which was flooding from the northern end of the channel. Soon afterwards we were back into deeper water, and in the middle of the afternoon came abreast of the Sea Hill pilot station at the entrance of the Fitzroy River, where I decided to anchor as there was no wind out in the open water beyond. *Moonbie* motored off into the distance after I had arranged to meet her again at South Molle Island in a few days' time.

Instead of just sitting aboard *Trekka* waiting for a breeze, I put the dinghy into the water and rowed ashore to go for a walk. I walked up over the hill near the lighthouse and soon afterwards met the coxswain of the pilot station, Mr. Price. He took me along to his house where I met his wife who, in a matter of moments, had the table laid with a mouth-watering selection of scones and cakes. There were three families living at the station and I think the womenfolk missed a bit of company, for it was not very often that they had visitors. They told me of other yachts that had called there, some of which I knew quite well, and we were pleased to have mutual friends.

When I returned to *Trekka* late that evening after a most enjoyable visit ashore, the dinghy had a pile of magazines aboard and some fresh provisions, eggs and lettuce. This is the kind of hospitality I received so often and remember so well. Perhaps it was easier for me to meet new friends being single than if I had a crew along, for two people can be more of a handful to entertain than one.

From here right on up to Torres Straits I would be able to sleep soundly every night, for there were good anchorages all the way and there was no need to sail at night any more.

Early the following morning I motored out of the Fitzroy River and once outside found a gentle breeze. The motor was stowed away in the aft locker and I got sail up. There was little wind, but just after noon we were close to the Keppel Islands which looked so attractive that I decided to stop at Great Keppel and go for a swim. I anchored *Trekka* just a few yards off a wonderfully white sandy beach and went ashore in just a pair of swimming trunks for a walk. I saw a couple of homes among the trees but no sign of anyone on the island. Perhaps it was because this was the first of the many islands *Trekka* would call at as we threaded our way up inside the Barrier Reef, or perhaps the island was particularly outstanding, but I remember that anchorage as being one of the most perfect places I've ever seen. The island obviously belonged to someone, but it must have been a vacation home as there was no sign of anyone being there recently. At any rate I certainly enjoyed stopping there. As the sun went down that evening, I made an omelette out of the Sea Hill eggs and enjoyed it while listening to the radio news, sitting in the cockpit. The air was warm now that we were in the tropics, and it was good to know that I should have this kind of weather for the next few months, almost all the way to South Africa.

The charts were most interesting now. The Great Barrier Reef itself was about fifty miles offshore here at its southern extremity, but close to the Queensland coast were many groups of islands scattered about the calm water, a few of them with people living there but most of them uninhabited.

Sailing along a strange coastline and passing new islands is always exciting, but to do this with perfect weather, sitting out in the hot sun all day without any need of clothing and with no schedule to worry about, complete in the knowledge that time is of no importance, this to me is perfection, life does not come any better.

The next couple of days were spent working north up the coast in bright sunshine but with little wind. The night of 25 July saw us snugly anchored inside Island Head Creek, a very lovely anchorage indeed. The moon came up over the hill, full and so bright that I was able to sit in the cockpit and read a few pages of a book. From the shore the strange call of some tropical bird carried across the still water and I reflected that this section of the coast was completely unspoiled; this is how Captain Cook saw the Australian coastline, and somehow I think it will be many years before any of this is changed.

I left early the next morning as I wanted to reach Middle Island in the Percy Group for the night. It was a distance of nearly fifty miles, and though there was little wind to start with, as the sun climbed higher the breeze freshened and *Trekka* danced along. We did not arrive until after dark, but the moon lit the way into the little crescent-shaped bay where I anchored close to another yacht. Soon after anchoring I was fast asleep in my bunk.

I was awakened in the morning by a voice alongside *Trekka*. I scrambled out of my bunk and stood in the hatchway blinking into the morning sunshine. Sitting in a somewhat battered dinghy was a smallish elderly man with a grizzled beard and bright blue eyes.

"Sorry to wake you up," he apologized in an English accent, as I grasped his hand. "I'm Norman Young from the *Diana* over there. We're leaving for Mackay in a couple of hours but would like you to come and have some breakfast with us."

I looked up and saw the yacht I had seen faintly in the moonlight the night before, a stout-looking vessel which I later learned was a Falmouth quay punt and had been sailed by Mr. Young with a great variety of crews.

A few minutes later I met the four young men aboard who were the present crew. I gathered that they had joined the ship in Brisbane, but that three of them were only going as far as the Whitsunday Islands. The fourth member of the crew was a young Queenslander named Gary Turpin, a stocky athletic lad with an infectious grin who later was to become a very firm friend. He was to sail many thousands of miles aboard *Diana* before he left her in South Africa.

Over an immense breakfast of porridge, bacon and eggs, toast and coffee, I learned more about *Diana* and her owner. Norman Young had retired from the Civil Service after many years with the Treasury Department and had decided to spend his remaining years cruising in his beloved *Diana*. He was a bachelor and had no ties, so that his yacht was his home as well as being the magic carpet by which he could journey anywhere his fancy chose. He had originally left England for the West Indies with two other elderly men, and was somewhat proud of the fact that the average age of all on board for that Atlantic crossing was in excess of 65 years. This was quite remarkable when you take into consideration the type of boat *Diana* was, for the gear aboard was very heavy compared with a modern yacht. With her big gaff mainsail I could not see how three elderly men could ever have got it set, but they managed, and the three of them stayed together until Panama was reached. From then on, *Diana* collected dozens of different crews, some staying aboard for months, others getting off at the next port. Norman Young gave many young men their first taste of ocean cruising, and some of them later left to buy or build boats of their own to follow in *Diana's* tracks.

I was pleased to hear that *Diana* was bound for South Africa now, so that there was a good chance that we would meet many times along the way. Soon after I returned to *Trekka*, my newfound friends got sail up, hauled their anchor aboard, and slipped out of the bay bound for Mackay where I promised to meet them in a couple of days' time.

Middle Island was the home of a Canadian family named White who lived there year round in a homestead up in the center of the island. They had the reputation of welcoming stray yachts, and outside a small shack at the head of the beach was a telephone with a notice above it saying simply, "Please Ring." Later in the morning when I went ashore, I cranked the phone handle, and when a voice answered the other end of the line, told him who I was.

"Good, good," the voice answered, "we heard you were on your way up the coast, please come up and visit us. Just follow the telephone line and you'll find us. It's about a half an hour's walk."

I set off, following the trail, which soon began to climb quite steeply up the timbered slopes. I gathered that this White family must also be humorists, as there was a little notice along the side of the trail which read "TIRED YET?" and a little farther, a very effective "BEWARE OF THE BULL."

I hurried along the trail and before very long the ground levelled off and I saw the homestead among the trees. A few moments later I met Harold White, a great barrel-chested man with an oddly falsetto voice. He crushed my hand as he greeted me. Then he took me along to meet the rest of the family. There were Claude, who was Harold's younger brother and like him big, and two old friends who lived with them, Dolly and Syd.

I asked Claude why they chose to live here on top of the island instead of the beautiful little bay where *Trekka* was anchored.

"Well, for one thing, it's more healthy up here," he replied "Cooler too, I reckon. But I guess the main reason is because of the sheep we run. All the best pasture is up here and we can look after them better where we are, almost in the center of the island, than we could down on the beach."

This family was almost self-supporting. They grew their own vegetables and had an almost inexhaustible supply of meat. The few things they needed from the outside world were available from Mackay, but it seemed to me after talking to them for a while that they had just about everything they wanted right on the island. The five of us sat down to an enormous lunch and I realised that these were outdoor people after seeing their appetites.

In the afternoon Harold took me for a tour of the island in their car, a 1926 Whippet that appeared to be as sound mechanically as the day it was bought. We bounced and jolted along a few trails on the island from which superb views of the coast and other islands in the Percy Group were visible. I was shown a grove of trees where the two brothers had pit-sawed the lumber to build their boat, which they had constructed at the homestead using temporary fastenings, before dismantling the whole hull and then transporting everything down to the beach for the final assembly. Harold said that this had saved them no end of time in the long run, for they were able to work on the boat at odd moments at the house, whereas had they been building close to the beach, much time would have been lost walking to and from the homestead.

Later in the afternoon I saw the boat and was able to appreciate some of the effort that had gone into her building. She was very similar to Harry Pidgeon's famous *Islander*, having a V-bottom and very strong construction. She was moored alongside a little jetty in a lagoon which was entered through a narrow channel at the northern end of West Bay where *Trekka* was anchored. The lagoon was quite undetectable from the open sea and was one of the few natural harbours along the Queensland coast that was completely cyclone-proof.

Both Harold and Claude wanted to see *Trekka*, so about four o'clock that afternoon I said goodbye to Dolly and Syd, then walked down the trail with Harold to the little bay. When we arrived we found that Claude was with a party of fishermen and a fine-looking fishing vessel was anchored near *Trekka*.

The fishermen were also keen to see *Trekka*, and as all of us were such big people, we had to make it in two trips of the White's runabout. Then we all went aboard the fishboat, *Trade Winds*, where Jack the skipper cooked us a fine fish supper. We talked long into the night before we all said goodbye. Harold and Claude set off to walk back to the house and I returned to *Trekka* where I was soon asleep.

Though there was little wind in the morning I decided to leave for Mackay, but we had gone only a few miles when the sun burnt off what wind there was and I had to fasten the outboard over the stern and motor for a few hours. Instead of motoring on through the night, I anchored just north of the Beverly Islands in ten fathoms and was surprised when *Trekka* strained at the warp to see that the tide was flooding at nearly two knots.

By noon the next day *Trekka* was anchored close to *Diana* in Mackay Harbour, and I went off for some supplies to the town which is about three miles from the harbour. It is a pleasant little town with a wide main street which has flower gardens planted right down the center; at the time I was there the street was a riot of color.

The shops were all fitted with sun awnings extending over the sidewalk so that it was possible to stay in the shade when walking along shopping. I was able to obtain all the supplies and items I required and was fortunate in getting a ride back to the harbour with my purchases, for there was no bus service between the town and the harbour.

While in Mackay I bought ten gallons of fuel for the outboard as it had been used frequently the past few days, but I was not to know that the fuel would remain untouched for many thousands of miles until I reached South Africa months later. From Mackay north and across the Indian Ocean, the Southeast Trade Wind blew steadily day and night to drive *Trekka* ever onward.

Three days after arriving in Mackay we were off again, this time to the Whitsunday Islands. With a good breeze to send us along, *Trekka* arrived at Lindeman Island just after darkness and I anchored among some small craft near the tourist settlement. I went ashore in the morning to the

Trekka's dinghy was popular with the youngsters

resort where I met the Nicholson family who owned and ran the operation. They kindly invited me to use their facilities and eat with them whenever I wished, and it was not long before I was using their showers and doing some laundry.

The resort is set among palm trees at the head of a white coral sand beach on the southern side of Lindeman Island. Though it was not a large resort, the island had a landing strip and the tourists usually arrived by a light plane which operated a regular service with the mainland.

When *Diana* arrived and anchored close to *Trekka* the next day, it was not long before her four young crew members and myself were entering into the spirit of the resort. We played the various games and competitions which we somewhat unashamedly won from the guests who were paying for their holiday; I seem to remember coming away with a silver spoon for winning the table tennis competition, and between them the boys from *Diana* shared the rest of the prizes.

Early one morning I was awakened by Gary and one of the other lads from *Diana* who were going to hike to the top of the island to see the sunrise. I pulled a pair of shorts and a shirt on, and a few moments later the three of us rowed ashore leaving the dinghy on the beach. We set off through the palm trees, stumbling occasionally in the darkness, and shortly afterwards climbed into open grassland. The air had a pleasant

View from the 700-foot summit of Lindeman Island

South Molle Island was one of my favorite anchorages

chill to it, and as we brushed through the tall grass our legs were wet with dew. It was almost light when we reached the 700-foot summit, and as the shadows faded we were able to appreciate a magnificent view. Off into the distance stretched a string of islands like so many jewels on a necklace, then as we feasted our eyes on the scene the sun slowly lifted above the horizon to tip the island peaks in a pink glow. The three of us were silent as if each wanted to retain the memory of the unforgettable sight so that at some time in the future we could savor it. A few minutes later we reluctantly turned away and began to retrace our tracks back to the beach in the bright morning sunlight.

We arrived back at *Diana* to find that a massive breakfast was almost ready, and while we ate ravenously we discussed where to visit next. I was going on to South Molle Island and arranged to meet *Diana* there in a few days time, so it was agreed between us that the two boats would cruise together going north once we left the Whitsunday group.

After breakfast I rowed back to *Trekka* and a little later sailed out of the bay into the Whitsunday Passage. I steered *Trekka* close to Dent Island, which has a lighthouse on it, and was surprised a few minutes later when the keeper rowed out with his assistant in a small dinghy to come and have a chat. I learned the whereabouts of several yachts I knew, for the lighthouses along the coast were in constant radio contact. They invited me ashore, but I declined as the anchorage did not look to be a good one, the tide sweeps through the passage at a rate of three knots. I did not know what the holding ground was like so I elected to continue on to South Molle. Just before sunset I rounded the northern end of the island and shortly afterwards anchored close to Hal Evans's *Moonbie.*

Of all the places I visited along the Great Barrier Reef, I remember South Molle best. Like Lindeman Island, which it resembles in size and height, it is also a national park and has a small tourist resort situated in a bay on the northern coast of the island.

When I met Hal Evans ashore the following morning, he introduced

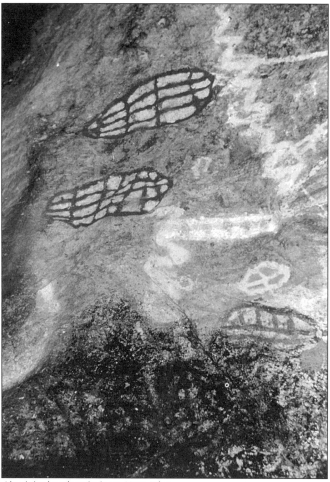

Aboriginal rock paintings, Nara Inlet

me to the Bowers brothers who were operating the resort and they told me to make myself at home and to use all the facilities.

So much of my time in the past few months had been spent alone or in the company of older people that I had almost forgotten what it was like to relax with someone my own age.

The resort on South Molle catered for young people, and now all at once I had plenty of companions both male and female to enjoy myself with. I played tennis in the mornings, usually before breakfast when the air was still cool, and enjoyed the lovely walks along the many trails to various beauty spots. Quite near the resort was a large colony of flying foxes which hung from the branches of some tall gum trees. Occasionally they would take fright, and the air was filled with their beating wings and sharp raucous cries as they circled about in alarm above the tree tops.

In the afternoons both _Trekka_ and _Moonbie_ sailed about the island with friends aboard. One day I took _Trekka_ over to Nara Inlet where I was told there was a cave with aboriginal paintings on the walls. The inlet is about two miles long and quite narrow, the shore rises rapidly on each side and is well timbered, so that it is not unlike a Norwegian fjord. I anchored _Trekka_ close to the head of the inlet and then set off through the brush to look for the cave which I found a few minutes later. It was small and a little disappointing as the paintings seemed quite meaningless. There were two drawings that looked not unlike snowshoe prints, about the same size, but the rest were just daubs of different colors, rather like some examples of modern art.

When we returned to South Molle just after dark, I saw that _Diana_ had arrived and was anchored nearby. I think Norman Young soon realised the dangers of a place like South Molle to his young crew and knew that too long a stay there could result in him losing them, so I was not surprised when Gary told me that they were departing next day for Cannonvale where the other three members of the crew were leaving the ship to return to Brisbane. This would leave just the skipper and Gary aboard to take the boat several hundred miles on to Thursday Island unless someone else could be found.

When I awoke the following morning and looked out of the hatchway, _Diana_ had gone. A feeling of restlessness swept over me and I knew that it was time for me to be moving along. I knew now what those friends in Brisbane had been warning me about when they mentioned the dangers along the Barrier Reef. There was a fine yacht moored just a few yards away that had been bound overseas, but her owner had found his green hills here at South Molle and his voyage had been abandoned.

I spent the day ashore knowing that it would be my last one and walked the trails taking photographs of the various bays and headlands. From the summit of the island the view is quite spectacular and unforgettable. I watched a large freighter coming north along the Whitsunday Passage, a white trail on the face of the sea. Then she passed and disappeared beyond North Molle Island. I knew that before another day passed *Trekka* would be following in her wake. At daybreak the next morning I got the anchor aboard, a gentle breeze smoothed out the wrinkles in *Trekka's* mainsail as we gathered way. Hal Evans stood in *Moonbie's* hatchway watching, and I knew that he, too, had found his earthly paradise in these Whitsunday Islands. He lifted his hand in salute as *Trekka* glided by, then I eased the sheets and we pulled away from the bay out into the open water bound for Townsville.

CHAPTER *16*

Sailing in Company

A S THE MORNING PROGRESSED the Trade Wind strength-
ened and *Trekka* surged along before it with a bone in her teeth. By
darkness we had covered over fifty miles, and as the course to Townsville
was relatively free of dangers, I decided to keep going all night. During
the hours of darkness I set the twin-staysails and was able to rest in my
bunk for a couple of hours. The light on Cape Bowling Green was abeam
just before daylight, and when I had eaten some breakfast I went on deck
to set the mainsail which soon had us going at near maximum speed.

At noon we were in Townsville where I found *Diana* already berthed
in the river near the center of town. Mr. Young and Gary helped me
secure *Trekka* alongside *Diana*, and I learned that they had arrived late the
previous day. The absence of the rest of the crew did not appear to worry
these two very much.

I checked in with the Customs and soon completed the forms which
would be handed in at Cairns, the next port up the coast that I would be
calling at.

Gary and I went off shopping and returned to the yachts with arms
full of packages. Townsville was a good place to shop and we were able
to obtain all the necessary items on our lists.

After two days' stay in Townsville, I decided to continue on up the

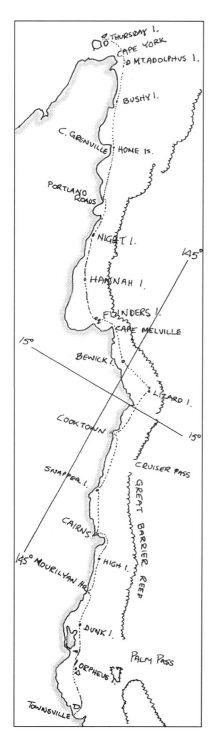

coast and arranged to meet *Diana* at Cairns some 150 miles farther on. It was now the middle of August and I was becoming a little concerned at the way time was slipping by. I had traversed less than half the length of the Barrier Reef to Thursday Island so far, and if I wanted to avoid cyclones in the Indian Ocean, I had to reach South Africa, over 7,000 miles away, before Christmas. From now on *Trekka* had to keep moving.

From Townsville I sailed to Orpheus Island where I spent the night with tropical raindrops drumming on the deck, but though it was still raining the following morning when I left, the sky cleared later and I had a most enjoyable day's run to Dunk Island.

Farther south it would have been safe to have kept sailing at night, but the route was becoming more tricky as we went up the coast, and as there were good anchorages in the lee of the many islands along the route, there was little point in sailing after the sun had set. This was most interesting and enjoyable cruising inside the Barrier Reef and I was not going to spoil it through lack of sleep. Providing I left early in the mornings it was possible to sail fifty miles without strain and find an anchorage for the night before it was dark.

I was off again early in the morning, but the wind, which had been steady for the last few days, faltered and we made poor progress, so that by the middle of the afternoon we had covered only twenty miles. I had intended to keep sailing that night, as the course was clear of dangers and there was little choice of an anchorage farther on, but on looking at the chart, I decided to go into Mourilyan Harbour instead.

This little harbour is really the mouth of the Moresby River and has a narrow entrance between two headlands which are each over five hundred feet in height. Rocks extend out from each shore so that the channel is only about 170 feet wide, and at springs the tide runs in and out of the harbour at seven knots. The Pilot Book warns strangers not to attempt entering without a pilot, but on checking with the Tide Book and noting that it was almost slack water, I decided to go in with the outboard motor.

Having safely negotiated the narrowest section of the channel, I was congratulating myself on my daredevil pilotage when I was shocked to see a large freighter moored to the wharf inside. I stared at it, quite unbelieving that this ship could have entered through such a narrow channel, and for a moment was sure that there must be another entrance to the harbour. I learned later that there were plans afoot to blast away the rocks in the narrow section of the channel. With this done it will be a safe harbour and provide excellent shelter during the cyclone season. While ashore I got talking with the navigator of the freighter and he invited me aboard. He was most interested in my voyage and showed me his method of working out the longitude, a far quicker way of doing it than the method taught to me by my father years before.

I returned to *Trekka* later with a full stomach, the result of a fine meal from the cook, and some charts, a present from the navigator. At slack water in the morning I motored out of the channel, and once clear of the entrance, stowed the motor and got sail up to a steady southeasterly breeze. The coast was backed by thickly-wooded hills, and in the distance the peaks of the Bellenden Ker mountains, which rise to an altitude of 5,000 feet, were clearly visible. At the end of the day I anchored behind High Island on Tobias Spit, but it was an uncomfortable anchorage and *Trekka* rolled about violently during the night to the swell which came round both ends of the island. I was not sorry when daylight arrived and I could proceed on to Cairns, where we arrived in the afternoon to find that *Diana* had beaten us in by a few hours, having passed *Trekka* during the night when I was attempting to get some sleep.

Cairns was a disappointing stop for me. This was the last big town along the Queensland coast until Thursday Island and I had quite a list of shopping which should have been available, but apart from foodstuffs I had very little success. Mr. Young and Gary also complained of similar failures, and we just had to face the reality that we would have to man-age without many items. Disappointed with our shopping efforts, we decided to take a day off and visit the underwater observatory at Green Island, one of the true coral reef islands of the Barrier Reef. Instead of sailing the fifteen miles to the island, we went across on the ferry boat, the motion of which was so completely different to *Trekka*'s that I felt quite seasick, and had the crossing been much longer, would undoubt-edly have disgraced myself in front of my two companions.

The observatory was nothing more than a large tank beneath the sea which had glass portholes in the sides. It was entered through a shaft of

Diana keeps me company along the Great Barrier Reef

stairs from the pier but was well worth the visit, for the view out of the portholes was completely natural. As the water was so clear, it was possible to see quite intimately the living coral and brightly colored reef fish which frequently swam up to the portholes to examine the strange creatures within.

Later on we walked round the island which is about a half-mile long and only a few feet above sea-level. The colors of the sea were a delight to behold—from the palest of greens close to the white coral sand beach, they ranged to every conceivable shade of green and blue. Shadows moved across the kaleidoscope of colors as the Trade Wind clouds drifted beneath an incredibly blue sky.

We returned to Cairns on the ferry boat which resumed its drunken rolling as soon as it left the shelter of the island, and I made a mental note to apologize sincerely to *Trekka* for thinking that her antics had been violent at times.

Cairns held little to attract us, so we speedily completed buying provisions, some of which would have to last until South Africa as we could not depend on obtaining very much at Thursday Island. On 23 August the two boats left Cairns together and sailed in company constantly for the next five hundred miles. Perhaps I remember this stage of the voyage best for the wonderful sailing it produced, day after day of exhilarating surfing, with *Trekka* going at her very best to stay up with her larger companion. The miles seemed to fly past, each one memorable for the very joy of it all. *Diana*, rather like a sedate old lady, picked up her skirts and really waltzed along in a welter of foam; *Trekka*, not to be outdone, surfed and skidded down the face of the curling waves in a most unladylike manner, thoroughly enjoying the excitement and sometimes making me shout aloud in admiration of her antics.

We arrived at Snapper Island in the middle of the afternoon, and as there was no anchorage farther on that we could reach that day, both boats stopped here for the night. Like the High Island anchorage this was rather an uncomfortable one, for the swell swept round both ends of the island to keep the two boats rolling constantly.

The next day's stage was quite a long one, as we hoped to reach Cooktown which was a distance of 55 miles, so we all turned in early that night to get some sleep. I was awakened by Gary's hail at four o'clock in the morning, and when I stuck my head out of the hatchway saw that he had already got *Diana*'s anchor aboard. It only took me a few moments to do the same for *Trekka* and before I was fully awake had all sail up, too.

There was not much wind at this hour of the day, but once the sun showed itself above the horizon the breeze increased until it was blowing a fine steady twenty knots. I set the spinnaker later in the morning and under this sail *Trekka* had the edge in speed over *Diana*. The hours went by with the sails stretched taut, the mainsail pressed hard against the spreaders and shrouds, while the little blue spinnaker bulged out beyond the forestay, threatening to burst apart at the seams. Everything held together, though, and by four o'clock that afternoon both boats had negotiated the tricky entrance to the Endeavour River to anchor off the little settlement of Cooktown.

On the shore stands a monument to commemorate the landing here of Captain Cook in 1770 where his ship the *Endeavour* was repaired after striking a reef and nearly foundering. Cooktown was at one time a prosperous little town due to gold being discovered nearby. But as with many Australian boom towns, the alluvial gold was soon worked out, and though gold is still mined inland at the Palmer Goldfields, Cooktown when we were there was little more than a ghost town.

We walked along the main street passing empty derelict buildings that the bush was trying hard to regain. The place had an air of hopelessness and decay that was unsettling. We found a couple of shops where we bought some fresh fruit and bread and a small post office where I posted off some mail, knowing that this would be the only opportunity until we reached Thursday Island.

It was at Cooktown at the small jetty that I first saw the dreaded stonefish. This repulsive-looking creature usually lies on the bottom among stones, and its naturally brown and greenish body is covered with a dirty coating of slime which makes it very difficult to see. It has thirteen strong dorsal spines which all have a double poison sac, and should some unlucky person step on one and have the poison enter the wound, the resulting pain is so immediate and agonizing that people have been known to commit suicide rather than bear it. The fish is usually sluggish in its movements, and for this reason is dangerous to bathers who could tread on one. Sometimes stonefish are caught on a line, as was the one I saw, and you need to take great care in removing them from the hook; moreover, they can live for several days out of the water, so they should not be underestimated. Whenever Gary and I went swimming we always wore a pair of tennis shoes if we were wading out into the water from the shore.

On 26 August, after a day and a half in Cooktown, *Diana* and *Trekka* left for Lizard Island, fifty-odd miles up the coast. Another day of fast sailing saw us anchored behind the island well before darkness, but the strong wind which swept off the land prevented me from going aboard *Diana* at the end of the day, and I had to be content with my own cooking for a change.

The wind was just as strong in the morning and I knew we were in for another fast day's run. The course was almost west today, and it was a change to have the wind coming over the port quarter after so much sailing on the starboard tack.

Diana's mainsail was not in use today. It had been made by one of the best-known sailmakers in the world and was made of flax, yet although it was only two years old, the material had so little life in it that Gary maintained that every time he hoisted it he had to sew half of it back together again. Norman Young blamed the Auckland gas works for the ruination of his sail and said that *Diana's* berth in that city had been in the lee of the gasometers; it was his firm belief that the gas fumes had rotted the cloth. This was an interesting theory, but I thought the fumes from the particular brand of tobacco he smoked were far more powerful and probably more noxious than any the Auckland gas works could emit. With the wind above 20 knots, it was suicide to set the sail which would only rip into tatters and self destruct. In any case, Gary flatly refused to hoist it, knowing that he would have to sew it together again, and Mr. Young was quite incapable of getting the heavy sail up by himself. I was constantly amused at the silent battle of wits these two engaged in and found their company entertaining.

Of all the sailing along the Great Barrier Reef, I remember the day's run from Lizard to Bewick Island best. The wind was a steady 25 knots once we left the shelter of Lizard Island, and even without her mainsail, *Diana* with her longer waterline began to pull away from *Trekka*. She was using two big headsails boomed out and her mizzen, while *Trekka* had her usual working staysail and main up. It would have been almost impossible for me to set the spinnaker by myself in these conditions, but there was a chance that I might be able to set the masthead genoa and boom the staysail out with one of the twin poles. *Trekka* was doing 6 knots as it was, and I had to be quick on the foredeck to get the genoa hanked on and hoisted before she came up into the wind or gybed, but all went well and I reached the tiller just as the sail filled. *Trekka* hesitated for a brief moment, then like a racehorse that has the bit between its teeth she bolted toward the fleeing *Diana*. In a series of fantastic surfs on the curling waves, when her speed must have gone beyond 10 knots for seconds at a time, *Trekka* tore through the water at a rate that left me gasping with excitement. I found that by throwing my weight forward at the correct moment it was possible to get her planing on practically every wave, and using these tactics, it was not long before we caught *Diana* and came up under her stern. At this moment, *Trekka* caught a wave and began to surf down the face of it. I had the momentary vision of Mr. Young's startled face and was certain that we were about to disappear down *Diana's* hatchway, then at the last moment we sheered away, just missing her transom as we rushed past. I saw Gary shaking his head in astonishment, so then I had to show him my new sport. Waiting for the right moment, I ran forward on to the foredeck in the same manner surfers in Hawaii do on their large boards. This had the effect of making *Trekka* stay on a wave even longer and soon we had left *Diana* quite a long way astern. At three o'clock that afternoon *Trekka* was anchored behind Bewick Island, having covered the 43 miles from Lizard Island at a speed of just under seven knots. This was probably the fastest sailing she ever did.

As it was still early in the day, Gary and I went spear fishing from *Diana's* dinghy. Both of us were so leery of sharks that, when we had the dinghy anchored, the conversation went something like this:

"Water feels quite warm, John."

"Not very clear, though. Don't you think we'd be better farther in?"

"Well, it's not very deep here, John. Let's see you go in and try it."

"Oh no, I went in first yesterday. It's your turn today, Gary."

"Well, maybe it would be a bit better closer to the shore."

And so the whole operation was repeated closer in. After much looking under the dinghy, we stepped over the side into the knee deep water, and as our courage came back, we gradually worked farther out. We never did see a shark, but we were not sorry about that. All about us swam gaily-colored reef fish which darted in amongst the coral whenever they became alarmed. It was not very often that we got a fish for we had doubts whether many of these colored ones were edible, but it was enough for both of us just to look at this beautiful world beneath the sea. The two of us had become firm friends and these excursions away from the two boats gave us an opportunity to talk young men's talk out of earshot of the old man. I think Gary in particular needed this, and I suspect Mr. Young appreciated having the boat to himself for a couple of hours after a brisk day at the wheel.

The old man invited me to eat aboard *Diana* whenever I wished and I would frequently do this, for it was far more enjoyable preparing a meal and eating with the two of them than making a meal for myself on *Trekka*. In the evenings we got the charts out and discussed the route for the following day, deciding where to anchor for the night.

I had no means of knowing without becoming intrusive why there was no woman in Mr. Young's life. He always sailed with men crews but not for one moment would I think he was gay. I suspect that he was rather unattractive to the opposite sex, being small in stature with a permanent stoop and a somewhat rodent-like manner. He had some good stories which I enjoyed, to Gary's disgust, and was well travelled long before he got into sailing. I think he somewhat enjoyed the new listener and told a few tales that Gary confessed he'd never heard before. Some of the others he could recite by heart with all the mannerisms and would keep me in fits of laughter.

Early the next morning we were off again and the miles were soon slipping past, though not at the previous day's rate, past Barrow Point and North Bay Point, where the Great Barrier Reef is only four miles off the coast. Then soon afterwards we rounded Cape Melville, where in 1899 a cyclone swept the entire pearling fleet ashore, drowning over three hundred men.

In the early afternoon we anchored near a sandspit off the western end of Flinders Island and went ashore to examine a rather dilapidated hut which stood nearby. This proved quite interesting, for marked on the walls were the names of many yachts and other craft that had called here. We dutifully added ours and then left in *Diana*'s dinghy, powered by *Trekka*'s outboard motor, to have a look at a wreck which we had noted on Stanley Island about a mile away. The wreck turned out to be a landing craft which had been stripped quite thoroughly, but we were left wondering what had become of its crew, for none of the islands in the group were inhabited.

After eating aboard *Diana* that evening, I was about to return to *Trekka* when we noticed that she had dragged her anchor and was fast disappearing downwind and out to the open sea. Gary and I pursued her in the dinghy with the motor and soon afterwards we both scrambled aboard and got sail up for the beat back to the anchorage. This time I made sure there was enough warp out when I anchored and the rest of the night passed uneventfully.

From Flinders we went on to Hannah Island where we found four Thursday Island luggers at anchor. They were stout-looking ketches about 50-60 feet overall with a pronounced sheerline giving them low freeboard amidships. Good-looking boats but very roughly built. As we got farther north we frequently passed others anchored in the open channels with their mizzens set riding head to wind while their native crews dived for pearl or trochus shell. I was interested to note that a forestay was rigged to the top of the mizzen-mast when they were laying like this.

A surprising amount of shipping was using this route inside the Barrier Reef. Not a day went by without some freighter or tanker passing us, and we usually got a cheery wave from the officers on the bridge who examined us closely through their binoculars. I'm sure that the sight of the two yachts must have given some of them a twinge of envy, for it would be difficult to find a yacht in more perfect conditions than these.

Another day's run of 45 miles saw us at Night Island, and then we were off again in the morning to Portland Road where there is a jetty and a couple of buildings ashore. We met three white men who lived together in a small house, but they were rather surly and unfriendly, almost as if they resented our intrusion into their privacy. One of them offered the information that a crocodile had killed his dog a few days before and advised us to stay away from the creek that emptied into the bay near where the two yachts were anchored, but apart from this they ignored us completely, leaving us puzzled as to what they were doing there.

The following day we reached Cape Grenville and anchored behind the Home Islands for the night. Gary and I went skin-diving in the afternoon and found the water unusually clear. The coral formations here were excellent, perhaps because of the lack of sediment in the water.

Bushy Island, 50 miles farther on, was the next day's stop, and then we left for Mount Adolphus Island on what was the final day's run inside the Barrier Reef. In the early afternoon, we passed close to Quetta Rock

Living coral formations and reef fish

named after the British India Company's S.S. *Quetta* which in 1890 struck this rock and foundered with great loss of life.

The two yachts found a sheltered anchorage in Blackwood Bay, Adolphus Island, and soon after arriving we all went ashore to stretch our legs. We were in high spirits at having safely negotiated twelve hundred miles of reef-infested waters and, though it had all been enjoyable, I was beginning to feel the excitement of setting off across the wide expanse of the Indian Ocean.

In *Diana's* saloon that evening, we spread out the charts of Torres Straits, planning the following day's run to Thursday Island. We spent an hour or so attempting to work out the time of high water, as the tides in Torres Straits were reported to be strong, but at the finish we were in such a muddle that we decided to follow our usual practice and leave after breakfast.

Our worries about the tides were quite unnecessary for we had an easy passage to Thursday Island, arriving off Port Kennedy shortly after noon, and we anchored there among many pearling luggers near a long pile wharf. It was perhaps appropriate that we should have arrived at Thursday Island on a Thursday.

The island itself is dry and barren with little greenery to be seen anywhere. The town has that frontier look about it, the main street lined with dusty trees backed by a few featureless shops. The air was heavy with the thick red dust that penetrated everywhere. Whenever a vehicle went by, fresh clouds of it descended on everything. After a few hours ashore we were caked with the red grime.

Though the shops did not look very smart, they did have nearly all the supplies we had been unable to obtain at Cairns, but prices were considerably higher than in Brisbane or Townsville.

That evening, by way of a celebration, we dined ashore at the Royal Hotel which, though perhaps not quite so elegant as the name would suggest, did provide an adequate meal. The proprietress let us use the hotel's somewhat primitive showers, and they were much appreciated.

I had hoped to haul *Trekka* out of the water and anti-foul her bottom on one of the slipways here, but the prices quoted were too much for my pocket. I had a word with the harbourmaster who thought that *Trekka* might lie alongside the wharf at neighboring Horn Island; so, a couple of days later, I motored *Trekka* over to the island where I found two wooden piles close to the wharf that had four feet six inches alongside them at high water. At the very top of the tide that evening I managed to get *Trekka* alongside the piles, and began painting the bottom at five o'clock the following morning when it was still dark. The morning tide was not high enough to float us off and I had to wait until nearly midnight before we floated into deeper water. *Trekka's* bottom had been quite clean, but with South Africa still over 6,000 miles away, I was pleased to have the opportunity of doing so before Mauritius which was still a long way away.

Though Mr. Young and Gary had managed *Diana* by themselves since the Whitsunday Islands, they were not keen to go on across the Indian Ocean without another person aboard. It had been arranged that one of Gary's friends from Brisbane would join *Diana* at Darwin when she reached that port.

A couple of days later I watched *Diana* leaving for Darwin, Gary cranking the anchor chain aboard while Mr. Young looked after the engine controls from the cockpit. They were an odd pair to be sailing a big heavy boat like *Diana* together, one a small, indomitable man approaching his seventieth year, very set in his ways, who was quietly sailing around the world in his own vessel as though it was the most natural thing to do, and his companion, a young lad of nineteen whose spirit of adventure had led him to *Diana*. He was starting out on a great journey, not knowing what the future held or where it would lead him, and I admired his pluck, not many his age would have the motivation and energy to go. I remembered the contrasts of their accents and couldn't help but smile, wondering which one would eventually win, the precise English of an ex-Civil Servant or the intriguing drawl of the young Queenslander. I was sorry to see them go for I knew that I was going to miss both of them very much.

On the morning of 10 September, our third anniversary away from Victoria, B.C., *Trekka* left Thursday Island for the Cocos (Keeling) Islands, 2,800 miles away. This was the longest passage I had attempted so far in *Trekka*, but with favorable winds I hoped to be there in a month.

We rushed out of Normandy Sound on a six knot tide with a fine easterly breeze pushing us along. In the early afternoon Booby Island was abeam, the last land I saw for the next month. At dusk the twin-staysails were set and I left *Trekka* to steer herself toward Cocos.

CHAPTER 17

The Kindly Indian Ocean

I WAS STANDING IN THE COCKPIT a couple of nights later when I felt something crawling up my leg. Perhaps it was the surprise that made it feel so horrible, for when I shone a flashlight on it, I saw it was a creature rather like a shrimp with long feelers, a transparent body, and shaped not unlike a grasshopper. I promptly flung it overboard. On reflection it probably was a shrimp and had made a home for itself in one of the cockpit drains; even so it gave me quite a start as it was so unexpected.

We passed many sea snakes during the next few days. They were quite small, seldom being more than three feet long, with a black back and head and a yellow underbody. They were excellent swimmers and wriggled away on the surface of the sea when *Trekka* approached. I tried many times to photograph them but never succeeded.

We had two 24-hour runs of 115 miles and then the wind rapidly eased off. I saw that we had crossed the Gulf of Carpentaria on the chart and it almost seemed as though we had come into the lee of the Australian coast. For the next week we had very little wind, but the strong favorable current boosted our mileages and *Trekka* kept going along steadily. What wind there was came from the east so that *Trekka* could steer herself with the twins, but these two sails were meant for blustery Trade Wind sailing

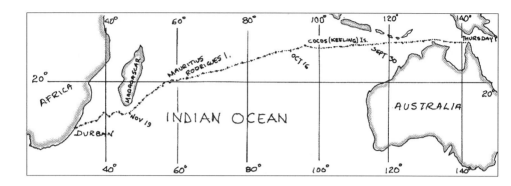

and in these light airs they were not large enough to be really effective. Then I got the idea to increase the sail area by using the spinnaker above the twins, flying it from the masthead with the sheets led through blocks attached to the ends of the twin-poles and secured to cleats on the mast. The result was perfect, the twins did the steering while the spinnaker did most of the pulling. *Trekka* immediately picked up speed and it was largely due to this rig that she was able to make such fast passages later on.

It was very hot indeed during the day. The temperature in *Trekka's* cabin was a steady 98 degrees F. and out in the sunshine it was 20 degrees higher. Though I was a sun-worshipper, there was a limit to what I could stand and it became necessary to rig a sun awning over the cockpit to make it bearable on deck. I was also concerned about fresh water, for our total capacity when I left Thursday Island was twenty-four gallons, quite enough at the normal rate of consumption, but with this heat I was drinking more than half a gallon a day. To stay cool, I frequently doused myself with a bucket of sea water and as I wore not a stitch of clothing, this was a simple and most enjoyable operation.

I was sitting in the cockpit a couple of nights later when I heard a muffled report like a small explosion. I looked round and saw a bright green light falling across the sky until it entered the water. I heard no splash and thought it might have been a Very pistol flare, but there was no sign of shipping about so perhaps I had seen a meteor.

On 25 September we passed about twenty miles south of Roti Island off the southern end of Timor, but the horizon was hazy so I did not see the island. A couple of times the superstructures of tankers showed above the horizon and a plane passed overhead high up, but apart from these signs of civilization this was a very peaceful part of the ocean.

The calm weather continued and I wondered what had become of the

Southeast Trade Wind. I had read that the Indian Ocean was a rough place for small boats, yet here we were drifting along day after day with just the gentlest of breezes.

At midnight on 1 October we approached what appeared to be a frontal system, a wall of low cloud extending across the sky from horizon to horizon. As we reached this cloud the wind changed direction to the southeast and almost immediately we were enveloped in a tremendous downpour. The rain eased later, but the wind held steady so that by noon there were 98 miles on the log.

The sky stayed cloudy and frequent rain squalls wet the decks. I caught enough water in the canvas awning during one rain squall to fill up all the water bottles, and once I had done this my worries were over. The wind increased until it was blowing a fine, steady breeze reminiscent of the winds along the Barrier Reef, and *Trekka* went along as she had never gone before. On the third, she ran 118 miles to noon, and the following day she set a record day's total of 125. Not content with this, she made her best run ever the next day with a wonderful 133 to which was added the favorable ocean current which brought the figure to 146 miles. Considering that she was steering herself for the twelve hours of darkness when I had to reduce sail to get her to sail herself, this was extremely good going. The next three days gave us runs of 125, 120, and 127, so that in a week *Trekka* had run 845 miles on the log and made good 910 miles. Toward the end of the week the favorable current left us, but with this kind of sailing we did not really need it.

On the night of 8 October, I hove *Trekka* to about 30 miles east of Cocos to wait for daylight before trying to locate the island. Sun-sights in the morning showed that we were southeast of the atoll; after sailing for three hours on the new course, I saw the tops of coconut palms shortly before noon. After closing the shore and running along the coast of Direction Island, we rounded the western point of the island to enter the calm water of the lagoon. I furled the mainsail and beat up to the lee of the island close to where a landing-barge and crash-boat were moored, and was about to pick up a mooring buoy when I saw a young man coming out in a small boat to show me where to anchor. He was one of the Cable Station staff, and after directing me to anchor close off the beach, he took me ashore to meet the members of the Cable Station.

Cocos, I learned, was an important station and was a kind of crossroads for the ocean cables which connected it with Rodrigues Island,

Singapore and Perth. The staff usually spent eighteen months on the island and only the manager and his second in command were married and had their wives on the island.

Dan Griffin, the eldest of the single men remarked, "We're all exiles here, John, and we don't see many new faces. Please eat in the mess with us and make yourself at home."

I enjoyed the company of all these single men who were much the same age as myself, but I noticed that the conversation invariably settled down to one topic, sex. One of them said quite ruefully, "Hell, there must be a lot of people think you are living an odd kind of life, sailing single-handed round the world spending days on end alone, but think of us here on this ruddy island, we don't get off for eighteen months at a stretch!"

I gathered that most of them chose to spend their holidays in Singapore, and I asked one of them what kind of place it was.

"Never seen it," he chuckled. "I spend my entire holiday in the hotel making up for eighteen months here!"

Cocos, I was sure, would be an interesting port of call for a yacht with an all-girl crew, which would probably be a more effective method of putting the station out of action than the efforts of the German raider *Emden* during the First World War.

The doctor on West Island, where the air-strip is, came over to Direction Island to give me an injection of gamma globulin the following day for there was an outbreak of hepatitis on the island which he did not want me catching.

A couple of days later I got to visit West Island with one of the young men from the Cable Station. We sailed the six miles across the lagoon in a small boat which the staff used for recreation. It took an hour and a quarter and was a most enjoyable sail across the sheltered water. The airstrip was built during World War II and was presently being used by Qantas Airlines for their service from Australia to Johannesburg. The next stop from Cocos was Mauritius, and I was told that this route was the longest regular commercial flight over the sea in the world. At the time I was there, Qantas was using Lockheed Constellations on this route, and the stage to and from Mauritius was always done at night so that star-sights could be used for the navigation. I was impressed at the number of personnel needed for servicing the aircraft and manning the airstrip and wondered at the enormous overhead costs needed to run a modern airline. West Island's personnel were obviously better off than those at Direction for fresh provisions, milk and ice-cream were flown in regularly. I had a meal in the spotless canteen that would have done justice to any good restaurant anywhere, and I learned that there were movies and entertainments to keep the men from feeling too remote. I seem to remember that the Qantas flights were every two weeks, with the plane returning from South Africa three days later. Some of the sexually-frustrated young men on Direction Island would make the visit to West Island every couple of weeks just to have a look at what they called the "hosties" or flight attendants.

I was able to collect some mail from the Post Office on the island and was pleased to receive a chart of the Indian Ocean which Mrs. Smeeton had sent from England and which I had been unable to obtain at Thursday Island.

Back on Direction Island, I played tennis with the men and went skin-diving in the clear water of the lagoon. Skin-diving was one of the most popular pastimes and many of the young men owned aqualungs and took their diving quite seriously. Some collected shells, and I saw their collections which were truly beautiful. Many hours had been spent cleaning the shells and some of them shone like the finest bone china.

Dan was trying to tell me about someone he knew from Canada, "You may know him, as he comes from Victoria," he said.

I wondered how many times before someone had asked me the same thing.

Leaving Cocos for Rodrigues Island   Dan Griffin

"I'm trying to think of his name," Dan went on, with his eyes screwed up in concentration, "Bill something. Bill . . . Bill. . . . " I thought of the only Bill that came to mind and suggested, "Bill Barber?"

"Yes, that's the man. See? I knew you'd know him," said Dan, and proceeded with his story as though it were the most natural thing that I should have known his friend.

Cocos had seven yachts call there in the year when *Trekka* visited the island, compared to only one the previous year, Irving Johnson's *Yankee*. One of the first to call this year had been Commander Clarke in *Solace* which he and his West Indian crew had really driven after leaving Cocos, making the 2,000-mile run to Rodrigues in fourteen days, a very fine effort. *Havfruen III* had called two weeks before, but there were two other small yachts ahead of her, *Larrapinta,* a 38-foot ketch from Sydney, and *Vixen,* a 36-foot cutter from Miami.

After spending a pleasant five days at Cocos, I was ready to tackle the 2,000 mile stage to Rodrigues. So that I would not run out of reading material, my friends ashore presented me with a pile of worm-eaten books that the library would otherwise have thrown away. With these stowed in a plastic bag and my water bottles topped up, I was all ready to go.

On the morning of 14 October I set the new Terylene sails, because many of the men were going to take photographs from the crash-boat that was going to accompany me as far as the lagoon entrance. Dan promised to send me any good pictures he got; a few minutes later we were off. *Trekka,* as though eager to be on her way, quickly slipped along over the calm water until, off the lagoon entrance, my friends turned back. I waved for the last time and then ran over toward Horsburgh Island where there was a bit of a lee, and proceeded to remove the new sails and replace them with the old cotton suit. When sailing off the wind there was little point in wearing out the new ones when the cotton suit did the job equally well.

A few minutes later we were sailing again, and I streamed the log over the stern. An hour later, Cocos was out of sight and we had the ocean to ourselves again. I went below to get the first worm-eaten book, so that I could steer and read at the same time.

The weather was quite perfect with just the right amount of wind, a clear sky, and the normal ocean swell. I thought that if these conditions lasted for a few days we'd be able to make some good runs.

Looking back on this passage to Rodrigues I am amazed how easy it was. This was by far the fastest port-to-port passage *Trekka* ever made.

The weather was perfect, day after glorious day, and our track across the chart seemed to leap in great jumps with each noon position. By the end of that first week, *Trekka* had covered 858 miles with the worst day's run being 115 miles. This was the mileage recorded on the log and run through the water; it proved to be the best she ever did. There was little or no helping current on this passage so the mileage on the log was what we made good.

I followed my usual practice of steering throughout the day and then letting *Trekka* manage herself when the sun went down. The twin-staysails, mainsail and mizzen were the usual sails set, but sometimes I set the mizzen staysail when I thought the speed was falling off. At night it was easy to furl the mainsail and hook up the twins to the tiller, but I only used one pole for the weather twin, the other one being set as an ordinary staysail. The mizzen was also used as the wind was well on the quarter instead of aft.

On 23 October we were becalmed for a few hours and the day's total sank to 81 miles. This was the only poor day's run we made on the passage.

At night the radio picked up South African stations, faintly at first, but as the days went by with increasing strength. The following evening there was Christmas pudding on the evening menu for we had passed the halfway point to Mauritius. This was a custom I looked forward to partly because it was such an easy meal to prepare. Christmas pudding was served with custard, a whole potful of it, and this comprised the entire meal. There was no filling up on potatoes or stew beforehand, for this was a celebration and I started with the best thing first.

Trekka continued to surge along westwards beneath the Trade Wind sky, and though we couldn't quite match that first week in mileage, we still made remarkable progress.

On 31 October at sunset, just 17 days and 7-1/2 hours from Cocos, I sighted Rodrigues about twenty-five miles off. The wind had fallen light so I let *Trekka* drift on toward the island with the twins up during the night. In the morning the island was near at hand, looking wonderfully green and inviting. It is surrounded by extensive coral reefs but there is an anchorage among them on the northern side of the island in Mathurin Bay. As we approached the bay a motor launch appeared from the shore and guided me into the anchorage between the reefs. The anchor splashed down into ten fathoms to complete the run from Cocos for an average of 111 miles a day—surely a record for a boat of *Trekka*'s size.

The motor launch returned to shore and brought out the Resident Magistrate, M. Touteau, who welcomed me to the island, saying that he had heard I was on the way as the Cable Station had received news from

Cocos. I went ashore with him in the launch and soon met his charming wife who had soap and towels ready—apparently other boating people had called here before. Then the Toureaus drove me in their jeep to the summit of the island, 1,300 feet high, from which one can see splendid views of the island and surrounding reef.

It had been some time since the last steamer called at Rodrigues and because of this I was asked by the Post Office if I would carry the mail to Mauritius. This was an honor I was delighted to accept; indeed I was so keen to do so that I decided to leave the following day for Mauritius, and I was pleased and amused to see a formal notice outside the post office saying that all mail would close the next day at noon as *Trekka* was carrying it.

I went along to the Cable Station and met some of the young men there. One of them asked me if I would like to send a message to Cocos, so I wrote out a brief message to Dan Griffin and watched with interest as the young man wrote it down in "cablese," the form of writing which is abbreviated so that the message can be sent quicker and with less expense. A few moments later I was handed Dan's reply in which he said that the photos of *Trekka* had been developed and that he was sending them on to South Africa for me.

The manager of the station and his family invited me to lunch and presented me with some fresh vegetables for *Trekka*'s larder.

The day after arriving in Rodrigues we were off again. I wanted to get to South Africa and spend some time there with many of my old friends and perhaps enjoy Christmas with them.

The green mail-sack was stowed away up forward and some fresh strawberries and vegetables from Madame Toureau put in a safe place, then I got the anchor aboard and hoisted sail.

There was very little wind and I knew I should have waited for more settled conditions. A huge black cloud approached from the south and for a few hours we experienced some squally weather. *Trekka* crashed and banged along with just the staysail and mizzen up, but by the morning the sky had cleared and the wind went back to the southeasterly quadrant.

A couple of evenings later a plane passed overhead going toward Cocos and this showed we were not far off course.

On 7 November the high mountains of Mauritius were in sight and throughout the day we steadily closed the shore. The island looked very beautiful from the sea with the land rising rapidly in the center to heights of over 2,000 feet. Port Louis, the main harbour of Mauritius, is on the western side of the island and I elected to sail around the north coast to get there. Extensive sugar plantations were visible from the sea, some of which were being burned off. The smell from them when we came into the lee of the land was as sweet as the cane itself.

At ten o'clock that night we beat up the harbour, passing two lanes of shipping, and then the Customs launch spotted us and came alongside to pass me a tow line. We were towed into the inner harbour where I anchored and then handed over the mail-sack from Rodrigues. The authorities cleared me in the morning, leaving me free to go ashore and explore what Port Louis had to offer.

Havfruen III, the big English ketch, was in Port Louis, having been in dry dock for a few days, and I was pleased to see Batch and Ann Carr again and hear how they had been getting on since we last met in Brisbane. I was offered a berth at a private wharf owned by Blythe Brothers which I was very glad to accept, for it was far more convenient than rowing ashore in the dinghy. The offices of this firm stood close to the wharf and, before leaving Mauritius, I took a somewhat unusual picture of *Trekka* from the top office balcony.

Doug Reid, the young New Zealand crew member from *Havfruen III*, took me out to the yacht club at Grande Bay, surely one of the most attractive dinghy-sailing clubs in the world. I was trying to write mail at one of the tables in the patio, but soon became aware of delightful young French girls walking past clad in bikinis. My concentration wavered, and finally letter-writing was abandoned in favor of admiring the beautiful scenery.

A young Frenchman

Moored in Port Louis, Mauritius

took Doug and me to the races, explaining that this was something we should see. The only horse races I had ever seen were the Hollywood variety or perhaps the occasional news-reel of the Grand National. If you went to the Mauritius Races to see the horses you would probably be wasting your time, I had seen better-looking horses on the beach at Jersey giving rides at sixpence a time. It was the people at the races, dressed in their finest, who were worth seeing. There was a grandstand which was capable of holding almost two hundred people, and if you were anyone of any consequence in the community, you stood there with the rest of the island's elite. Yet it was not the grandstand that caught my attention, it was the mass of Indians in the center of the course that completely fascinated me, for whenever one of the four horses in the race went by there was a frantic rush by everyone to see it go by on the back stretch. I expected to see bodies trampled into the ground as each horse passed, but these racing fans were obviously dedicated ones and used to these goings-on. The center of the course was a riot of color. Indian women dressed in gaily-colored saris while the menfolk wore European clothes. Refreshment stands in the Indian style were scattered among the crowd selling various tit-bits which were fried in a pan over a small fire. At odd intervals people rushed across the track after a horse had gone by to reach this mass of humanity and I began to appreciate the caliber of the jockeys who faced the obstacles on the two circuits of the track, for if the wrong horse was leading, a torrent of abuse, lemonade bottles and other such handy missiles were hurled at the riders. The three of us made our way through the crowd thoroughly enjoying it all, for it was impossible not to be caught up in all the excitement. Horse-racing has never appealed to me very much, but I did enjoy attending the Mauritius Derby.

Although Mauritius has been British since 1814, most of the population are of Indian or French or mixed descent. French is the language more commonly used, but in Port Louis most of the storekeepers speak English.

I was frequently asked by Indians in Port Louis for work. This was usually from tailors who were probably eyeing my frame and calculating how much extra material would be needed. But quite often I got demands for my laundry, too. The applicant always had a printed card and references from other satisfied customers. These cards usually stated that the man was a very good tailor or laundryman who took very special care in his work, "Signed A.J. Smith (Royal Navy Stoker)."

I would have stayed longer in Mauritius and enjoyed its wonderful beaches, climate and scenery longer but for my desire to spend more time with friends in South Africa. *Trekka*'s pantry was stocked with fresh vegetables and fruit, and being in all respects ready for sea, we left Port Louis on the afternoon of 12 November bound for Durban.

There was a gentle northeasterly wind blowing once we were out in the open sea, so I set the twins and then retired below to cook the steak I had bought just before leaving. Another ocean hop was beginning.

By the following morning the enormous bulk of the French island of Reunion was plainly visible, towering up 10,000 feet into a cloudless sky. As the hours passed clouds began to form about the summit and slowly but surely hid the island from view while the rest of the sky remained clear.

The wind was becoming lighter the farther south we went, and it was obvious that we were nearing the limit of the Southeast Trade Wind. I was sorry to see it go for it had been a good friend driving *Trekka* so well these past few months. The Indian Ocean must be the best of all oceans for good sailing weather. Perhaps we were fortunate and had exceptional conditions, but I was left with the impression that this ocean has a far worse reputation than it deserves.

There was great excitement one morning when a freighter, the *Crofter* of Liverpool, appeared over the horizon and altered course to come and have a look at us. She came close alongside and an officer hailed me from her bridge asking if I was all right. When I waved back that all was well, he promised to report me in Durban which I later learned he did. I watched the bulk of her disappear over the horizon and wondered what *Trekka* must look like from the bridge of a large ship.

On 18 November, just 175 miles from Madagascar, we passed a trot line in the water similar to the Japanese ones in the Pacific. A line of glass buoys, each with a bamboo stake attached, stretched as far as the eye could see, but there was no sign of a boat or ship about. Perhaps it was indeed a Japanese line, for their vessels are reported to be fishing all over the world nowadays.

The wind piped up and *Trekka* started to fly again; by noon the following day we had run 132 miles in the past 24 hours and a favorable current had boosted this to 155 miles, which surpassed the 146 miles total for a day's run on the way to Cocos. The wind kept increasing and I had to heave to for a few hours until it moderated enough for us to continue. When it did ease the sea went down very quickly, and by noon the following day we were sailing to a northwesterly breeze 60 miles off the coast of Madagascar. For the rest of the passage to Durban the wind was constantly changing direction, so that my sleep was frequently broken at night by having to go on deck and change sail. Fortunately I was so used to *Trekka's* gear by this time that I could change any sail on the blackest night without getting into a tangle.

Trekka's larder had been particularly well stocked on this passage, the fruit that I had bought green in Port Louis was ripening steadily. There were apples, papaya and oranges, as well as litchis, a small fruit with white flesh, a brown stone in the center, and a thin brown shell covering the whole. They taste rather like grapes and are delicious. Another interesting buy had been bottles of sterilized milk packed in South Africa. This tasted the same as fresh milk and I enjoyed it with cornflakes at breakfast time.

The currents in the Mozambique Channel are strong and quite unpredictable. One day would find us set thirty miles north of the course and the next far to the south. It was all very confusing and I was pleased that there were no islands or reefs in the vicinity for us to hit. I stood well to the northward of the track to Durban, knowing that the Agulhas Current runs strongly down the African coast and on 1 December sighted land near Cape St. Lucia. We were running along the coast with a nice following breeze when I noticed a tiny black cloud on the horizon ahead. It quickly grew in size and I realised there was a lot of wind behind it. The northeaster held steady until the cloud was almost upon us, then it faltered and there was a brief lull lasting no more than a minute during which time I hastily furled the mainsail. There was a sudden blast of cold air and *Trekka* heeled to the onslaught of the elements. This kind of weather is typical along the Natal coast and is very similar to the southerly "Busters" experienced along Australia's New South Wales coast.

A few hours later the wind was back to northeast again and *Trekka* romped along on the last few miles to Durban. At dusk we were abreast of Umhlanga Rocks with the lights of the hotel there clearly visible. Then a few miles farther on the illuminations of Durban came into view. It was a wonderful sight after spending twenty days at sea, the lights from the many hotels and traffic completely obliterated the feeble efforts of the navigational beacons marking the approaches to the harbour. But this was familiar territory to me now, and at 10 p.m. *Trekka* entered the channel between the two long breakwaters and ran into the calm water of the harbour. The signal station on the Bluff fired a salvo of Morse at me with a signal-lamp and kept at it until I did my best with a flashlight, remembering the code from Boy Scout days, and told them who we were. Amazingly, they were able to read my fumbling efforts and a pilot boat appeared out of the darkness to direct me to an anchorage for the night. I was informed that the port doctor and officials would clear me in the morning.

CHAPTER *18*

Penny Whistles and the Cape of Storms

W HEN I HAD BEEN cleared by the authorities next day, the Customs launch escorted *Trekka* to the yacht basin where she lay for the rest of her stay in Durban. There I was handed two letters which offered me honary membership during my stay to the Point Yacht Club and the Royal Natal Y.C. This was a gesture which I much appreciated, especially as it resulted in me making a lot of new friends. It was wonderful to be in Durban again, for it is a pleasant city and one that is easy to enjoy with its permanent holiday atmosphere.

Havfruen III was moored only a few yards away and it was not long before I met the crews of the other visiting yachts, Peter and Lesley Mounsey from Sydney on the 38-foot ketch *Larrapinta* and Jim and Jean Stark in *Vixen* from Miami. Four overseas yachts in port at once was a record for Durban, but a few days later *Diana* arrived to make it five.

Gary and his friend Brian were sporting beards that put Mr. Young's to shame, but after I had photographed them they both shaved them off after getting a good look at themselves in the Yacht Club washrooms.

Durban at Christmas time was unforgettable, the stores all gaily decorated and the very buildings themselves appearing to smile. The thing

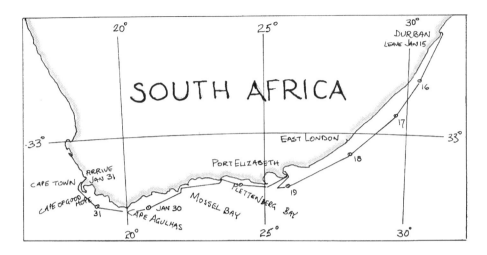

I remember best about the city at this time of the year is the music, not the dreary old Christmas carols which are paraded forth every year and which grind on monotonously in the same honeyed tones, but the bubbling happy music of the Zulu Kwela tunes that make even my feet twitch to their wonderful rhythm. After the day's work in the city, Zulu boys get together with their instruments and form small bands which play in the streets to passers-by for the odd coins which are tossed their way. These bands usually number no more than six or seven musicians, and the instruments are usually guitars and penny whistles made out of a length of metal tubing. Sometimes other instruments are used, like a saxophone or clarinet, but some of the best bands get the most magical effects with only the simplest instruments. Whatever restrictions these people of color may have in their everyday lives it certainly does not appear in their music, and anyone hearing it for the first time could not help but remark that these are a happy people. Gary and I were listening to one of these bands from the second-floor windows of a friend's apartment, the sun had gone, and it was that time of day just before night. A young Zulu girl dressed in black and wearing white shoes was dancing in the street with an open hat in her hands held out for contributions. As the light faded, it became impossible to see her at all against the dark background of the street except for the pair of white shoes. We watched quite fascinated as the shoes appeared to dance by themselves among the passers-by to the steady rhythm of the music. There are few places in the world today where you can hear the true music of a people, and I felt humbled and privileged to hear these Africans who had far more talent than many so-called stars.

After the Indian Ocean crossing, *Trekka* was in need of some attention and I spent several days repainting and varnishing her until she looked more like her former self. The best time of the day for this kind of work was early in the mornings when it was still cool. This also meant fewer interruptions from interested passers-by, for I have been told that I am a poor conversationalist when busy.

In the workshop of the Point Yacht Club I made a small teak table which fastened to the base of *Trekka*'s mast between the two bunks. It could be swivelled out of the way when not needed or easily be detached and stowed if necessary. This table was most useful, and once it was installed it was difficult to imagine how I had managed without one before; meals and letter-writing were much easier operations with the new addition.

Face-lift in Durban   John Vigor

A few days were spent visiting old friends in Pietermaritzburg where I had lived six years previously. It was good to see them all again, yet as so often happens when you return to a place after a long absence, it seemed as though it was not the same as you remembered it and I was pleased to return to my little floating home in Durban.

I met a young South African named Charles Kennedy who had recently returned from Vancouver, Canada. He told me about a young man he had met up there a few years before who was building a small boat. I listened carefully and burst out laughing, for it was me he was talking about! We had forgotten each other, as it had been a casual meeting during the Empire Games in 1954. Charlie became most interested in my voyage and eventually joined *Diana's* crew when she continued on across the Atlantic. He later returned to Vancouver where he married, built his own boat, and with his family sailed around the world. I like to think that part of the inspiration of that voyage was due to him seeing *Trekka*.

Gary, Doug Reid and I sailed *Trekka* in a couple of club races held in Durban Harbour. We suffered from a lack of local knowledge and ran aground on several of the many shoals in the harbour partly due to flying a spinnaker borrowed from a 30-square-meter-class friend. When this sail was full and drawing well, I had to lay down on the foredeck and lift a portion of the foot to see where we were going. Sometimes my directions became a little confused in the narrow channels and we spent a lot of time extracting ourselves from the mud-banks. We did have a lot of fun though and I think the local sailors had a good laugh at our antics.

Gary told me that he had decided to leave *Diana* and join the Mounseys on *Larripinta* which was going on to England. I was sorry that we were to part company for he was a good companion even though he appeared to be addicted to macaroni and cheese, the only meal he would ever cook on *Diana*. Our paths were to cross again four years later in England where he met and married a lovely English lass named Jeannie.

Doug was staying on *Havfruen III*, and as the ketch was bound for the West Indies, we were sure to meet up again before too long.

My thoughts were somewhat preoccupied on the next stage of the voyage down to Cape Town, and I suspect bets were being laid as to my chances of making this leg successfully.

Durban sailors had a somewhat morbid sense of humor when the passage to Cape Town in a small boat was mentioned, and many of them told me of the trouble and strife other yachts had encountered while attempting to round the "Cape of Storms." I met Ray Cruikshank who had crewed with Tom Steele in the *Adios* when they had been rolled over during a storm on this passage. I had also met Tony Armitt and Brian Loe in New Zealand after their successful circumnavigation in the 28-foot *Marco Polo* which had suffered storm damage near Port Elizabeth during this leg of the voyage. Until *Trekka* completed her trip, *Marco Polo* was the smallest yacht to circle the globe.

The accounts of these bluewater sailors of their experiences off the coast of South Africa indicated that this could be a most unpleasant trip if the weather conditions were against you.

There were many other tales of woe that set me thinking about the Cape. Was it always bad? Or were most of these other hectic voyages made at the wrong time of the year? On checking I learned that most of these horror stories had an element of unpreparedness about them—the boat was not in the best condition or it was an unfavorable time of the year. Yet the "Wilderness Coast" does have quite a reputation and there have been some major shipping disasters occur between Durban and the Cape. It was not surprising that the crews of the other four visiting yachts were eyeing one another wondering who would be the first to attempt this leg. We all discussed the 900-mile passage and argued about the best tactics: was it better to stay in close to shore or venture farther out? The Agulhas Current was the main bogey. This mass of water flows down the African coast toward the Cape at the rate of about 50 miles a day, but under certain conditions it can double that speed. A gale from the southwest against the current kicks up a vicious short sea which is dangerous to any shipping, and particularly small craft.

My plan on this stage was to keep *Trekka* as light as possible, for although the motion was sometimes quite violent when she was light, she got hit less by the sea than when laden. I put aboard only enough stores to get me to Cape Town and saved quite a bit of weight by filling only three of the water bottles. Knowing that there might be some hard sailing on this stage, I bent on the new suit of sails as the old cotton suit would not stand much rough treatment. They had become so baggy from the constant use that it was becoming difficult to beat to windward with them. The old cotton mainsail had stretched nearly eighteen inches over the original luff length of 22 feet, 9 inches, and it had become necessary to roll a couple of turns of the boom if it was to be sheeted in hard, otherwise the boom rested on top of the dinghy.

On Wednesday, 15 January 1959, the weather had cleared after two days of strong westerly winds. These conditions are usually followed by three days of easterly wind so I quickly collected a clearance from Customs and within the hour was drifting down the harbour and out to the open sea with a faint easterly breeze smoothing the wrinkles out of the sails.

A long swell rolled up from the southwest, and it was not long before my shore-softened stomach paid its toll. *Trekka* began to edge out offshore for I wanted to take full advantage of the favorable current during this spell of fine weather.

By noon next day we were 100 miles down the coast and 30 miles offshore, but during the night the wind suddenly switched round to the southwest and began to blow hard. The sea became quite steep, but *Trekka* seemed to have the situation under control and after a few uncomfortable hours we were able to proceed under sail again toward the southwest. Sights the following day showed that, during the time we had been hove-to, we had in fact been set over fifty miles to windward by the current—little wonder that the sea had been steep!

The wind switched around to the east again and *Trekka* surged along down the coast carrying all the sail she could. At noon on the fourth day we had passed Port Elizabeth, but that evening the breeze fell away and I noticed that the barometer was falling—a sure sign that another depression was on its way. When the wind returned it was from the west, and all too soon it had kicked up the sea to such an extent that we were forced to heave to again. It seems that the winds along this section of the African coastline either blow up or down it, but never off or on to the land, so that there appears to be little danger of being blown ashore.

During the hours of darkness, the loom of the light on Cape Recife was clearly visible, and rather than be tossed about like a rag doll waiting for the wind to change, I decided to run back to the promise of shelter in Port Elizabeth. The passage to Cape Town had now been cut in half and we had done the worst bit, for the section of coastline from Durban to Algoa Bay is barren of any shelter apart from the Port of East London on the Buffalo River. From Port Elizabeth onward there are several bays that give good shelter during westerly weather, and if I watched the barometer, there was a good chance of avoiding gales if I sheltered in time.

I moored *Trekka* close to some other craft near the Navy landing. The harbour of Port Elizabeth was designed for liners and freighters rather than small craft, but this was a case of "any port in a storm." Soon after arriving I went ashore and bought a large piece of beefsteak as a celebration which I rounded off nicely with a full eight hours of sleep.

In the morning the westerly wind had gone, to be replaced by a gentle breeze from the southeast, and I lost no time in getting back to sea again. The breeze strengthened and we sailed down the coast steadily getting closer and closer to the southern tip of Africa. After being so long in the tropics I was feeling that this was something like Cape Horn, but the latitude of Cape Agulhas, the southernmost tip of Africa, is only 34 degrees 50 minutes as compared to the Horn's 56 degrees.

On the afternoon of 24 January, I motored into Plettenbergs Bay as the wind had gone and it seemed likely that when it returned it would be from the west. Soon after I had anchored, two Navy vessels, a frigate and a Fairmile, entered the bay and anchored about a mile away close to the settlement ashore. They were still there the following morning when I attempted to leave, and as we sailed close by the frigate *Good Hope,* an officer on the bridge hailed me with a loudspeaker and asked the name of the yacht and where we were from. He seemed quite surprised when I told him.

The wind was still undecided and I saw that it would be a waste of time to try and sail with so little; rather than try my patience, I returned to our anchorage under the cliffs on the southwestern side of the bay. Soon afterwards, a whaler came toward me from the *Good Hope.* The coxswain said that the officers would like me to have lunch with them, and if it was all right they would come and collect me later. I gladly accepted, and when the officers duly arrived rowing a whaler and clad in shorts, I realised that I did not need to feel too much of a hobo in their company. Soon I was enjoying a hot shower and then lunch with these friendly young men.

The sky had a threatening appearance to the west, and soon after lunch I was taken back to *Trekka* with some spoils for her larder, some fresh bread and a pound of butter. I had just got the anchor up and laid on deck when the first quick breaths of the black-looking squall reached us. I wanted to return to the anchorage under the cliffs, which would provide more shelter, and I got the mizzen and staysail set, then a terrific gust of wind hit us and *Trekka* heeled right over, pots and pans clanking away merrily. It was difficult to estimate what the wind force was in that puff but I would guess it must have been fifty miles an hour. *Trekka* fled to the shelter of the cliffs and soon afterwards I had the anchor down and both sails stowed. By the following morning all was peaceful again, a clear sky and a breeze from the east promised good sailing and I lost little time in getting sail up. The two Navy vessels left shortly before me bound for Port Elizabeth, while we departed in the opposite direction toward Cape Town. I had intended looking in at the little harbour at Knysna; indeed the navigator on the *Good Hope* had given me a chart of the entrance of the little port, which looked most attractive, but as we were carrying a fair breeze, I decided to continue on and try to reach Mossel Bay instead.

Throughout the day *Trekka* kept going down the coast, each mile registering on the log, and by nightfall the lights of Mossel Bay were abeam. The distance to Cape Town was now about 250 miles, and as the breeze was holding, I passed the bay and set a course for Cape Agulhas. Three hours later a strong westerly replaced the helpful easterly, and as shelter was close at hand, I put the helm up and headed back to Mossel Bay. I spent two days sheltering in the little harbour of Mossel Bay, feeling very pleased with myself for it was blowing great guns out at sea.

Leaving *Trekka* snugly anchored, I set off to see what the settlement ashore had to offer and found it quite a pleasant little place. The main street climbs steadily up the hill and is lined with many cafes and small restaurants, for this is a popular seaside resort. I noticed photographs in a couple of shop windows of black marlin which had been caught in the waters off the coast and learned that this was a popular spot for keen anglers. Perhaps it was because of the black marlin that the settlement reminded me a little of New Zealand, and even the scenery was reminiscent of parts of the North Island.

On the morning of 29 January 1959, I left Mossel Bay with a fine, steady easterly breeze driving *Trekka* along close to her maximum speed. By darkness we had covered 60 miles, but unfortunately the sea was getting up and the wind continued to increase. I kept reducing sail until at last the tiny storm-jib was as much as we could carry. By this time the wind was blowing extremely hard, but it was a fair wind and I didn't want to waste it so I spent all night at the helm in an effort to help *Trekka* along. The depth of water here on the Agulhas Bank was less than 50 fathoms, but the short seas did not appear to be troubling *Trekka* at all. Steering was not difficult, though as the hours wore on, I grew very tired.

Daylight revealed a somewhat more cheerful scene, though it was still blowing very hard, and the little storm-jib was ample sail area for these conditions. I climbed stiffly down the hatchway and prepared some breakfast, continuing to steer from inside the hatchway by simply reaching the tiller with one hand while the other prepared toast and hot coffee. *Trekka* was the kind of boat in which you could do that!

We were well off the coast, and a haze about the horizon hid the land that should have been visible, but according to the log we passed Cape Agulhas, the southernmost tip of Africa, at four o'clock that afternoon. The Pilot Book said that after one passes the Cape the weather will often change, and fortunately for me it proved to be for the better. The wind rapidly eased off until, just before darkness, my hand-held wind indicator showed it to be 22 knots. This was still a little strong for the twin-staysails, but as it was easing I set them all the same, and soon afterwards, with *Trekka* surfing along steering herself, I thankfully turned into my bunk and fell asleep almost immediately.

At daybreak I was up, greatly refreshed, and looking out for the Cape of Good Hope which, according to my reckoning, was about thirty miles off. I had to wait until noon when the coastal fog lifted enough to show the Cape clearly eighteen miles off. By the late afternoon we were sailing up the lovely Cape Peninsula in the lee of the mountains named the Twelve Apostles. White clouds spilled down off their peaks like water-falls, and ahead I could see that Table Mountain was also wearing its "tablecloth." This is the sign that the southeaster is blowing, but here in the lee off Seapoint we were just moving along very quietly. Darkness fell and we drifted past the Green Point light toward the light on the end of Cape Town's long harbour breakwater.

The view of Cape Town at night from the sea is superb; lights from houses, street lamps and traffic climb high up the slopes of Table Mountain. This scene seemed all the more unforgettable because I was so elated at having safely rounded the Cape of Storms. Suddenly, a terrific blast of air hit us and *Trekka* staggered from the blow. I thought it must just be a williwaw from the mountains, but I soon realised that this was continuous. With *Trekka* heeled far over, I crawled along the deck and got the mainsail down, then I went on beating with the staysail and mizzen toward the harbour entrance, now less than a mile away.

The furious blast of wind was the famous Cape southeaster sweeping around the end of Devil's Peak. During the summer months it blows almost continuously, often with great velocity; one gust at Table Bay Docks Lookout Station was recorded at 102 miles an hour. *Trekka,* well over-can-vassed, beat her way up the harbour with spray flying. Sizeable waves were slopping against the wharfs in Duncan Dock, and as it was getting late, I anchored close to a Union Castle liner that gave a little protection to the lat-est arrival from the open sea. With the big 27-pound anchor down, I turned into my bunk knowing that *Trekka* would not wander during the night, even with the gale of wind that was whistling through the rigging.

In the morning the wind was gone and Table Mountain was clear of cloud. A police launch came over toward us and shortly afterwards *Trekka* was towed to the small yacht basin by the clubhouse of the Royal Cape Yacht Club.

On this lovely clear Saturday morning, many yachtsmen were potter-ing about with their boats and several of them came over to have a look at *Trekka*. One of them remarked how clean she looked, and compared with some of the other craft in the basin she really looked like a little jewel. The sheets and halyard tails were bleached white with the sun, and the paintwork, fresh in Durban, looked as new.

"She won't look like that very long here," remarked one of the passers-by. This puzzled me at the time, but the following day I saw what he meant when the wind returned. The Yacht Club was unfortunate to have a large area of open lots, railway sidings, and shunting yards immediately behind it, and when the southeaster was blowing, grit and dust from the lots and soot from the locomotives descended on the unfortunate yachts. It is not surprising that paint and varnishwork could not stand up to this treatment for very long. The finishes of the yachts were literally sand-blasted away.

Offshore sailing in South Africa is a pretty rugged sport and I was pleased to meet these keen yachtsmen at Cape Town. Some of the older members had met my father when he sailed his ketch *Our Boy* out from England 25 years before, and one couple could even remember the wee three-year-old who had been aboard and remarked that I had grown somewhat since they had last seen me.

I was most interested to meet Mr. C. Bruynzeel, the owner of *Zeeslang*, an extremely light-displacement little sloop designed by E.G. Van de Stadt. Mr. Bruynzeel was probably the most experienced ocean-racing yachtsman in South Africa, having owned several large yachts, among them the lovely *Zeearend* and the light-displacement *Zeevalk*. We had a lively discussion as to the merits of light boats and heavy ones; I was interested to hear of his plans to build a 72-foot ketch incorporating his years of experience. This new boat, which was of laminated wood, became one of the most successful ocean-racers in her day under the name of *Stormvogel*.

Boatbuilders and woodworkers are familiar with the plywood which is produced in Holland under the Bruynzeel brand; they know it to be a first-class product which was designed to be used in a marine environment by a man who knew what going to sea was all about.

By the time I arrived in Cape Town, *Trekka* had very little aboard in the way of supplies. Cairns in Australia had been the last place where I had bought a sizeable amount of canned food, but now with the Cape safely behind me, it was time to see about buying stores. Food prices in South Africa were the cheapest I found anywhere during my voyage, and this particularly applied to canned goods, so I tried to put enough aboard to see me all the way back to Canada. *Trekka*'s designed waterline steadily sank deeper and deeper as every available bit of locker space was filled with cans and boxes.

The Yacht Club gave me six two-gallon polythene bottles which allowed me to carry more fresh water, for there were some very long stages before me in the Atlantic and Pacific when extra water would be needed. Of course, space had to be found for this, too, and though *Trekka* was deeper in the water than ever before, she was not complaining too bitterly.

There was not much needed now before I could sail from Cape Town except charts. These I had ordered from England on my arrival at Durban but they had still not arrived, and as the days passed I became increasingly impatient to leave. During this waiting period I pulled the mainmast out of the boat and gave it a couple of coats of varnish which had not been done since Thursday Island. The commodore of the Yacht Club, Basil Lindhorst, heard about my delay because the charts had not turned up and came along to tell me that there was a pile of outdated charts in the club that had been presented by one of the shipping companies. He gave me a key to an upstairs room and told me to pick out what I wanted. There was a great pile of charts and Pilot Books from which I was able to select the few that I required to get me back into the Pacific.

There had been little work to do on *Trekka* aside from loading supplies, so I had been able to spend much time visiting friends and seeing the wonderful scenery about the Cape Peninsula. What with swimming and walking and sightseeing, the days quickly sped by, and after being in port for two weeks I was ready to put to sea again. The people at the Yacht Club had been most kind to me and I hoped that someday my next boat would visit this happy port.

On the afternoon of 14 February 1959, two years to the day after *Tzu Hang*'s dismasting in the Southern Ocean, *Trekka* edged away from the dock bound once more on another ocean crossing. A cannon at the club fired a salute, and under main and staysail we quickly drew away from a group of friends who had come to see us off.

Trekka's motion felt strangely different because of the weight of stores in her—she had certainly never been this low in the water before. We shot down the harbour and went out between the pier heads into the open sea with a fine blustery southeaster filling the sails. It was a glorious day to be leaving. The sky was clear and this good breeze drove us along very quickly. Robben Island was soon left astern as *Trekka* waltzed along to the northwest, where 1,700 miles away the lonely speck of St. Helena lay. That evening the twin-staysails were set and *Trekka* began what was to be one of the easiest passages she ever made. The wind stayed southeast for days on end, and *Trekka* under her twins steered herself all the time. Whenever the wind eased, I set the small spinnaker from the masthead above the twins with the sheets led through blocks on the end of the twin poles. This soon became my favorite rig, for the addition of the spinnaker certainly slowed the motion down, making life aboard much more comfortable. With the boat self-steering so much, I was able to catch up on writing mail on the new table, and friends in Cape Town had given me a pile of books and magazines which are always good companions.

As we got farther north the weather gradually became warmer. We were making very good time, averaging over a hundred miles a day, and not having to steer at all. I liked this kind of passage very much.

One of the things that impressed me was the total lack of bird life. Previously, on other passages, there had always been the odd petrel or bosun-bird (Tropicbird), but there seemed to be no birds at all over this part of the ocean.

The radio was providing me with a lot of entertainment. My favorite serial, *No Place to Hide,* was rapidly reaching the climax and I hoped that I'd hear the finish of the story before we got too far away to pick up the station. Every night it was a little more difficult to hear and finally I had to acknowledge defeat. I never did hear the end of the story.

The B.B.C. was now very clear and I noticed how many of the requests in the programme "Listener's Choice" came from St. Helena or Ascension Island.

Leaving Cape Town bound for St. Helena Island

It was wonderful to see how the little boat kept moving along, the three blue sails without a wrinkle in them hauling us along hour after hour. Every once in a while *Trekka* surfed off a wave, and sometimes sprays of flying fish fanned out in all directions, some of them gliding over a hundred yards. Others, in a panic to get out of the way of the monster that was bearing down upon them, shot straight up into the air, and a few landed on deck but usually managed to flap back into the sea again.

The decks were dry all the time and as I was not steering, I did a little bit of varnishing. The cleats around the cockpit were not in use these days, since the sheets were made fast to the tiller, so I was able to sand them down and give them a couple of coats of varnish besides touching up a couple of other places that needed doing.

CHAPTER 19

Two Dots in the Ocean

JUST BEFORE NOON on 2 March, I sighted the steep cliffs of St. Helena dead ahead. We were still about 30 miles off, but slowly the island became more distinct until late that afternoon we were rounding the black cliffs of the "Barn" at the northeastern end of the Island. St. Helena looks a grim and forbidding place from the sea. The steep greyblack cliffs fall sheer into the water like the walls of some medieval fortress;

The steep, forbidding cliffs of St. Helena

nowhere is there any green apparent and it looks a very dismal place. I can quite understand how the Emperor Napoleon Bonaparte felt when he first saw those cliffs.

The anchorage at James Bay is on the northwestern side of the island which, during the regular Trade Wind weather, is the lee of the island. It was almost dark when we rounded the

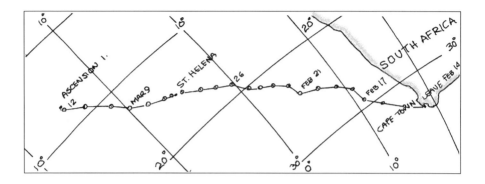

north point and tacked down the coast to the bay. A few lights ashore
were visible and in the darkness I could just see the shadowy forms of
some lighters moored near by. I anchored close to them in 10 fathoms
with my big 27-pound anchor. I didn't want *Trekka* drifting away here,
she might take quite a bit of finding.

In the morning the port officials and the doctor came out to clear me.
They thought *Trekka* had done very well to make the passage from Cape
Town in 16 days. The harbourmaster knew all the names of previous
yachts that had called here and how long they had been at sea from the
Cape. I went ashore with the officials who told me that there was a boatman who would take me out to *Trekka* whenever I wanted without having to use my dinghy.

Landing in a dinghy would have been quite a hazardous operation in
any case and, in mine, almost impossible. The landing place was at the
northern side of the bay near the end of the sea wall. A strong surge was
setting into the bay and when we got to the landing I could see the water-
level rising and falling as much as eight feet. The boatman was an old hand
at this, though, and I watched with interest how he approached the landing stern-on and, at exactly the correct moment, brought the stern up to the
steps. When the next swell came along, the stern was lifted almost level
with the top of the steps and most of us stepped quickly ashore. As the boat
fell into the trough, the boatman pulled away slightly and the next swell
brought the stern in the same position as before. It looked quite easy but I
realised that the St. Helenans were excellent boatmen. Later on I saw them
launch a whaleboat from the quay by lowering it into the water with the
crane. It was a similar exhibition of clever work, for the slightest mistake
and the boat would have been smashed to pieces against the quay in the sea
that was running. *Trekka* appeared quite safe where she was anchored,
though her masts were describing great arcs in the sky as she rolled.

The little settlement of Jamestown is entered through the gate of the fort which stretches across the great gulch from one side of the bay to the other. Situated on the cliffs and commanding the approaches to the bay are all the old fortifications. In years gone by this was an important call for the big sailing ships, both commercial and Royal Navy, to stock up on fresh provisions and water. When steam put an end to sail, the island fell on hard times for there was no need for the smoke-pots to call. The islanders had been poor ever since, and there was little industry on the island except growing flax for making rope, and the odd bit of fishing. A few years before a small canning plant had commenced operations, but as fish catches were not regular the venture closed down. Perhaps with good equipment it could be made to pay, but the problem of no harbour was a difficult one to get over, for the weather can become bad at certain times of the year and westerly storms sweep into the bay, and all craft had to be lifted out of the water with the crane.

Jamestown itself is rather like a small English village. I have seen similar places in Devon and Cornwall, but if one looks up the great volcanic slopes, the illusion is lost immediately.

I met two keen anglers who had come from South Africa to try the sport fishing. They had to make do with the simplest of boats and were without the usual fighting chairs, but one of them had managed to land a small black marlin weighing just under 200 pounds.

The anchorage at James Bay

At the time I was there, the only regular service with the outside world was the monthly visit of a passenger boat, and I gathered that this was a most looked-forward-to event. Many of the womenfolk made fine embroidery work after the fashion of the Madeira work. What I saw was not as fancy as the Madeira embroidery, but the materials were probably better as the St. Helena women used only the best Irish linen.

On my first day ashore I climbed the great flight of steps known as Jacob's Ladder. Six hundred and ninety-nine steps lead up the side of the gulch to a fort at the top, which was now serving a more useful purpose as the school for the island's numerous children. Every school day these youngsters climb the steps, and though it may look easy to anyone who has never been up them, I can assure you it is a stiff climb and took me a good ten minutes to reach the top. There was an iron handrail on each side of the steps which gave a little sense of security, for a tumble could easily cause broken limbs. The children have devised a good means of descending by lying on top of the handrails with their arms spread wide and feet on the opposite side, then sliding sideways down the rails which have become well polished over the years. I have no doubt that some of the mothers wondered how their offspring managed to wear out the backs of their clothes so quickly.

Of course no visit to St. Helena is complete without seeing Longwood, the house where Napolean was exiled. Much of it had been attacked by borers over the years, and the house has been repaired so much that little of the original is still standing. Some new teak floors had just been laid and they were very beautiful, though at the time I felt that it was something of a shame to use teak for this. Situated in one corner of the main living room was a globe of the world which was made in 1808; it was interesting to compare the coastlines of the world as known then to present day ones. I noticed that a rock was marked about 40 miles due south of the southernmost tip of Africa, Cape Agulhas. Somewhere close to that spot an 8-fathom patch was discovered a few years ago and I wondered if there was any connection between the two.

In Mrs. Benjamin's store in Jamestown I found all kinds of wonderful buys—one-pound cans of New Zealand butter and some very fine English margarine, also in cans, which kept better in the tropics than the butter. Both these items had been unobtainable in South Africa. I was on the hunt for some good ship's biscuits, similar to Pilot Bread, as an alternative to loaf bread. My large tin of biscuits which I had bought in Auckland was almost finished, but the only type I had been able to get was cream crackers.

While in Mauritius, I had bought some "hardtack" from a ships chandler there. They were enormous biscuits, an inch thick and seven to eight inches across. I tried all kinds of ways to eat them but never found the knack. When they were broken into small pieces it was like chewing stones. I soaked one in fresh water for three days and then had a go at it, but only the outside had softened a little. The inside was still as hard as rock. I considered putting them in the pressure cooker, for by this time I was wondering just what kind of supermen ate these things, but I still had

The great flight of steps known as Jacob's Ladder

other biscuits left and eventually threw all the Mauritius ones away except for a couple kept for conversation pieces. One I gave to Gary aboard *Diana;* he went to the dentist the next day, but he confessed that he hadn't even been able to put a mark in the biscuit.

I met two elderly English ladies who had settled on the island and learned from them that there were quite a number of people who had come to the island to stay. Cost of living was very cheap for retired people, and the one hotel in Jamestown was charging only five pounds sterling per week all found.

On 5 March, after a very pleasant three day's stay, I left St. Helena. Next stop was to be Ascension Island, another lonely dot in the ocean some 700 miles away. I left my two fishermen friends waving in the boatman's tender. I think they would have preferred to sail with me than on the liner that was calling the following week.

Once clear of the island, I set the twins and spinnaker and let *Trekka* take care of herself. I had swapped my store of books with one of the English ladies and was soon settling down to one of her books. There was no doubt about it, sailing was terribly rugged these days!

The wind was light for the first two days, but it freshened until it was back to the normal Trade strength, and we went along as we had on the passage to St. Helena. It was much warmer now, and I began to notice a few birds about, mainly the white bosun-birds with their long tail feathers. There was plenty of fish life, the flying fish shot out of the water in clouds, and I never got tired of watching the dorados chasing them.

One day we had a school of big black porpoises swimming with us. They were the type known as blackfish and I watched them for a few minutes before going below for my camera. Suddenly *Trekka* jerked and pulled up sharp and I realised that we had hit one of the porpoises. We got going again and a few seconds later did the same thing. These creatures are usually so nimble that I was surprised at colliding with one; this was the only occasion *Trekka* ever did so.

The twin-staysails had done quite a lot of work recently and the stitching on one of them was starting to let go. I have found that the old saying, "a stitch in time saves nine," is very true, especially with sails. I had the port twin down for about an hour one day so that I could sew up some of the seams. It will be a great day for the ocean voyager when the seams of sails are welded together; perhaps for synthetic cloth that day is not too far off.

At nine o'clock on the morning of 12 March, Ascension Island was in sight just over thirty miles away. The peak was clear and the island looked very small from a distance. But as we approached, it grew out of the sea until I was able to distinguish various points about the island, and the tall rock of Boatswain Bird Island which I approached quite closely.

Ascension Island is a strange-looking place. It is volcanic and numerous craters and lava flows are scattered about the island. Only the top of Green Mountain has any vegetation on it at all, the rest is barren and resembles a lunar landscape.

I arrived off the anchorage at Georgetown at four o'clock that afternoon and anchored near a landing-barge and a couple of other similar military craft. A few minutes later I saw a boat being lowered into the water at the end of the quay; when it arrived alongside soon afterwards I met Mr. Harrison who was the Resident Magistrate as well as being the manager of the Cable Station. He told me that he was expecting me to arrive that day as he had been notified by the Cable Station in St. Helena of my departure and he guessed that the passage would take about a week. Yachts that had called before had usually taken seven days.

We landed at the foot of some stone steps and it was a similar operation to landing at St. Helena. There was also a large swell rolling in, but the men handling the boat were St. Helenans and good boatmen, so we scrambled ashore without any trouble.

Mrs. Harrison was most kind and insisted that I have a fresh-water bath, though I knew water was rationed on the island. After a long sea voyage, that first fresh-water bath feels really wonderful, although you invariably find that all your suntan goes down the plug-hole when you have finished washing.

The Harrisons had been stationed at Bermuda and Barbados. I thought that after being there Ascension must seem somewhat lonely, yet both of them liked it very much. Certainly the climate is wonderful, the island is only eight degrees south of the equator and right in the heart of the Southeast Trade Winds so that there is always a breeze to keep the temperature down. With an ideal climate like this there were no apparent pests, flies and mosquitoes, and the island was very healthy, but there is no denying that it is a pretty remote spot in the ocean. Not everyone would care to live there.

Apart from the Cable Station there were no other people on the island except for the American base. The landing strip was constructed during World War II and must have seemed an impossible task at the time. The desolation and contours of the island have to be seen to appreciate the magnitude of the exercise. The only available site was the nesting ground of millions of "wide-awake" birds (Sooty Terns) with a hill right in the middle of it. Apparently the hill was easier to remove with bulldozers than the birds, and millions of nests were destroyed before the birds eventually found quarters elsewhere on the island. With the advent of American guided missiles, the base was manned again and Ascension Island became a monitoring station for rockets from Cape Canaveral in Florida.

It was rather amusing to come from St. Helena, where everyone seemed to talk of Napolean and the old days, and then hear conversation on "Snark" guided missiles and rocket engines. I got invited to the American Base by the Base Commander Captain Duch of the U.S.A.F. Though I was not allowed to see anything secret, it was interesting to see how the base was run. Just about everything was flown in from the States, and I had a fresh steak that night that had arrived by the Globemaster transport that day.

There were quite a number of men at the base but no women. To compensate for this wages were very high, but as one man said to me, "That don't help at all."

The mascot of the base was a donkey named "Hardaway." He had learned to drink beer right out of a can and spent his day bumming drinks off the men. He was drunk from morning until late at night and had such

The lunar landscape of Ascension Island

a solemn look on his face that everyone kept offering him drinks. His diet seemed to agree with him, for he looked in very good condition, though one man was convinced that beer was no good for him, and swore that he was developing a "gut" from drinking so much.

The Harrisons took me to the farm at the top of the mountain one day in their jeep. The road winds up the mountainside and is very steep and narrow. The hairpin bends were very tight and I thought it would make a splendid course for a keen hill-climb motorist. We stopped at one of the bends where greenery was starting to grow and looked at the desolation below. Everywhere were the fantastic colors and hues of the craters and ash. Higher up the mountain it became pleasantly cool. Grass and a few trees grew by the side of the road, and when we arrived at the farm it was difficult to believe that this was the same island. A fine drizzle drifted down on us for a few minutes and I realised that it was the moisture from the Trade Wind clouds. No wonder everything was so green up there. I met Peter Critchley and his wife who were running the farm. As there was only the Cable Station staff to cater for, Peter grew crops of every-thing—potatoes, onions, carrots, lettuce and cabbage—as well as many other vegetables. There were poultry and pigs, and in fact it could easily have been a little farm in the Channel Islands or some part of Britain.

Staying at the farm were two ornithologists, Dr. Bernard Stonehouse and his wife Sally. They were part of the party that were studying the "wide-awake" bird for the International Geophysical Year. They asked me if I had seen any birds on the way up from St. Helena, but I told them that aside from a few bosun-birds and storm petrels I had not seen very many. They told me that the wide-awake bird returned to the island every nine months to nest but disappeared after staying on the island for three months. No one seemed to know where they went, but Dr. Stonehouse thought that they might stay out at sea somewhere, only returning to the island to nest.

I wanted to walk to the summit of the island to see the dew-pond at the top and Sally Stonehouse offered to come with me. We set off along a trail which wound around the mountainside, circling the summit and giving wonderful views of the rest of the island. The trail became very muddy, but when we were nearly there we entered a thick grove of bam-boos. A few steps more and we came to the very top of the mountain. There among the bamboos was a lily-pond about twenty feet across with a few goldfish swimming lazily about. It seemed most unexpected to find a pond on the summit of a mountain. The moisture from the clouds con-denses on the bamboos and provides water for the pond. Close by was a piece of old chain, and Sally said that she had been told that if you held the chain and made a wish, your dream would come true. I know it works because my wish came true one day in September six months later.

When we returned to the farmhouse breathless and hungry, Mrs. Critchley had a wonderful spread for afternoon tea. She seemed genuinely pleased when she saw the massacre of her cakes and pastries.

Before I left, Peter put some potatoes, onions, a large stalk of bananas, and some lettuce in the jeep for me. These were most appreciated and I think Peter would have been pleased to know his potatoes were the finest I've ever tasted. I still had some left when I reached Hawaii four and a half months later. They had kept perfectly.

Mr. Harrison was a keen yachtsman and I took him for a short sail in *Trekka* one afternoon. I guessed he didn't get much chance to sail while living on Ascension, and I knew that this was one of the things he missed very much.

CHAPTER *20*

Fish Friends on the Way to Barbados

O N THE AFTERNOON of 15 March, I left for Barbados in the West Indies. The Harrisons came to see me off and I sailed close to the quay so that they could get a picture of *Trekka* under sail. With a fine, steady Trade Wind blowing, we were soon putting the island below the horizon as we set off on the longest stage so far, 3,000 miles. The twins and spinnaker pulled away like a team of horses and the log clocked the miles away constantly.

Trekka had been growing some weed about the waterline, but I noticed that while she was anchored at Ascension, some small black fish had been eating the weed and it was almost gone. They were curious little fish and would eat just about anything I threw into the water. I tore some paper up and threw that over the side; they loved it.

We continued running before the wind for the next four days, by which time we had covered 430 miles. The wind was starting to get very light now, though, and toward the north I could see heavy black clouds. That night I could see flashes of lightning in that direction, too, and I realised that we were approaching the Inter-Tropical Front. Instead of continuing to the northwest, I altered course to the west and ran parallel

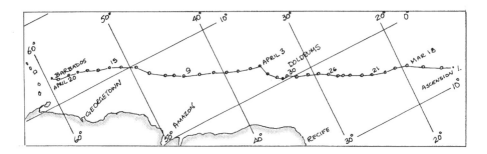

to the cloud, hoping that we could find a narrower belt of doldrums
toward the South American coast. For the next few days I edged farther
toward the west, staying close to the same latitude. The wind was light
and fluky but there was a nice current under us that was giving our daily
runs a boost of about 15 miles every day.

I had a look over the stern at *Trekka*'s bottom one day and noticed that
it was starting to foul up with goose barnacles. I remembered how they
had grown while crossing the Tasman Sea and I hoped they would not
slow us down too much. This passage was going to be long enough as it
was. I noticed that whenever *Trekka*'s bottom had marine growth on it, we
started to collect a family of fish friends that followed the boat for hundreds of miles. Two yellow-finned tuna had joined the company; they
were large fish and would have weighed nearly a hundred pounds apiece.

The sea was very calm and just the lightest of breezes pushed us along,
but it was most enjoyable to be out in the sunshine all day. It was quite
hot at midday for we were getting close to the Equator now.

One evening I noticed something odd about the moon. There was a
big piece bitten out of it and I wondered what had happened. On checking the nautical Almanac I saw there was a partial eclipse of the moon on
that night. A few minutes later it was back to its usual shape and I felt
somewhat easier.

When we were about 450 miles from Cape São Rocque, the easternmost point of South America, the wind steadied in the southeast, so I ran
before it for the next couple of days, determined to cross the doldrums at
about 33 degrees west longitude.

The sky clouded up and soon afterwards the rain was teeming down
in solid sheets. I had to replace the twins with the working rig and make
use of the occasional squalls that blew hard for a few minutes before leaving us slatting around in a jumble of a sea. The wind was trying to go
around to the northeast, but it was still very uncertain and I had to constantly adjust the sheets to make the most of each breath that came along.

I was amazed at the bird life about the boat. We passed thousands of wide-awake birds and I thought Dr. Stonehouse would probably be interested to know about all these. Perhaps he was correct that they remain at sea for nine months.

On 30 March we crossed the Equator and left all the squalls behind. The sky cleared and we were left becalmed on a still and silent ocean. The water was like glass and I got my face mask and inspected the bottom of *Trekka* again. She was fouling up quite quickly and I wondered if I should attempt to scrape her off before I got to Barbados. Almost as if to answer that question I saw a shark slowly circling the boat. It was brown in color with white-tipped fins and tail. I decided the bottom would be quite all right for another couple of weeks.

All about the boat were hundreds of fish, mostly dorado with their young. They circled around slowly as though asking why we had stopped. I noticed one with a scar on his side that kept close to the shadow of the hull. He was an easy fellow to recognize and I immediately christened him "Scarface." The two big tuna were still with us, and an ugly-looking barracuda, nearly five feet long, stayed practically motionless well below the surface. The shark tried to catch some of the smaller fish which rushed to the protection of *Trekka*'s hull. The rudder jerked over and I felt the shark beneath the boat trying to get at the little fellows. I felt quick anger that he

Old Scarface stayed with us, day after day

should try to eat one of my little friends and quickly got one of the twin poles with which I managed to poke him on the head. He looked quite offended and slunk away, leaving us all in peace.

When the wind came back it was from the northeast. Gently at first, a faint air stole across the surface of the water, then ripples began to spread, so I quickly got sail up and soon we were ghosting along over the calm swells. I set the genoa in place of the staysail and away we went toward Barbados, still 1,700 miles away.

All the little fish had gathered astern just behind the transom. It appeared that the wake of *Trekka* pulled them along so they did not have to swim to keep up with us. Sometimes a Portuguese man-of-war drifted by and a dozen or so of the little fellows would dart off to investigate it. Then there would be a mad rush to get back to *Trekka*. Very often they couldn't make it and the number of tiny fish slowly dwindled until there were less than a dozen.

The dorado and old Scarface stayed with us, day after day, swimming along at their own stations, some out ahead, others on each side and astern. Every once in a while a cloud of flying fish erupted from the water and I saw dorado chasing them at terrific speed, swimming on their sides and keeping an eye on an airborne fish until it could glide no farther. Then there was a quick splash and the dorado returned to *Trekka*, flicking their tails with satisfied looks.

The dorado were sudden death to the flying fish and sometimes got so excited that they leaped out of the water in great jumps of twenty feet or more in their efforts to catch up with the speedy flying fish.

The wind increased until it was blowing quite freshly, the sea was right on the beam, and every once in a while a wave lopped aboard and wet the pages of the book I was reading. I had to roll a reef in the mainsail a couple of times and the staysail was quite big enough for a headsail these days.

At night-time I usually stowed the mainsail and let *Trekka* go along steering herself with just the staysail and mizzen set. There was plenty of wind to keep us going and the runs each day were quite good considering the state of *Trekka*'s bottom.

I had been so amused at all the radio requests from St. Helena and Ascension Island on the B.B.C. "Listener's Choice" programme that, just before I left Ascension, I wrote to the B.B.C. and asked them to play a tune for me. I had the radio tuned in one evening and was busy getting my main meal of the day ready when to my delight I heard the pleasant voice of the lady announcer with my choice. "Calling John Guzzwell of the yacht *Trekka*, who asked us to play a request for his friends aboard the two other yachts at sea in the South Atlantic, *Diana* and *Havfruen III*. The record is 'The Breeze and I,' sung by Catarina Valenta." Neither of the crews on the two yachts heard the programme, but I know that many of my friends at St. Helena and Ascension did.

Trekka had been chasing the sun north for days and our latitude was almost the same as the sun's declination. The days came when I couldn't decide if the sun was north or south of us. The sextant read eighty-nine degrees forty-five minutes, and by the time I had turned around to look at the southern horizon I noticed that the sun was lower in the west. I have had this happen a couple of times. Noon-sights are not easy to get when the sun is directly overhead, and if you are not careful it's very easy to miss a latitude sight. Trying to work a position-line after noon is not much better, either, for with the sun immediately overhead, the line runs north and south, giving a longitude but not a latitude.

The following day we were north of the sun, and as the days went by, we gained on it so that the sextant angle decreased and the noon-sight became easier.

I saw the pole star for the first time in *Trekka* since I crossed the Pacific on the run down to Fanning Island. Our latitude was eight degrees sixteen minutes north and I wondered how close to the Equator it was possible to be and still see the star. So often cloud about the horizon hides it from view.

As we got more to the west the wind slowly became more easterly, which brought it farther aft. I was able to set the twin staysails with only one boomed out, so that *Trekka* could steer herself at night-time with the wind on the quarter. The wind was also lighter as we got farther north, and sailing was not such a wet business as it had been a few days before.

Each night the West Indies radio stations and Radio Demerara in British Guiana came in a little stronger on the transistor portable, and I realised that we were getting close now. Only another week and I would be snug in Barbados.

The dorado were still swimming along beside *Trekka*; they had followed us for over 1,200 miles now and Scarface was still among them. It occurred to me that I might try to catch one for a meal. I had some line and lures that a keen fisherman had given me when I was at Lindeman Island on the Great Barrier Reef. I had never caught anything on them, but with so many fish about it should not be too difficult, I reasoned.

I secured a good-looking lure to a stout nylon leader, then tied this to a strong hand line. The lure no sooner hit the water when a big dorado took it. He swam up toward the stern and fixed me with a questioning look as if to say, "What's the game, buster?" Then he gave a brief flick of his head and swam away with the lure still in his mouth. I pulled the line aboard and saw that the nylon leader had parted. But my fishing instincts were aroused now. I thought there could be no finer thing for dinner that night than fresh dorado and I was determined to get one. I spent quite a while unlaying some spare rigging wire to make a leader, but although I hooked several more there was no way that I could land one, they were simply too big for the equipment at my disposal. Their colors were lovely to look at and changed from green through silver and almost white, and then to the most wonderful electric blue. Some appeared to have brown stripes down their sides, but they changed colors so often it was difficult to say exactly what color they were.

My stock of lures was soon used up and I saw fish swimming alongside with the silver spoons hanging from their mouths. Fortunately for them they were not stainless hooks and it wouldn't take too long for them to rust through and free the fish of the encumbrance.

On the night of 20 April I sighted the light on Ragged Point, the easternmost point of Barbados. As we closed the land I could see the breakers on the reef, clear in the bright moonlight. I stayed up and ran along the coastline round the south end of the island. Then early the following morning, we rounded Needham Point and came into Carlisle Bay where I anchored not far from a big freighter. There was still a little darkness left, so I went below to snatch a couple of hours' sleep. *Trekka* had taken just under 37 days for the 3,000 miles.

I was awakened by the port officials who wanted to know why I didn't have my yellow flag up. They were not a scrap interested in papers or passport but seemed rather annoyed that I was not flying a quarantine flag. I told them I had only arrived a couple of hours before and was very sleepy and had forgotten all about it. They accepted this story without too much disbelief, and I promised that if ever I came again I would fly my little yellow flag. The doctor looked at me a bit doubtfully, then said I was fit enough to go ashore. The other port officials told me to go over and anchor off the Yacht Club and pointed toward the southern end of Carlisle Bay where I could just see some small craft moored off the beach. I tacked up the bay and anchored close to the Aquatic Club. A Dutch yacht was anchored close by. She was of the barge type with bluff bows and lee-boards, and I thought her crew must have been pretty plucky to have sailed her from Europe.

It was a delightful anchorage just off the beach. I went ashore in the dinghy and was offered honorary membership of the Aquatic Club for the remainder of my stay. This was very handy as there were showers to be had there, and it was possible to get meals, too.

The following day I met Ian Gale and his wife, Margaret. Both of them were young people around my age and very keen on sailing. Ian was the Commodore of the Dinghy Sailing Club which was right next door to the Aquatic Club. He had a little 26-foot schooner named *Simbie* which was built for him in Bequia. She looked a trim little vessel and was kept beautifully. We decided that we'd take both boats for a sail and try and get some good photographs of them before I left.

Simbie, Ian Gale's 26-foot schooner, was a trim little vessel

In the warm Barbados waters, scraping the weeds off *Trekka's* hull was a pleasure

Bridgetown, the main town on Barbados, was a fascinating place. I used to love to walk along the waterfront and see the big trading schooners unloading their cargoes from other islands. Many of these schooners had been fishing on the Grand Banks for cod before they were sold and retired to a warmer climate. They make a fine sight under sail, beating up to the island from Martinique or running down the coast, perhaps from Georgetown.

The narrow shady streets of Bridgetown, with the crowds of gaily-dressed West Indians, were a riot of color. Fruit vendors sold oranges and limes on the street corners, and all the while I was conscious of laughter and gaiety in the air. I found good produce in the market near the bus depot and was interested to see many of the island crafts on sale here, too, from plaited shopping bags to steel drums all tuned up and ready to play.

Early one morning I saw *Havfruen III* motoring up the bay toward us. She had just arrived from Ascension Island, too. Later that evening I joined Batch and Ann Carr with their crew to celebrate the completion of their voyage around the world, for *Havfruen* had crossed her outward track at Barbados to finish her circumnavigation. She was bound for England a few days later via Bermuda, so this was to be the last time the two boats were to share an anchorage together.

There was something very satisfying about returning to the beach late at night after visiting friends ashore, pulling the dinghy into the water, then rowing back home to *Trekka*. She was ridiculously small to be sailing around the world, but she was home to me, and once aboard, I felt completely independent. I could have a wonderful time ashore and meet lots of friends, but I was never sorry when it was time to return to *Trekka* where I had everything at my fingertips, no worries, a very good deck over my head, and plenty of food.

I cleaned off *Trekka*'s bottom while she was anchored. The water was delightfully warm, and swimming about with fins on my feet and a face-mask on was a pleasure rather than work as I scraped the barnacles off with a broad knife paint-scraper. The bottom needed painting again, but I thought it would last until I got to Panama where I wanted to anti-foul it before taking off on the final leg of the journey.

One lovely sunny afternoon, Ian Gale and his wife, Margaret, brought an attractive young lady along with them to crew for me so that we could get some photos of each other's boats during the afternoon sailing. It was a pleasant change to see someone else enjoying the feel of *Trekka*'s tiller, and I was able to change sail up on the foredeck without the usual scramble aft to bring the boat back on course. This type of day sailing is quite different from ocean sailing and I enjoyed the afternoon very much. For many larger cruising boats it was just too much trouble to bother with these brief afternoon excursions, but on a little boat like *Trekka* it only took a few minutes to have sail up and be away.

CHAPTER *21*

Panama and the Pacific Again

AFTER A WEEK'S STAY at Barbados, I was ready to leave for Panama. I had collected all my mail and had bought fresh fruit and vegetables. I still had cases of canned goods aboard, enough to see me to Hawaii, anyway.

On the morning of 29 April, I left Bridgetown and sailed past *Havfruen III* for a final farewell. Both boats had put a few thousand miles behind them since they first met in the Bay of Islands in New Zealand, and I was sorry that this was the parting of their ways.

Cristobal, the port at the Atlantic end of the Panama Canal, was 1,200 miles away. The passage started off with light winds and wonderful sunny weather, but a few days later the sky clouded up and there was much rain.

I was startled one afternoon by what sounded like breakers on a reef. It was thousands upon thousands of porpoises, breaching and leaping out of the water as they made their way rapidly across the horizon. It was truly a remarkable sight and one I fear will never be repeated due to the terrible toll commercial fishing has had on these unfortunate creatures.

Another day we were running with the twins and spinnaker set when I heard a roaring sound. I looked around the boat, then saw a disturbance on the water less than fifty yards away. The water was being whipped

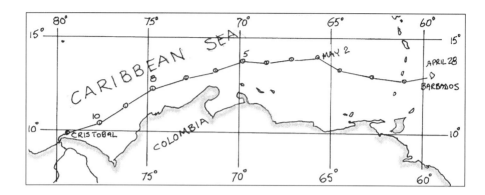

about over quite a small area, and as I watched, fascinated, a waterspout began to form. The spray was rising from the water so that it was a hollow tube about eight feet in diameter. It was spinning about like a dust-devil and moving across the sea at about eight to ten knots. Though we were so close to it, the wind held true, but I got the spinnaker down in record time in case it came closer.

The spout overtook us; when it was a couple of hundred yards ahead, it seemed to disappear suddenly. This was the only time I had seen a waterspout and I was left with the impression that a small one like this

Thousands of porpoises made their way rapidly across the horizon

would not cause much damage to a small boat apart from making the sails flog around briefly.

I was starting to see plenty of shipping about, and though it would be very unlikely for a ship to hit *Trekka* at sea, I decided to light the lantern and hang it in the rigging at night, just in case. We were close to a shipping track all right and the sea was full of rubbish. I saw paint tins and boxes floating about and quite a few large planks which I thought of when we were sailing fast at night-time. *Trekka*'s cedar planking would not need to have a very hard knock to have a hole smashed through it.

As we approached Panama, I saw more and more ships and I hoped that the lantern was visible, though I had some doubts. We were running with the twins and spinnaker set early one morning when I saw a ship coming up astern on the same course as *Trekka*. She had strangely familiar lines and I thought she looked a bit like one of the refrigerated cargo ships that operated between New Zealand and Britain. When she got closer she altered course a little so as not to approach us too closely, and I was able to read her name, *Taranaki*.

As this is the name of a beautiful part of New Zealand's North Island, I was sure my guess was correct. The officers on her bridge waved cheerfully, and I wondered what they thought of seeing a small yacht steering herself and running right on course while her skipper sat atop the dinghy waving back.

A couple of days later, after arriving in Cristobal, I met these same officers and had lunch aboard the *Taranaki* while repairs were being made to her engines. The men said that *Trekka* looked very lovely but also very small. I would have liked to have seen her this way for it's so very seldom you get to see your own boat sailing.

I arrived at Cristobal just after daylight on 12 May after a 14-day passage from Barbados. There was only a breath of air when I arrived and we drifted in past the breakwaters with barely steerageway. A Pilot Boat came over to check up on the new arrival and offered me a tow. I said that we had a motor and got it out of the aft locker to bolt it over the stern. It was pretty rusty, but after all it had not been used since Plettenbergs Bay in South Africa. The Pilot looked out of the wheelhouse window and I could see from the doubtful expression on his face that he did not think I had a hope of starting it. It was a British motor and had marked on the tank somewhere beneath all the rust, "The best Outboard Motor in the World." It was a somewhat dubious claim but I felt a stir of national pride as I looked at the battered old thing. The Pilot asked good-naturedly, "What's that, an egg beater?" I knew what he meant but refrained from answering, determined to uphold the boast of its makers. I flooded the carburetor and mumbled a few prayers over it before pulling the starter cord. It fired immediately and roared into life. The expression of amazement on the Pilot's face was reward enough and I wondered how many other makes of outboard would have withstood the neglect and abuse as well.

I had been anchored only a short while when the doctor and measurer arrived. The doctor said I was fit enough and could go ashore to report in to Customs later. Then I helped the measurer to get *Trekka*'s dimensions so that he could work out the tonnage by the Panama Canal rule, as dues to transit the Canal were computed on a vessel's tonnage.

Later that day I moved *Trekka* to the Yacht Club in Cristobal. It was a handy place to moor and had water and power laid on at the dock. I was soon joined by a ketch named *Sundowner* with a crew of young high school students from Newport Beach, California. We were soon all good friends, and as the boys could speak Spanish much better than I could, I waited until one of them was going up to Colon before going to do any shopping.

About the only job I wanted to do here was paint *Trekka*'s bottom, and the morning after I arrived, *Trekka* was sitting up on the slipway at the Yacht Club and was having two good coats of anti-fouling paint applied. The next stage was going to be a very long one and I didn't want the bottom covered in barnacles again as it had been on the run from Ascension.

The Panama Canal Zone, the narrow strip of territory on each side of the Canal, was kept free of flies and mosquitoes by constant spraying of insecticides, and I saw large tanker trucks equipped with spray guns moving along the roads spraying the trees and bushes. Once across into Panamanian territory, the contrast was amusing. Papers and filth were allowed to remain in the streets, which looked as though they were never swept, and I wondered what the American Health Department in the Zone thought about the situation.

With *Trekka* back in the water, I wanted to get through the Canal and back into the Pacific again as soon as possible. I learned that if I could find someone with a launch-operator's licence, I need not take a Pilot, but it was necessary to have two other men on board as line handlers for going through the locks.

I had read various accounts of other ocean voyagers who had taken their yachts through the Canal and some of them sounded a little scary to me. The general opinion was that it was best not to transit the locks against the side of the lock walls and many yachts opt for center lockage. To do this, though, you need four good lines, each at least 100 feet long, and a man to handle each line. This was asking a bit much of *Trekka*, so an alternative was to lock through alongside one of the banana boats, motor launches that make frequent use of the Canal.

Jim Gloss, a young man whom I met at the Yacht Club, had a licence and he kindly offered to come with me through to Balboa. One of the young men off *Sundowner* also said he'd come. Jim told me that there was a tug locking through the following morning and we could go alongside her.

I went along to the Harbormaster and told him that I wanted to go through the following morning and I was taken upstairs and introduced to a Mr. Peterson as Captain Guzzwell of the *Trekka*. Mr. Peterson was talking to the Captain of a freighter and I heard enough of the conversation to know that the dues for that particular vessel ran into a few thousand dollars. A few moments later I was being taken care of.

"Well, Captain Guzzwell, so you want to make the transit tomorrow, do you? I'm sure that will be all right. Has your vessel been measured?"

"Yes, she was measured when we arrived here but I do not know what the tonnage is," I replied.

"Oh, if she's been measured I can soon find that out. Will your agents here be paying the dues or will you?" he asked.

"No, I would like to pay myself, now," I said. "I have no agents here."

"Very well, just a moment, I'll phone and get the figure of the measured tonnage so that I can work out the dues."

I watched him pick up the phone and heard the following one-sided conversation.

"Hello? Oh, I've got Captain Guzzwell of the *Trekka* in the office here. The *Trekka* is making the transit of the canal tomorrow and I need the measured tonnage figure so that I can work out the dues . . . Yes, *Trekka* . . . What's that? . . . Three? . . . Three what? . . . Three thousand or three hundred? . . . Just three!" He turned to me with a puzzled expression on his face and said, "They say three tons . . . is that right?"

I nodded, "Yes, that's about right."

"But three tons at seventy-two cents a ton . . . Why that's only two dollars and sixteen cents!" he said unbelievingly.

I did not argue about it but paid up quickly. It was good value instead of going round Cape Horn.

The following morning Jim arrived with his outboard. He said mine was not the best-looking he had seen and did not inspire him with confidence. "Where did you find it?" he joked.

"Hey, before the day is out you'll change your opinion about my old motor," I answered confidently.

With the young man from *Sundowner*, we set off and reached Gatun Locks an hour later, after I had set the main and staysail, too.

We were almost an hour early and found a banana boat that was about to go through. Jim asked the skipper if we could go alongside him and he said it would be all right.

I had borrowed four car tires to use as fenders and these were ready to hang over the side. A few minutes later we motored into the great canyon of the lock and secured alongside the banana boat and astern of a German freighter, the *Perseus*. The huge lock-gates closed behind us, and a moment later the calm surface of the lock began to boil as water gushed into the lock through the eight-foot-square manholes in the floor. *Trekka* was tossed about against the banana boat but the tires saved our paint. A few minutes later the gates ahead opened and we followed the *Perseus* through into the next lock to repeat the operation. Once more we did the same. Then we left the locks behind and motored out into the fresh water of Gatun Lake, some 85 feet higher than the Atlantic.

This was supposed to be the rainy season but the weather was perfect. There was a nice little northeasterly breeze and it was quite hot. Jim sug-

We follow the *Perseus* into the next lock

gested that we make a quick stop at the Gatun Yacht Club for some ice before setting off across the lake to Pedro Miguel Lock. We pulled in one of the floats, and before I could say anything, Jim was off bucket in hand to get ice and some sodas.

We were soon on our way again with the outboard running like a watch, never missing a beat. But the speed was still too slow for Jim so I put every possible sail up, too—the masthead genoa, staysail boomed out, main, mizzen staysail and mizzen. Jim knew the "Banana-boat Passage," a narrow channel that is a short cut and saves a couple of miles. It was rather frightening to me to see all the tree stumps sticking out of the water on each side of the channel so poorly marked. I went below so that I wouldn't have to look.

"While you're down there, John, make us another drink and put lots of ice in it this time," ordered Jim from his station at the helm. This was his fourth rum and coke and he was starting to enjoy the outing. Presently we were back in the main channel again with shipping of all sizes passing us in each direction.

"Hey, John, these drinks are starting to catch up with me," said Jim a few minutes later, "I need to use your toilet." I did not know quite what to say and just looked at him.

"You do have one, don't you?" he asked seriously, conscious of my hesitation.

"Jim, I haven't got room for one of those on *Trekka,*" I explained weakly.

"Well, what do you use, you must use something?" he asked. "Hell, even a bucket will do, give me a bucket!"

"I've only got the one bucket, Jim, and you put the ice in it," I said simply. He ended up peeing over the stern, but I noticed that there were no more calls for rum and coke for the rest of the afternoon.

We passed the Continental Divide and the Gaillard Cut and arrived at Pedro Miguel Locks at four o'clock that afternoon. There was some delay here, but we eventually locked through alongside the wall, going down presented no problems. When the gates opened, we raced across to the Miraflores Locks which would see us out into salt water again. It was getting dark when the last gate opened and *Trekka* motored out onto the waters of the Pacific. I felt that I was almost home again. Astern, the *Perseus* slid out of the lock to overtake us. She had not made the transit any quicker than we had.

With the motor still purring contentedly, we moored alongside the gas dock near the Balboa Yacht Club, where the three of us were soon having a barbecued steak in celebration of *Trekka's* return to the Pacific. Jim shook his head over my outboard and admitted that for such a horrible sight, it certainly ran very well.

At Balboa, I met Wally Pearson and his wife, Anbritt. They were keen sailors and Wally had built his own boat, a very fine Alden-designed ketch named *Tondelayo*. They had recently returned from a cruise to the Galapagos Islands and had really enjoyed cruising among those unique islands. They strongly recommended me calling there and I was tempted, as it would have reduced the length of the passage to Hawaii by about a thousand miles, but I also knew that a visit to the Galapagos would require more than a few days and I was keen to get back to Canada before the summer was over.

Sundowner arrived the following day and moored close to *Trekka*. The boys had stopped here before and knew their way around Panama City quite well. I went shopping with them there and bought some fresh vegetables and more potatoes as my Ascension Island ones were getting low. Mrs. Pearson got me a few items including canned pumpernickel bread and some canned cakes from the Commissary, which could only be used by employees of the Canal Company.

CHAPTER *22*

5,400 *Miles Across the* *Pacific*

THE SAILING ROUTE from the Canal to Victoria, B.C. is a difficult one. It is well-nigh impossible to go up the coast, for the winds are very light and head ones at that; the currents are against you on that route, too. It seemed to me that the easiest way, though by no means the shortest, would be best. This was to go right out to the Hawaiian Islands and then on up to British Columbia. It meant one very long stage, about 5,400 miles, or nearly double the previous longest stage, and then from Hawaii another 2,600 miles for the final leg. Looking at the weather charts confirmed this to be the best strategy for, although the first stage was pretty long, it would be done in a region of good weather and any trip with Hawaii at the end of it has to be all right. There are few more pleasant landfalls to look forward to.

Sundowner was off back to California; because she had a good engine the boys planned to motor up the coast and refuel at Acapulco. We planned to leave together.

On the afternoon of 21 May, the two yachts left Balboa in company and *Trekka* accepted a tow from the other yacht as there was very little wind and I wanted to be well offshore before nightfall without using up my few precious gallons of fuel.

This stage had quite a thrill attached to it, for if *Trekka* reached Hawaii

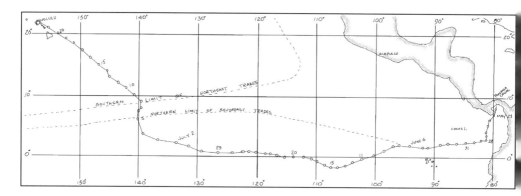

safely, she would complete her circumnavigation of the world and become the smallest vessel ever to do so.

As the light was fading, the boys on *Sundowner* slowed their engine and cast off the tow line. We shouted goodbyes to each other, and I wished that we could have continued our companionship. I felt a little lonely as they motored off into the last of the sunset, then I set about getting some sail up.

The first stage of the voyage would take us close to the Galapagos Islands where I hoped to pick up the Southeast Trade Wind, but before I got there we had to sail nearly 900 miles over a piece of ocean that has a bad name for sailing craft. Between Panama and the Galapagos Islands, the winds are fluky and the currents strong and unpredictable. Some yachts have been weeks trying to reach the islands. Although there would still be over 4,000 miles of ocean to cover once we reached them, I was not too concerned about this stage for I felt this was one passage that would suit *Trekka* very well. She was a light boat and needed very little wind to get her moving; with the new suit of sails bent on, I knew she could outpoint most cruising boats. All we needed was just a little wind.

That first night out, thunder crashed and lightning lit the sky about us. Rain fell as only tropical rain can, in solid lumps, but a faint breeze from the southeast allowed *Trekka* to sail herself toward the south and Cape Mala.

The sky had cleared the following day, and we slipped along over a very calm sea. I decided that whenever the wind dropped and the conditions were favorable to do so, I'd use the outboard motor to keep edging south out of this doldrum-like weather. Though the sky had squall clouds all about the horizon, none seemed to come near us and we stayed in the sunshine all the time. I was a little worried about fresh water on this stage because I only had 35 gallons aboard and little idea of how long the passage was going to take. Knowing that this was an area famous for its rain squalls, I made a little canvas tray that fitted underneath the main boom so that I could catch rain water from the mainsail. Later that day, a brief squall came along and I saw that the tray collection scheme worked perfectly. Once some of the containers were empty, it would be quite feasible to refill them from passing rain squalls.

My plan for the first part of the passage was to get south as much as possible before going out west to the Galapagos Islands. On the second day out we passed Cape Mala and I noticed that we had a nice strong favorable current giving us a boost when I worked out the distance run on the log and the actual miles covered.

Quite often we passed through strong ripplings in the sea, almost as if we were on some enormous river. Eddies and small whirlpools tugged at the keel, but *Trekka* kept on working her way south in beautiful weather and over a very calm sea. I wished that there was more fuel aboard, for with the sea so calm the motor could have been used for long periods.

On the fifth day out the wind went into the southwest and freshened. *Trekka* was soon going fast to the south, and at noon that day we passed to the east of Malpeo Island, just a lonely lump of rock in the ocean, the home of sea birds only. The sea in the vicinity of the island was very confused and lumpy, almost as though we were in shallow water. The following day, although we had made a good run on the log, I noticed that we had lost thirty miles to a strong northerly-setting current. It would seem that the rough sea near the island was the meeting place of two currents in opposition to each other.

On the seventh day out of Balboa we were down to latitude 2 degrees 57 minutes north and were finding the current very strong. In the past 24 hours we had run 94 miles on the log and only made good 35 miles. It was time to try the other tack, yet the wind remained firmly in the southwest. I put *Trekka* on the port tack, letting her work herself as close to the wind as possible. It was rough and uncomfortable sailing over a lumpy sea and at times we leaped from crest to crest, testing the boat and her skipper. It took another two days of this discomfort before there was a change, with the wind backing a little more to the south. Just being able to ease the sheets a little made a great difference. When the weather changed from sunny cloudy conditions to a grey cold drizzle, I sensed that we must be approaching the colder waters of the Peru current which is an offshoot of the Humboldt, that mighty stream of cold water that flows up the west coast of South America and eventually turns westward in the vicinity of the Galapagos Islands.

I kept taking the water temperature which had been a steady 82 degrees ever since leaving Balboa. Now I noticed it had dropped to 80 degrees. It took another four days of close-hauled sailing before we finally worked out of the opposing current. The wind had remained quite steady, allowing us to make daily runs in excess of a hundred miles a day, but all that time had been against the current. It was not until 4 June, when the day's 24-hour run to noon was 121 miles, that I noticed we had finally left the contrary current behind. From now on I could expect the current to be with us.

Later that afternoon the two small islands of Wenman (Wolf) and Culpepper (Darwin), the northernmost of the Galapagos Islands, were in sight. We sailed between the two and close to Wenman, but it was very barren, being volcanic in nature, and I doubted if it would be possible to land. The chart was very sketchy and the Pilot Book somewhat vague so I decided to keep going.

It was as well that the current was helping us now, for the wind became very light, the sea was calm, and the weather really beautiful. The nights were quite cool though we were close to the Equator. This was due to the water temperature which had dropped from 82 degrees F. in the Bay of Panama to the present 74 degrees F.

It was lovely peaceful sailing. The days were wonderful with blue skies and a gently heaving ocean. I sat in the cockpit reading most of the time without a stitch of clothing on, as my shorts had the seat worn out of them from constant rubbing on the fiberglass deck. I preferred to sit on a sail bag instead.

Trekka was starting to grow a fine crop of barnacles on her bottom. This was most disappointing as I had anti-fouled the bottom in Cristobal two months before with two coats of a good American brand paint to make sure she'd stay clean on this passage. I knew that it wouldn't be long before I'd have to do something about it.

On 11 June we crossed the Equator, and I noticed that the current had given us a boost of nearly 40 miles during the past 24 hours.

According to the chart, I was just about in the middle of the South Equatorial Current, the continuation of the Humboldt Current.

A few days later I found to my dismay that the current had vanished. Worse was to follow, when it turned against us and set to the southeast. I started to edge north in the hope that I would find the favorable current that had been such a help a few days before.

The light conditions persisted, and during this time I made some repairs to the sails, re-stitching some of the seams. I also continued working on writing an article for the New Zealand yachting magazine, *Seaspray,* which had printed previous accounts of the voyage.

When just 25 miles south of the Equator, the sea became very calm and I decided that the time had come for me to do something about all those barnacles on *Trekka*'s bottom. The idea of going over the side by myself was not an attractive one, for if there was one thing I was scared about it was sharks. It is seldom that you see any at sea but that does not mean they are not there, and it did not stop my imagination from working either. I had a mental picture of what the scene looked like to a shark some fifty feet below the surface—*Trekka*'s round red bottom with the keel and rudder slung below it, and a figure in the water alongside with just body and legs visible, splashing about as if in distress. So it was with considerable reluctance that I lowered myself over the stern of *Trekka* armed with a very rusty old knife and a paint-scraper. A quick glance about below the surface indicated that I was safe enough for the moment, so I scraped away around the rudder, watching the grey stalks and shells of the barnacles gradually drift down into the blue depths below. With no sail up, *Trekka* was rolling slowly to the ever-present ocean swell. As I hung on to her toe rail, my shoulders would sometimes be pulled out of the water as I attempted to scrape down right beneath the bilge.

Much time was spent with one eye over my shoulder, yet after about fifteen minutes I had cleared off quite a large area on both sides of the hull. It was not a very good job but the bottom was a lot cleaner than before. I climbed back aboard thankfully and hoped it would not be necessary to do it again. After getting sail up again, I noticed that the boat was moving much faster through the water now that so much of the drag had been removed.

The wind returned the following day, and it was more like the Southeast Trade Wind of the Indian Ocean. *Trekka* was soon going well to the westward, staying about on the Equator but slowly edging farther north, where I hoped to find more current.

The wire halyard from the masthead which I flew the spinnaker on had chafed badly at the splice and I had a difficult couple of hours repairing this as the boat rolled along under the twins. This masthead halyard was for the genoa and was never designed to accommodate the spinnaker which should have had a block at the masthead and a simple all-rope halyard. It was one of those jobs I had meant to do and yet had neglected. My arms were very tired from renewing the splice some six feet above the deck and I was pleased to complete the job and end the discomfort without losing any of the tools over the side.

I celebrated my twenty-ninth birthday with an evening meal of canned steak fried with onions, followed by one of the cans of Australian Christmas puddings with custard. Coffee was served in the cockpit as the sky faded and I was treated to a wonderful tropical sunset that would have measured force 8 on the Richter Scale. The stars began to wink one by one, and I sat there leaning against the upturned dinghy, very much at peace with myself. It is impossible to describe the beauty of these sunsets at sea when the boat is steering itself and everything is well on board. When I am away from the sea and caught up in the rush of everyday life, I shall try to remember these moments for they are among the most beautiful I have known.

The little portable radio was giving me a lot of entertainment at night, being alive with stations. Some of my old favorites like Radio New Zealand and Radio Australia were back on the air again after many months and several commercial stations in the States were coming in loud and clear. I listened in to the sensational heavyweight title fight between champion Floyd Patterson and the Swedish challenger, Ingemar Johannsen, from a Los Angeles station. I was surprised another night to hear the South African weather forecast from the S.A.B.C.

On 27 June, we were 47 miles north of the Equator and I decided to have another go at removing more of those barnacles from *Trekka's* bottom; our progress was slowing down again and the past few days had shown that the unfavorable current was still with us.

I was in the water for nearly half an hour, and by the end of that time had made quite a good job of cleaning off the bottom. The hull itself was clean, although there were still a few barnacles left between the keelbolts that were difficult to remove.

The Equatorial Current had been playing hide-and-seek with us the past few days, but now it started to give us a mighty shove to the west. At noon on the 29th, *Trekka* had made good 147 miles in the preceding 24 hours, and as the wind was holding steady, I thought that here was the chance I had long waited for. Every skipper wonders how far he can drive his ship in 24 hours, and I had long speculated on what *Trekka* could do given the best conditions and a good current to help her. The greatest distance she had covered in a day was 155 miles off the east coast of Madagascar, but it looked as though I might be able to beat that now. *Trekka* kept boiling along hour after hour, and though the wind was quite strong, I decided to hang on to the spinnaker that night and see if we could set a record run.

Sleep was quite impossible, though I lay in my bunk trying to rest, and I finally got up and stood in the hatchway looking at the gear, the quarter-inch nylon sheets were stretching like rubber bands in some of the stronger puffs. The entry in the Logbook at midnight reads:

"A-never-to-be-forgotten night! *Trekka* roaring along with a phosphorescent wake shooting off into the darkness like the tail of some big rocket. Sparks of green fire blast away as we plunge through the night or is it space? I hope the gear holds, the twins are getting ripe for this kind of thing, it's not yet one o'clock and the log reads 70 miles; if everything holds we should have a record run."

The governor-wheel on the log would suddenly spin into life and then slow for a few moments before going crazy again.

Hour after hour she kept going at top speed, surfing and sliding along, rolling and bouncing so that the supplies in the lockers below rattled away and the mast squeaked where it came through the deck.

After breakfast I took over steering in an effort to keep her running truer, as sometimes she would sheer off a wave and collapse the spinnaker, which shook the whole boat when it suddenly filled again.

By noon the log read 132 miles but sights showed that we had covered 175 miles with the current added. That night I took the spinnaker in so that I could get some sleep, but *Trekka* kept on sailing herself under the twins, heading toward Christmas Island.

I altered my watch an hour every 15 degrees of longitude so that the sun passes the meridian between 12 noon and 1 p.m. On 3 July the clock was put back another hour (there was five hours' difference between Panama time and Hawaiian time) and we had a twenty-five-hour day. I worked out the sun-sights I had taken and found the latitude close to what I expected, but the longitude was nearly sixty miles out from my D.R. position. I took fresh sights and checked the watch with time-pips on the radio, but always got a position farther ahead. I finally concluded that the sights must be correct, though it was difficult to believe, for *Trekka* had covered the remarkable distance of 192 miles in 25 hours.

The track chart was now a pretty sight, with the past few days' runs contrasting sharply with those on the way out to the Galapagos.

On the chart at longitude 140 degrees west I had marked in a position which I had named Point X. This was where I decided would be the best place to turn north and cross the doldrums before heading directly for Hawaii. I had been tempted to turn north days before, but Point X marked the narrowest belt of doldrums in this area, so I held on until we were only 30 miles short of the position, when I thought we were close enough as the current was still flowing very strongly to the west.

On the afternoon of 4 July, I gybed *Trekka* over on to the starboard tack and we went along to the north to try and find the Northeast Trade Wind. *Trekka's* daily runs continued above the 150-mile mark, and in one week she covered the extraordinary distance of 1,101 miles, surely a record for a boat of her size and one that would have been quite impossible but for the current.

We kept going north, but on reaching latitude 7 degrees 30 minutes north, the weather changed and I realised that this was the end of the Southeast Trade Wind. It was like losing an old friend. She had driven us along for thousands of miles, sometimes boisterously, sometimes gently, under skies dotted with white cumulus cloud or beneath overcast ones, with the occasional rain squall to darken the faded blue twins and wet the decks. I wondered if *Trekka* would ever know her caress again.

The next two days were typical doldrum weather. Rain fell in solid sheets from the lowering sky, beating the sea flat, only for the next squall to kick it up again. We were now in the middle of the Counter Equatorial Current which is about 180 miles wide hereabouts and sets to the east at a rate of about 30 miles a day. I motored for a few hours, using up the last of the fuel, and then stowed the motor away in the locker with the tank quite empty. A faint breeze came out of the northeast and gradually strengthened. *Trekka* could just lay the course for Hawaii, 1,300 miles away.

On 12 July, at latitude 13 degrees north and longitude 145 degrees 7 minutes west, the wind had increased to such an extent that I decided to drop all sail and wait for the weather to moderate. I did not like the look of the sky which had changed from its normal Trade Wind appearance; the sun also had a ring around it like a halo and this was not a good sign.

This was the first time since rounding the Cape of Storms that *Trekka* had been hove to because of bad weather. The wind increased until it was blowing with gale force, and I watched the barometer tumble down as the depression approached. I noticed that the wind was backing all the while, and when it was northwest it seemed to be at its hardest, but it continued round to the southwest where the fury went out of it.

This storm was probably one of the Mexican hurricanes which spawn along the southwestern coast and shoot offshore toward Hawaii in the summer months. They can pack winds well in excess of 100 knots but are usually small in extent. I was lucky to be south of its track in the safe quadrant.

After being stopped for nearly 20 hours, I was able to get going again and resume the course for Hawaii over a very lumpy sea. After the beat out to the Galapagos Islands, I had replaced the good suit of Terylene sails with the old cotton suit. These were the sails I had left Canada with nearly four years previously, and it was not surprising that they were becoming pretty ripe. After the rough treatment just before the gale, the mainsail gave up the ghost by tearing badly where it rested against the upper spreaders. Instead of trying to mend it, I replaced it with the new Terylene sail. Soon afterwards the old staysail tore badly, too. I had to set the new one and had just finished doing so when I noticed that the mizzen also had a hole in it, so that was changed, too.

The sails were not the only items that needed attention. I myself was starting to look in need of some grooming. My hair had not been cut since I left Barbados and because of water considerations I had not shaved since leaving Panama. It was time to do something about this situation. I knew that there was a pair of scissors on board somewhere and after a lot of rummaging through the lockers they were eventually found. There was still some fiberglass stuck to them to remind me of glassing the hull in New Zealand over a year before. The scissors had to be sharpened with a file before they would cut hair, but once everything was ready the job did not take too long and my appearance in the mirror indicated a considerable improvement.

On 20 July I had been at sea for 60 days and was looking out for the top of Mauna Kea, the 13,825-foot mountain on the island of Hawaii. We were still 60 miles off, but had the horizon been clear it would have been visible as I had sighted it from a distance of 85 miles on the run down from San Francisco nearly four years before.

A plane passed overhead going toward North America, and a couple of hours later I saw a small tanker also bound for the States. She passed about a mile away.

That night was a very special occasion and I had my last can of Australian Christmas pudding to celebrate it, for *Trekka* had just crossed her outward track and completed her voyage round the world, the smallest vessel ever to do so. I felt very proud of her.

The next morning when I scrambled out of the hatch, there were Hawaii and Maui peeping out of the morning haze. *Trekka* closed the shore and we romped along the northern coast of Maui while I feasted my eyes on the lovely green slopes that swept down to meet the edge of the sea. Past Kahului we went, where I had made *Tzu Hang*'s mainmast and where her southern voyage had been planned, and then on to Molokai, lit by a lovely sunset.

I stayed at the helm that night, running along the coast of Molokai with a bright tropical moon to light the way. It was wonderful to be back in familiar waters again. With the stage almost completed, I treated myself to a good wash in fresh water, then had a shave afterwards.

With the first light of dawn, we were entering Molokai channel with about 50 miles left to Honolulu. The spinnaker was pulling steadily, and a couple of hours later the mountains on Oahu became clearer. The lighthouse on Makapuu Point came into view, and early that afternoon we passed it and sailed into more sheltered water.

Toward late afternoon we rounded Diamond Head and came up to the entrance to the Ala Wai Yacht Basin. I tacked up the channel with just enough wind to fill the sails, and then moored against the gas dock where I waited for the authorities to clear me. It had been a very long passage, and the 5,400 miles had taken 62 days.

The next few days were busy ones for me. Apart from meeting many old friends and writing mail to others in various parts of the world, there was much to do on *Trekka*. The last time she had been painted and varnished was in Durban and the bottom needed anti-fouling again, so I set about trying to make her look a bit more shipshape.

Rubbing down the topsides at Honolulu

I got *Trekka* out of the water on to a cradle and went to work, rubbing down the topsides and painting them, and then cleaning off the bottom and anti-fouling it again. It was not long before the little boat was looking near her best again. Once she was back in the water I had many interested visitors to come aboard and sit beneath the sun-awning and swap yarns with me.

I met Jack and Peggy Burke who had lost their schooner *Venturer* on the reef at Lady Musgrave Island. They had a new yacht now, named *Shiralee*, which they had bought and sailed up from Sydney. There were many other friends, some of them I had met in my travels, like Buz and June Champion in their *Little Bear*. They had been in Sydney when I was there in *Tzu Hang*, and Lee and Anne Gregg, who had been in Whangarei aboard their little ketch, *Novia*. We had much to talk about for it had been a long time since we had seen each other.

I had a visit from Bill Horner who had sailed his *Brambling* out from England over much the same route as mine from Panama. He told me that he had been sitting at the Yacht Club with a group of fellow sailors over some beers discussing boats and people. The subject of small-boat voyages had come up and was being discussed heartily with each story topping the previous one. "If I had deliberately raised the subject and initiated the conversation it couldn't have been better," he said laughing. "Someone had mentioned a small-boat voyage and I said, 'Hell that's nothing, about four years ago John Guzzwell was here in his 20-foot *Trekka* which he sailed down from Canada; he's taking her around the world. As a matter of fact, if you look out at the boat channel now, here he comes!'"

I wanted to try and arrive back in Victoria, B.C. on 10 September which would make it exactly four years to the day that I left. To do this it would be necessary for me to leave no later than 5 August, as the passage was 2,600 miles and would probably take us about 35 days under normal conditions.

By the evening of the 4th all was ready, fresh fruit and vegetables were aboard; as some of my canned goods were getting low, I had bought a few more items to make sure there was enough for the passage. The water bottles were all full and Sonny Nelson, the local sail-maker, had repaired my oilskins. I figured that I was going to need them on this stage.

Although all was ready for a departure on the morrow, it never came to pass as I learned that a hurricane was rapidly approaching the Hawaiian Islands from the southeast. As it got closer, the weather slowly worsened, and the weather bureau reported that the wind force near the center was up to 135 miles an hour. The storm was given the name "Dot," and as it came closer to the islands, reports of strong winds, high seas, and the usual tales of storm damage were reported over the radio. Warnings were issued that the storm center might come close to Honolulu and residents were urged to be prepared for Dot's onslaught. I doubled up on *Trekka*'s mooring lines and wondered what kind of a mess there would be in the Yacht Basin if the eye of the storm passed over Honolulu. Some of the craft in the harbour were moored with lines no stronger than bits of string. The wind became very gusty as the eye moved closer and the Harbormaster's office flew the two red flags with the black square in the center as the official Coast Guard Hurricane warning.

The storm continued to approach, moving in a westerly direction at 10 knots, and when it was due south of Honolulu and moving on to the southwest, many people thought it was all over. A couple of yachts left to return to California but then, just as I had feared, the storm recurved and started back toward us. There was little I could do aboard *Trekka* to pass the time away. I wrote some mail and then walked up to the Waikiki Post Office clad in my yellow oilskins, sea boots, and wearing a sou'wester. The rain was driving across Kalakua Avenue in sheets and the street was littered with palm fronds from the trees along the sidewalk. A man who was soaking wet, wearing a short sleeved Aloha shirt, stopped me and said, "I can see you're one of the locals, I'm just a crummy tourist. They didn't tell me the weather could be like this here or I would have brought a raincoat or stayed at home."

That night the storm passed between Oahu and Kauai, and the latter island received quite a battering. The center had passed about 80 miles west of Honolulu and as the hours went by, the wind force slowly decreased. Although *Trekka* could probably have handled the storm, I was thankful we did not have to. These are situations that are best avoided if possible.

Because of Dot I was not able to leave Honolulu until 8 August. We could probably have left the previous day, but that would have meant leaving on a Friday and that is something many sailors simply refuse to do; it's considered bad luck and is one of the superstitions of the sea that I respected. The only time I had ever left port on a Friday at the start of a major voyage was aboard *Tzu Hang* from Melbourne for Cape Horn. I had no desire to repeat *Tzu Hang*'s pitchpoling in *Trekka*.

CHAPTER *23*

Home Run

IN SOME WAYS it was sad leaving Honolulu. This was now the last passage I would be making in *Trekka* for a long time, perhaps forever, and though I wanted to get back to Canada, part of me wanted to delay the homecoming.

Over the horizon some 2,600 miles away were the timber-clad mountains of British Columbia. *Trekka* seemed to know that she was headed home now to the land where she was born, home to the land where the pine trees scent the air and the white-capped mountains reach to the sky, home to the waters where the Coho and Sockeye run, where busy little tugs tow the log-booms, and the early morning fog hangs about the inlets. I, too, was looking forward to getting back, for no matter how beautiful another country may be and the time you spend there, it's not the same as returning home again after a long absence.

Oahu faded into the night, and soon only the light on Makapuu Point blinked a farewell to us. Our course was to the north, and *Trekka*, close-hauled on the starboard tack, kept working her way along a little east of north steering herself while the Northeast Trade Wind sang in the rigging. At times the wind eased and it was lovely sailing with the big genoa. At other times I had to stow the mainsail and go along with just

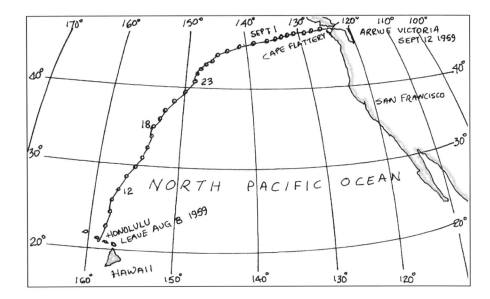

the staysail and mizzen up while crests slopped aboard into the cockpit and *Trekka* bounced along over a lumpy sea.

As we got farther north the weather began to get colder. At first it was just a slight chill to the air, but all too soon I had to get my old Cowichan sweater out of the locker to keep warm. Up into the thirties *Trekka* climbed, and each day saw the sun a little lower in the sky and the Pole Star higher at night.

At latitude 37 degrees north, we were not far from the center of the North Pacific High, the area of high pressure that has such an influence on the weather in the northwest of the American Continent.

There were some lovely cool days with clear skies and a very calm sea. *Trekka* ghosted along with masthead genoa set, going farther and farther north. The wind still remained northeasterly and I was still unable to lay the direct course for Juan de Fuca Strait. It was not until we were up to latitude 42 degrees north that the wind began to back to the north. I held onto a starboard tack for one more day, and then went about on to the port tack for the first time in eighteen days.

This was a wet, cold and depressing part of the ocean we were in now. For days we never saw the sun except for a brief glimpse through thick cloud. I had to wait for hours sometimes to get sights, and with the big swell that was running from the west it was often difficult to bring a hazy looking sun down on to a reluctant horizon.

I was awakened one morning just after daylight by *Trekka* hitting something. It felt just as though she had run aground, and I scrambled out of the sleeping bag and rushed to the hatch. She had collided with a huge waterlogged log that was encrusted with barnacles. Fortunately we were only moving along slowly, doing not much more than three and a half knots under twins and spinnaker. There was no damage, and the log drifted astern without fouling the rudder.

On 3 September I knew again the lonely feeling of a gale at sea. All sail was down and *Trekka* was riding the white-crested swell as buoyantly as the big gooney birds, the northern albatross, which had replaced the tropical sea birds. As the wind moaned through the rigging and the halyards beat a tattoo against the masts, *Trekka* climbed the desolate ridges only to plunge down the other side into the waste of a sea valley. Sometimes I braced myself in my bunk as I heard the hiss of a big sea approaching and waited for it to hit the hull. *Trekka* would lean far over like a prizefighter riding a punch as water swept across the deck.

We had been through all this before at various times, but I don't think it is possible to get used to riding out a gale in a small boat at sea, for each one seems different from the last, and I always know a great feeling of relief when the smoking seas have spent their fury. I have never forgotten the awful majesty of the seas in the Southern Ocean just before *Tzu Hang* was dismasted when she was running down the easting toward the Horn, and at the back of my mind is the knowledge that the sea could build up to the impossible height it reached on that occasion.

I was sitting below on the curved bulkhead seat looking out of the doghouse windows at the endless spectacle of the sea. I watched the crests approaching and the way my little vessel rode them so surely and bravely. I decided to make some tea and had just lit the stove when I glanced out of the window. My heart stopped beating and I saw as if in a nightmare a great monster of a sea advancing toward me. I watched hypnotized as it reared higher and higher and I knew that this was by far the biggest sea I had ever seen in *Trekka*. For a moment I was sure that it was going to be *Tzu Hang* all over again, then the brave little boat started for the summit with the courage of a Sir Edmund Hillary. Up, up, up, she went, then with a final flick of her stern she was over and plunging down the other side. I heard a great muffled boom as the sea broke, leaving a huge white swath to leeward. I had lost my appetite for tea and instead climbed back into the warmth of my bunk.

We were riding out that gale for 42 hours before I was able to get sail up again and continue on to Victoria. The wind was still fresh from the west and the sea quite high, but it was a fair wind, and *Trekka* surfed along under twin staysails steering herself. The barometer was still very low, and after checking in the Pilot Book, I reckoned that there was a secondary depression coming along. My diagnosis proved correct, for all too soon the wind was blowing with gale force again, and I had to pull all sail down and wait for conditions to moderate.

A few hours later the wind was easing and the barometer climbing steadily. With the twins up again we rolled along toward Cape Flattery, now only 165 miles away. On 9 September I could see what looked like land away to port, and on checking the chart found that it was the top of the mountains on Vancouver Island. Canada was in sight at last!

That night, thick fog closed down around us, and I dreaded the thought of another gale when so close to land and with visibility down to a few yards. Early the following morning I was in the cockpit, well bundled up with my sweater and oilies on, and wearing sea boots, too. I wanted to steer as accurate a course as possible so that I would not miss the entrance to the Strait of Juan de Fuca, which is only twelve miles wide. Even the great navigator, Captain James Cook, had missed the entrance of the Strait when searching for a possible route for the Northwest Passage. I could easily miss it too if the fog did not lift.

Toward noon the fog thinned a little, and soon afterwards it lifted completely. I went below to get the sextant, but I had used it for the last time, for when I looked ahead again, I could see the long-awaited sight of Cape Flattery, some twenty miles distant.

The wind fell right away as we closed the coast, and I decided to use the motor and try and reach the sheltered anchorage of Neah Bay on the Washington shore. We passed many fishing boats, all trolling for salmon, and toward late afternoon slipped past Tatoosh Island in company with some of the trollers that were also heading for Neah Bay.

The sun sank into the sea, leaving the sky a fading gold, the pine trees on the hills looked aflame, and then the colors faded to purple to violet and then to darkness. The anchor splashed down in the stillness and frightened a cormorant into the air. Because of Hurricane Dot in Hawaii, we were a little late in getting to Victoria. It was 10 September now and there was still fifty miles to go.

In the morning I went ashore and filled up my can with fuel at a garage, and soon afterwards we were running down the coast toward Victoria. Toward darkness we were close to Becher Bay on the Canadian shore, and

I decided to go in for the night and anchor so that I could get some sleep and get *Trekka* shipshape for the morrow. I moored to a jetty at the head of a small bay and was soon chatting to a man who was working on a small boat close by. He took me up to his house where I was able to phone a friend in Victoria and tell him that *Trekka* had come home again.

That night the press caught up with me and got the story. I was told to be at Ogden Point breakwater the following day at 1 p.m. where the doctor would give me pratique.

Unknown to me, a huge reception was being rapidly planned in which the Royal Canadian Navy was going to escort *Trekka* from Race Rocks into the harbour.

Trekka left Becher Bay the next morning under power with only 13 miles to go. Once outside the bay, the fog shut down all about us like a curtain but I was able to creep along the shore with the diaphone on Race Rocks to guide me through the passage.

William Head loomed up out of the fog, and then Albert Head. There was less than two miles to go now, when the fog started to lift a little and I saw a fishingboat heading toward us, the repeated blasts on its horn carrying clearly across the calm water. I saw figures standing in the bow, their hands waving excitedly, and as they came a little closer I saw that

Escorted by my friends, I enter Victoria Harbour

Jim Ryan

Trekka returns home after 33,000 miles, 4 years and 2 days

they were the same friends that had waved me goodbye four years before. A great lump rose up in my throat and I felt a flood of affection for them all. I gripped *Trekka*'s tiller hard and it seemed to quiver in my palm. We had known many adventures together in those years. They had been most wonderful years, and it was due to her that it had all been possible.

The fishing vessel slowed as she approached, and the voices of my friends floated clearly to my ears across the stillness. Faintly at first, then louder, "Welcome home, *Trekka*! Welcome Home!"

GUZZWELL SAILS HOME TO HERO'S WELCOME

Victoria newspaper headline describes the scene

Alan Lester

The Thermopylae Club presents me with their burgee   Jim Ryan

The city of Victoria honours me with a plaque

Epilogue

WHEN I THOUGHT of attempting to write this book and setting down on paper the account of *Trekka*'s voyage, there was one place where I knew all the happy memories would come flooding back, Russell in New Zealand.

During the northern winter of 1959-60, while *Trekka* was laid up with snow on her decks waiting for her skipper to return, I sat in the sun at Russell before the typewriter, remembering all the good times and some of the bad ones we had shared together. In the middle of March 1960, with a somewhat ragged manuscript stowed in my sea-bag, I returned to Canada aboard an Orient Line vessel bound for Vancouver. It was during this voyage home that I met a young lady who was to become my wife.

We spent our first few months together in Victoria where I got a job and attempted to be a normal human being. After the voyage this was not an easy role and I was often caught with a far-away look in my eyes.

Our spare time was spent sailing about the sheltered islands and inlets between Vancouver Island and the mainland, but *Trekka* was never conceived for these conditions and somehow she let us know that we had to take her to sea again.

In the spring of 1961, *Trekka* left for Hawaii where we spent several weeks cruising about the islands. During that time we came to realise that we really needed a larger boat as our family was soon to be increased.

We sailed *Trekka* to Los Angeles where we found a new owner for her who had long been an admirer and would look after her in the warm climate she had come to know so well.

It was not easy parting with *Trekka* after all the adventures we had shared together. She had taught me lessons in seamanship, and self-reliance, and had shown me what a wonderful life-style cruising under sail can be. They were lessons that would enhance me and my career in the years ahead when the course was sometimes difficult to steer.

Yet, as in life there has to be an ending, the time had come for us to part. Much of *Trekka*'s spirit was built into her successor, the 45-foot cutter, *Treasure*, which I built to Laurent Giles designs in England during the early 1960s and which has visited many of the places *Trekka* first showed me.

Although *Trekka* no longer holds the record, she was for many years the smallest vessel ever to circumnavigate the globe, and as such has earned herself a place in small-boat history.

Maureen and I relax aboard *Trekka* in Honolulu   Warren Roll

Afterword

Trekka Round the World went out of print about ten years ago, after several editions had been published. I was never able to determine how many copies were sold and, perhaps if I had engaged the services of an agent, it would have been to my benefit. Be that as it may, the book lay idle before repeated requests for the story prompted me to have a look at the manuscript and consider if it was worthwhile self-publishing a revised edition. With this in mind I spent a couple of weeks going through the text and had some help from a sailing friend, Molly Cadranell, in redesigning the format plus gathering together material that was not included in the original printing. This idea, like so many of mine, was thwarted by the lack of capital, and the book remained on a back burner until the spring of 1998 when I met Don and Réanne Douglass of Fine Edge Productions who approached me with a proposition to reissue the book under their label.

I immediately felt a great affinity with both of them for they are sailing people with four sons between them, and we share the uncommon experience of pitchpoling in the Southern Ocean at almost the same position though years apart.

Don and Réanne suggested that readers might be interested in knowing how my life continued after parting with *Trekka* in the fall of 1961, and what follows is a synopsis of the intervening years.

Clifford and Marion Cain from Monterey circumnavigated the world in *Trekka* during the 1970s, following much the same route as I did but knocking days off my passage times. During the years I lived in Hawaii, the boat again visited the Islands, this time owned by an English woman, Joanna Whipp, who set out with a male companion to follow *Trekka*'s well-trodden route. Joanna told me she needed more experience for this kind of voyaging, and eventually sold *Trekka* to Eric Abranovich, a young man who sailed the little boat in Hawaiian waters for about three years.

The Thermopylae Club—a group of businessmen from Victoria, B.C.—decided that the little boat deserved to be preserved in the city's Maritime Museum. They offered to buy the boat and donate her to the museum on condition that Eric sail her to Victoria for the handing over. I was living on nearby Orcas Island at the time and was contacted and asked if I would be willing to accompany Eric, once he arrived, into Victoria's Inner Harbour where the ceremony would take place. Naturally, I was delighted to be asked and it all went off very well. *Trekka* has been in the care of the Museum for nearly twenty years. If you would like to see the little boat, contact the Museum on Bastion Square.

Trekka Round the World was originally published in England in 1963, nearly four years after the completion of my voyage. The day it was released happened to be the day President Kennedy was assassinated in Dallas. Needless to say, it would have been better for me if Lee Harvey Oswald had picked a different day for his deed; my book's publicity was zero. I felt like Marlon Brando in the movie *On the Waterfront*. After he had been beaten by the mob he mumbled, "I could'a been a contender." But such is life and at the time I was happily building my 45-foot Laurent Giles-designed cutter in the small village of Sway in Hampshire's New Forest.

By the time *Treasure* was completed in 1965, our twin sons, James and John, were three years of age, and Maureen and I set out in December of that year to sail the boat to Australia where her family had settled after World War II. It was a time when the Australian Government was offering assisted passages to immigrants and we thought that we would be accepted as ideal settlers. We were young and had skills the country could use.

Our voyage took us across the Atlantic through the West Indies to Panama, on to Tahiti, Rarotonga and Fiji, thence to Sydney where we found to our chagrin that, because we had arrived in our own boat and did not need government assistance, the Customs Department expected me to pay duty on the boat, an amount that exceeded what I actually had in the boat. So after a short visit with Maureen's family, we turned eastwards where the New Zealanders gave us a kinder reception.

My skills as a joiner-boat-builder were appreciated in New Zealand and I had little trouble finding work. The children went off to school every day, sometimes on the Opua ferry but usually rowing themselves across the river estuary in the dinghy while I worked in the little boat yard at Tapu Point owned by my friend Richard McIlvride.

It was an idyllic time living in the Bay of Islands. We spent weekends exploring the many islands and anchorages the region had to offer at a time when there were still few cruising boats sailing those waters.

In 1969 we circumnavigated New Zealand following the same route Captain Cook had sailed in the *Endeavor* exactly 200 years before. At one anchorage in Fiordland where his men had set up an observatory ashore, we saw the moss-covered stumps of trees his men had cut to set up their equipment.

As a result of a yacht delivery job, I was offered a job in Hawaii in 1970, and we sailed *Treasure* to Honolulu where we lived for the next six years while I built two cruising yachts, one for Mr. Ronald Libkuman named *Sunrise*, a sister ship to my own boat.

Upon completion of the last boat I was forty-six years old, the boys were then fourteen, and I felt that they would benefit from a change to mainland living. I was also finding the climate too oppressive for the type of work I was doing, and I found on my return to the Pacific Northwest that the cooler conditions soon had me feeling more energetic.

We found some secluded property on Orcas Island with a large wooden building that had been constructed to service heavy equipment. It looked like an ideal opportunity for me and, for the first time in my life, I put myself in debt in order to acquire it. I picked up a commission to build a 37-foot cruising sailboat and it looked as though we were going to make it.

When the boat was finished, I got another order to build a sister ship. But somewhere along the way through all this work I lost Maureen who had been a loyal, loving wife and mother through some trying times. Living in a small island community had its own set of problems which can be devastating to relationships; ours was to end in a difficult divorce, and I buried myself with my two sons in more work.

Eventually I was to meet Dorothy Saunders who, with her two teen-aged sons, Steve and Jonothan, had moved to the island following the death of her husband in an airplane accident. Dorothy was then working with one of the owners of the Rosario Resort in organizing a salmon derby fishing contest which had a first prize valued at $10,000. She came walking down my driveway one day to ask if I would help in organizing the event which was to be held in mid-December of that year.

I confess that I fell under her spell immediately, but because she was introduced as Mrs. Saunders, I was not aware until the Derby that she was a widow and perhaps available. At fifty years of age I was not about to fool around with a long courtship; out of control and totally in love,

I lost little time in proposing to her. She became my wife two weeks later on New Year's Eve aboard *Treasure*.

I spent a couple of months remodeling the building on Orcas into a home for the two of us and the four young lads who had been thrust together by this union.

At this time I was involved with the construction of a large cold-molded yacht—the 133-foot *Antonia* being built in Brazil for a wealthy South American. Dorothy joined me in the town of Porto Allegre where a facility had been set up to construct the vessel.

On our return to Orcas Island where our four boys were living in the big house, we realised that some changes had to be made for all of us to survive the pressures of living together. My sons went north to Prince Rupert, Canada for the summer where they soon found work and Steve returned to school, also in Canada.

One fall evening almost exactly a year after our first meeting Dorothy asked me a hypothetical question, "What would you do, John, if someone told you that you had only six months to live?"

I thought about it for a moment and replied, "I think I would get on the boat and go spend the rest of my time in the South Pacific."

"If you feel that way," she said caught up with the idea, "why don't we do that?"

Two weeks later, after a lot of hurried preparations, we were on our way. Son Jonothan, just fourteen years old, was pulled out of Orcas Island High School somewhat to the displeasure of the football coach who was losing his star quarterback. Friends also must have felt a certain amount of concern for the boy and wondered what his mother had become involved with now.

To help in running the boat, I phoned Miles Smeeton in Alberta one evening to ask him if he would be interested in accompanying us as far as San Francisco since I had a green crew. We picked up Miles in Victoria and, with the prospect of fair winds, left immediately to get down the coast of Oregon.

Once into the open water of the Pacific, Dorothy realised that this was perhaps not one of her better ideas, and when the wind vane self-steering system broke, I knew that calling at San Francisco to have it repaired would result in losing my crew.

I had a quiet word with Miles in the cockpit and realised he had already pretty much summed up the situation. "Would you be prepared to sail with us to Hawaii rather than San Francisco?" I asked him without having to express my concern.

"I think that would be a very good idea, John," he replied with a twinkle in his eyes.

When Dorothy noticed that the compass heading had changed, she retired to the aft cabin for a couple of days and I gave her a lot of space. A couple of evenings later with the boat going along easily under auto-pilot and Miles, Jono, and me sitting in the cockpit "yarning" together, she appeared from her quarters. "All right, you buggers, you win. What would you like to eat tonight?" she asked, completely over her pique.

The rest of the passage to Hilo was wonderful and *Treasure* was indeed a happy ship.

Miles left us in Hilo. It was to be his last ocean voyage, and I thought that somehow our lives had come full circle. Years before, I had crewed for him and Beryl with their young daughter Clio, and now he had done the same for me.

We were to spend the next three months cruising the Hawaiian Islands and spending some time in Honolulu where Dorothy, who is a registered nurse, found temporary work at Kaiser Hospital.

We had decided to continue on to the South Pacific, and a couple of Orcas Island friends offered to stock the boat with supplies if they could join us for the trip to Tahiti.

I got back to the boat one afternoon after the two women had been shopping at the local Safeway store and noticed that the boat was a lot deeper in the water than when I left that morning. They had done a

Treasure in Tahiti

remarkable job in filling every available space to capacity with enough food to take us around the world.

It was a happy voyage and after Tahiti, with just the three of us on board now and fully competent to run the boat, we continued on to New Zealand with stops at Rarotonga, Tonga, and Fiji. We left *Treasure* on her old mooring off Dick McIlvride's boat yard for a year while we returned to the Pacific Northwest to earn some much-needed money.

A year later I arranged with Dick to sail the boat to Samoa where we could rendezvous with him. The timing was perfect, and Dick had done a great job in preparing the boat for our arrival.

The long uphill voyage home was in fact quite pleasant after the first 400-mile beat to Suvarov Atoll. We also called at Penryn Island and Honolulu before heading home on the last stretch back to Orcas Island.

A chance meeting in Honolulu with a man I had met briefly ten years earlier resulted in a job offer to help him finish an 85-foot schooner that was nearing completion in Fiji.

Soon after getting back to Orcas Island, I packed my toolbox and was on my way to Suva where *Whales Tail* was being built at the Whippy Yard. The owner, Paul Myers, had rescued his partially-built vessel from another builder on a neighboring island and had it towed to Suva where work had commenced again after years of inactivity. I was to find that the description of "nearing completion" was somewhat optimistic, but I was able to organize the work crew into a useful unit, and it was not long before we were making good progress.

Dorothy and Jono joined me later and we spent several months in Fiji until the project was finished and we returned home.

There is nothing like time spent away on a long sea voyage, or a project like this one, to what I call "blow away the cobwebs" of one's thinking mind. We returned to Orcas Island realising that the time had come to get back into the mainstream of life and out of this little backwater.

Accordingly, we moved to Seattle where I found more demand for my talents and it was not long before an opportunity to build a 65-foot sailing sharpie materialized. This boat, named *Lively*, was for Robert Haberman of New York. Designed by Bruce Farr, an ex-Kiwi who had set up offices in Annapolis, the boat was constructed mainly of Douglas fir marine plywood in the cold-molded manner using gallons of epoxy resin in the laminated construction.

At about this time, Dorothy decided that she wanted to become a flight attendant and was hired by United Airlines. She went off to Chicago to do her flight training and was eventually based in San Francisco.

I remember those days of hurried trips on weekends to see her, travelling on passes on a space-available basis, planning visits around her schedule while she flew off to various parts of the continent. On one of her passes we flew to Hong Kong and after several hours of exploring the countless shops, I finally said, "I need to rest up a bit. Why don't we go to the Yacht Club and check out the scene there?"

On arriving at the club we signed the guest book and within a short time were enjoying the view with some cool refreshment at hand. Not fifteen minutes later someone tapped me on the shoulder and asked, "Are you John Guzzwell? Because if you are, I have a project you might be interested in." It was David Higgins who, with his wife Lonnie, had set up the Marimed Foundation in Honolulu with the object of providing a Medical Service to the Marshall Islands using a sailing vessel to transport much-needed equipment to those far-flung islands. The project David had in mind was to build a large three-masted schooner of steel construction based on a design similar to that of the New Zealand sail-training ship, *Spirit of New Zealand*, designed by Ted Ewebank.

Jono and I flew to Auckland with David to see the vessel and meet with the designers. At this time it was assumed the new vessel would be built in the same yard taking benefit of the experience gained from building the *Spirit of New Zealand*. Although I could see certain advantages in doing this, it was obvious that most of the equipment aboard was going to be imported from the United States, and I was of the opinion that a U.S.-built vessel would cause fewer headaches to the Marimed Foundation in the future than a foreign-built ship.

After receiving estimates from several yards, the firm of Nicholls Brothers in Freeland, Whidbey Island, some 30 miles north of Seattle, was given the green light to go ahead with the building program. The vessel, named *Tole Mour*, is 124 feet on deck, with a beam of 30 feet and a draft of about 12 feet.

The Nicholls' yard produced the basic steel structure, and I was engaged as the manager to complete the finishing of the interior, installation of systems and hardware, and rigging the vessel.

It was quite a challenge. We were on a limited budget, and finding the right personnel for a project of this size was not easy. Among one of the many problems to solve was satisfying the U.S. Coast Guard requirements for a sailing vessel that they were unable to fit into a set category. We also had to meet American Bureau of Shipping standards—a problem that had not been anticipated by the New Zealand designers.

Eventually, by dint of hard work and perseverance, *Tole Mour* was completed and Dorothy and I were able to join the ship in San Francisco for the voyage to Honolulu. *Tole Mour* completed her three-year contract in the Marshall Islands where her experienced medical team delivered her much-needed services. At this writing, I believe she is based in Hawaii.

Dorothy was finally able to get based in Seattle which meant a lot less travelling time for both of us, and we eventually moved into a small condominium overlooking Lake Union.

About this time, I decided to build her a little sailboat in my spare time. Some years previously I had corresponded with the heirs to the Laurent Giles' design firm about the possibility of upgrading *Trekka*'s design for a limited production in fiberglass.

Lacking the necessary capital to float this idea, I drew up a modified set of lines based on her original design, but with a foot more beam and allowing the ends of the vessel to run out more. I had drawn these modified lines on a couple of sheets of plywood which survived several moves, and one day I took a good hard look at what they represented and made the decision to build the little boat in my workshop.

Dolly, as she came to be named after Dorothy's childhood name, measures 23 feet overall and is a modernized version of her famous predecessor. Aside from the increase in beam, I also gave her six more inches of draft, shortened up the keel to be more hydrodynamically correct, lightened up the structure for a better ballast ratio and increased the sail area by giving her a double-spreader cutter rig.

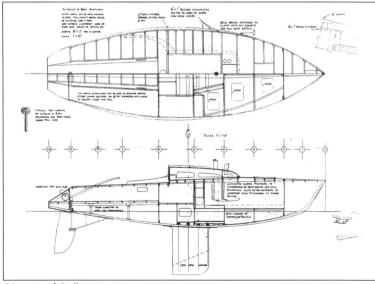

Diagram of *Dolly*

The little boat, which is finished bright, turned out very well and I gained enormous satisfaction in building her. I had almost forgotten what it was like to build something of my own creation instead of other people's dreams and consequently a lot of love went into *Dolly's* cold-molded hull. Featured in the 1994 July-August edition of *Wooden Boat* magazine, *Dolly* is a wonderful little boat for her size and I would have little hesitation in taking her offshore. She turned out better than I had hoped, floating right on her marks and weighing the 2,500 pounds I had aimed at.

On completion of the project, I drew up a set of plans of the design and, at this writing, two sister boats are under construction.

During the winter of 1993-94 I saw an event advertised in one of the yachting magazine. With the new Osaka airport in Japan scheduled to open the following summer, several yacht races to that city from various starting points were planned to commemorate the event.

One of those starting points was Los Angeles which would make most

Dorothy sails her beloved *Dolly* in Lake Union, Seattle

of the voyage in Trade Wind areas. I bounced the idea off Jono about doing the race in *Treasure* and asked him if he would be interested. He was, and I asked Dorothy how she would feel about our taking off for the summer. She was fully supportive and promised to visit us in Japan if we decided to do the race.

There was a lot of work in preparing for this event which required that the boat meet Category 0 ocean racing specifications. Safety equipment was the principal expense, but the race organizers promised that any boat which finished the course within a month of the lead boat would receive a grant of one million yen. I knew that *Treasure* was no race boat but neither was she that slow, and I felt sure we could get there in time to claim the money.

We talked fellow workmate Bruce Johnson into joining us, and we departed Seattle, April 2, to get to the starting line off Marina Del Rey on the morning of April 24.

The Oregon coast was still lively that early in the year. We spent a week weather-bound in Newport and another couple of days in San Francisco before finally arriving in Los Angeles in time for the pre-race inspection.

Osaka is a long way from Los Angeles. By the time you reach the Hawaiian Islands you have covered only about one-third of the distance. It was to take us 52 days to make the voyage during which time some of the old sails died. As it was, we collected a fine silver cup for third place in our class, plus the promised million yen which went toward the costs of outfitting the boat.

Bruce flew home from Osaka and, shortly afterwards, Dorothy arrived bringing the entire United Airlines flight crew with her. She looked wonderful!

With the prospect of typhoon season about to start, I was anxious to begin the return journey home which we planned via the Aleutian Islands. Jono and I left Tannowa Marina early in July and spent a couple of days at a small port near Shingu on the east side of Honshu Island before jumping off for the Aleutians.

The wind pattern forced us northward, and we eventually made a landfall at Attu Island, the westernmost island of the group. I had a copy of Miles Smeeton's *Misty Islands* on board and was full of admiration for his seamanship in navigating these waters years before us, without the benefit of modern electronic aids.

It was during this passage home that the idea of building a new boat for myself crystallized, and I began thinking that a return to the simplified sailing qualities of *Trekka* might be more attractive as I got older.

Dorothy flew into Kodiak and spent a few days with us, and we sailed in company with an Australian yacht that had done the Brisbane-Osaka race. We were off the usual track of cruising boats and I experienced a certain sadness that the voyage was nearly over.

Jono stayed with me across the Gulf of Alaska to Sitka and then flew back to Seattle, leaving me to bring the old ship the last few miles home. I came down the outside of the Queen Charlotte Islands and the west coast of Vancouver Island, arriving in Seattle on the last day of August 1994.

After returning from the 1994 Pan-Pacific Los Angeles to Osaka Yacht Race, I decided to build a new boat that was more competitive, easier to handle and fun to sail. At that time, the 1994 BOC solo around-the-world race* had just started from Charleston, South Carolina, and the yachting press gave quite a lot of information on the various competing boats in that event. I was particularly impressed with the 60-foot French boat, *Sceta Calberson*, sailed by Christophe Auguin, which was to win the event.

The shape of this particular boat intrigued me. Her French designers, Groupe Finot, had produced a hull shape that would surf downwind, yet have good upwind ability by using water ballast that could be pumped aboard into tanks on each side of the hull below decks. This extra weight, pumped to the weather—or high side of the boat—gave the boat a lot more power, reducing the amount of heel and allowing more sail to be carried.

There was no way I could afford to build a 60-footer, but a half-sized version of this boat was possible if kept simple, and as I had moved into a larger workshop, there was enough space to construct the vessel.

With some supplies remaining from building *Dolly*, I made a start on building this new 30-foot fractional sloop which was eventually named *Endangered Species*, partly in honor of the old-growth Sitka spruce used in her construction, and partly because few people today consider wood as being a suitable material for a lightweight racing yacht.

Using several magazine photos as a guide, I began lofting my version of this half-sized BOC boat, and ended up making four half-models of the hull which I placed on a mirror to get an idea of the complete hull shape.

By Christmas of 1994, the temporary hull mold was set up, upside-down, and I began construction of the hull itself. The hull is a cold-molded, laminated structure of five layers of 1/8-inch spruce, the inner four being laid diagonally and crossing each other at about a 90-degree angle, with the final fifth layer running longitudinally. Each layer of planking was set in a waterproof glue and held in place with temporary staples until

---

* The BOC Challenge is now called Around Alone.

the glue set. These staples were later removed with a special tool—a time-consuming task as there were over 100,000 staples used in the project. Because the staples showed marks on the planking, I elected to make the hull topsides out of teak which is harder than spruce and would look better when varnished since I was going to finish the hull bright. As with racing bicycles, the lighter they are, the more they cost. Most lightweight racing yachts today are built of exotic materials such as Kevlar or carbonfiber, with generous use of epoxy resin to bond the laminate together.

This technology was beyond my expertise and budget. Some years ago I became sensitized to epoxy resin which effectively barred my use of it,

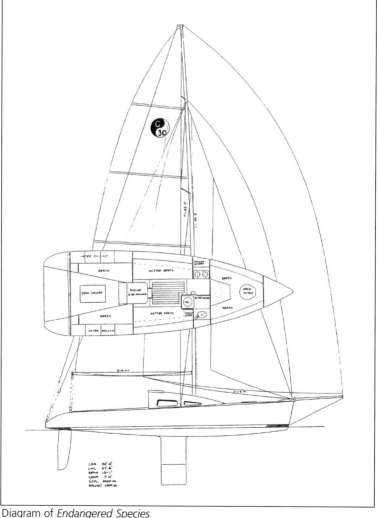

Diagram of *Endangered Species*

but I was convinced that if the wood was used as an engineering material and carefully put together—as with a violin or prized guitar—my hull would play a melody that the exotic materials could not. Some of the most satisfying days of my life were spent during the construction of *Species*, working out the details and assembling the various components into one homogeneous unit, so that each piece contributed to the overall structure. Without going to extremes in either time or materials, I was able to build a fairly light boat. At the time of launching, *Species* weighed 4,300 pounds, of which 2,000 were in the lead keel. With the addition of her rig and normal equipment, anchor, fenders, sails, and so on, her all-up weight is slightly over 5,000 pounds.

In August 1997, I took *Species* to the Wooden Boat Festival in Port Townsend, accompanied by my twin sons, James and John, who had sailed many miles with me as children on *Treasure*, but not as adults in their mid-thirties. It was a special weekend for me as we seldom get together, and there can be few better places to catch up on news and life than aboard a sailing yacht.

I knew that *Species* was a good boat from the way she handled, but I still did not know if she was competitive. The only way to determine that was to race her against other yachts of similar size. During the winter of 1997-98, I began making preparations to enter the 1998 Singlehanded TransPac Race from San Francisco to Hanalei Bay on the Hawaiian Island of Kauai. This 2,140-mile event, run every two years, is mainly a downwind run to the island.

I sent off for the particulars of the race and, on receiving them, found that several requirements would need to be realised in order to be accepted as an entrant. The main concern of the race committee was naturally safety, and only boats and skippers that had proven themselves in offshore conditions would be accepted. Although I myself had enough offshore experience, *Species* was in essence a virgin and, in order to pass the safety examination in San Francisco, the boat and skipper together must complete a 400-mile, non-stop passage, part of which must be at least 100 miles offshore.

My plan involved sailing *Species* to Victoria, B.C. for the 138-mile Swiftsure Lightship Classic race which took place over the Memorial Day weekend. I sailed this race with a friend, Jack Spriggs, and sons John and Jonothan, and we got a third in Class D, which showed the boat had potential.

The day after the race, I left Victoria alone for San Francisco, stopping at Neah Bay at the entrance to Juan de Fuca Strait to wait for a window of the right weather.

The passage down the coast took six days, and I learned a lot about handling *Species* and sailing her singlehanded. I was fortunate in having fair winds as this can be a rough, nasty trip.

I had fitted the boat with a windvane self-steering device and an electric autopilot—equipment which saves having to steer the boat manually but reduces the human element of anticipation. Although it does a wonderful job, there are certain conditions where it is best to hand-steer.

With *Species* safely in the marina at Sausalito, I returned to Seattle to make a new whisker pole to replace the one that broke on the way down the coast when the boat was running fast with a poled-out genoa. With the new pole strapped to the roof of my van, and loaded with tools and equipment, I drove down Interstate 5 in thirteen hours, something of a contrast to sailing the coast.

Dorothy joined me for the last few days in San Francisco and we shared some quality time together while she helped me with last-minute preparations. The night before the start of the race, son Jono also arrived, and it meant a lot to me to have them both there in a fully supportive role.

There were only twelve boats in the race plus Steve Fossett's radical trimaran, *Lakota*, in which he was to set a new record. The monohulls varied in size from the 60-foot *Etosha* to the little Moore 24, *Color Blind*, the only boat smaller than *Species*.

Each boat had been assigned a PHRF handicap—a measurement number applied to the boat's finishing time, similar to a golf handicap. This system allows different types and sizes of boats to race together so that all have a chance of winning, rather than just the big boats.

With a rating of 78, *Species* was expected to do very well. Only the 60-foot *Etosha* was more handicapped with a rating of 22. Looking at the other well-prepared boats, I knew that it was unlikely I could save my time against them, but I was determined to sail the boat as best I could, given the conditions.

The race start from the Corinthian Yacht Club at Tiburon at 11:40 a.m. June 27, was just five days after my sixty-eighth birthday. With a fresh westerly breeze and sunny skies, conditions were almost perfect, except for a strong flood tide which made beating out through the Golden Gate somewhat tricky. Most of the boats short-tacked along the northern shore to avoid the foul tide, before going onto a starboard tack which would last for the next 1,500 miles.

At mid-point in the race, *Species* was running neck-and-neck with the 38-foot *Giggles* which eventually won the event. At this point, I lost radio contact with the other boats and, as the wind came more aft, I had difficulty in keeping my asymmetrical spinnakers from overpowering the self-steering autopilot or windvane. Most of the latter half of the race was done with a poled-out genoa and mainsail and, from this point on, the longer boats gradually caught up with me.

Once into the Trade Winds, with air temperatures rising, it was great sailing with the boat surfing off the larger swells. The worst 24-hour run was 140 miles; the best was 179 miles.

Crossing the finish line early on the morning of July 11, *Species'* time for the course was 13 days, 18 hours, 24 minutes, 38 seconds which—on elapsed time—was right in the middle of the fleet but, on handicap, corrected to ninth.

Hanalei Bay is a beautiful place to visit by boat during the summer months when the bay provides sheltered anchorage to the normal Northeast Trade Winds. Having called there on several past voyages, I was interested in the changes that had occurred in the small community since I first sailed there in 1956. On this visit I was to meet several old friends who now live there permanently, and I wondered if I would ever decide to end my own days in one fixed place.

On the morning of July 19, eight days after arriving, I sailed out of the bay heading back to Seattle by myself. The weather forecast promised stable conditions for the next few days. With some fresh supplies on board and the 12-gallon fuel tank full of diesel, I was ready for the long windward passage home.

I was to find that *Species* goes well to weather, too, and for the next few days we beat our way northward over moderate seas under reduced sail. I did not attempt to sail too close to the wind which causes these light-displacement boats to pound, but rather let her fall off a little, knowing there would be ample opportunity later in the voyage to make the necessary easting.

As during past voyages over this route, I experienced some lovely sailing conditions when we came under the influence of the North Pacific high pressure system. The sea flattened out and the wind sometimes disappeared for hours at a time, then crept back over the surface of the water like little fingers reaching out to be grasped.

The days began to lengthen the farther north we went, and the cooler air of the north had me in warmer clothing during the day and a sleeping bag at night.

I arrived at Neah Bay on August 9, twenty-one days from Hawaii. After buying some fresh provisions, diesel, and taking a quick snooze, I left for Seattle making the overnight trip under power.

It was an emotional and nostalgic passage for me because I realise there cannot be too many more of these ocean voyages left on my calendar. I was also very grateful to the Good Lord in allowing me the space, ability, health and time to successfully complete the entire summer's voyage. Few are so lucky.

So, beware, dear reader. The sea has an enchantment that may captivate you and make you a bit of a misfit on land. It is perhaps the last place on the planet which remains unspoiled, with its moods and behaviours unchanged since time began. Like the moth to the flame, the sea has an attraction that defies explanation and those of us who come under its spell are forever changed.

I sailed out of Hanalei Bay heading back to Seattle

Appendix I

Trekka

The reader will not be surprised that I consider *Trekka* hardly the ideal type of yacht for a world voyage, but before crossing her off the list of successful designs, it is worthwhile considering her advantages together with her faults.

Firstly, cost: there can be no doubt that *Trekka* represents about the minimum investment for a world-voyaging yacht. Unlike many of her predecessors, she was brand spanking new when she left Victoria in September 1955, and she returned four years later in virtually the same condition. Most voyagers try to keep their vessels in good condition and looking smart, and perhaps in this respect I tend to be even more particular, yet friends on other yachts I met always envied the ridiculously small amount of work required to keep *Trekka* shipshape compared to their larger boats.

In most ports, charges are levied against yachts for moorage or port dues or, as in the case of Panama, making the transit of the canal. These charges are usually based on either tonnage or length and this was an area where *Trekka* really scored over her larger rivals.

Maintenance costs, hauling out on a slipway, paint and varnish, new sails and equipment, less time spent doing the maintenance, these were all advantages for *Trekka*. There are many more without belaboring the subject.

For a single-handed voyage, therefore, perhaps *Trekka* was not such a bad choice as some people may think. At sea she proved to be an excellent little sea-boat, making extremely good passages on many occasions, while not demanding excessive attention from her crew.

Naturally enough, *Trekka*'s chief disadvantage was lack of space. This was most apparent in port and never noticed at sea. In port the lack of space became a nuisance largely because of shore-side customs. Getting dressed into a jacket and trousers required me to become something of a contortionist, and the toilet arrangements were hardly as easy as when at sea!

One of the things I missed was returning some of the hospitality to friends who had been so kind to me on shore. Had I been able to invite some of these people into a more spacious saloon I would have done so, but two persons below in *Trekka* was about the limit.

However, on several occasions I was able to take friends sailing for an afternoon, which would entail much work aboard a larger yacht whereas on *Trekka*, bending on sails and letting go mooring lines took only a few minutes.

If I were to do it again single-handed? This is an interesting thought, and one that has passed away many pleasant hours on land and at sea. As

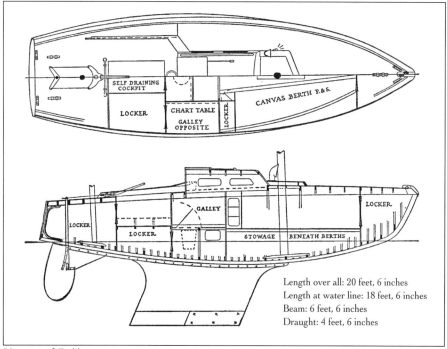

Length over all: 20 feet, 6 inches
Length at water line: 18 feet, 6 inches
Beam: 6 feet, 6 inches
Draught: 4 feet, 6 inches

Diagram of *Trekka*

a result of spending nearly three years living aboard *Trekka,* I used to think that any boat larger than twenty-five feet was quite spacious. However, space is like money, you think you never have enough. Because of this, my boat would be quite small, so that nothing would get out of hand and so that I could keep control of the gear and maintenance. It would be nice to have standing headroom, even if it was only under the doghouse, and I would also like to have a small inboard diesel engine instead of the out-board as used on *Trekka*. My main consideration would be that the boat be simple, yet this is perhaps the most difficult thing to attain as there is so much tempting equipment as well as systems available today in the marine business. One's ideas tend to change with the passing years, but I see a lot of people missing out on much of the enjoyment of boating by attempting

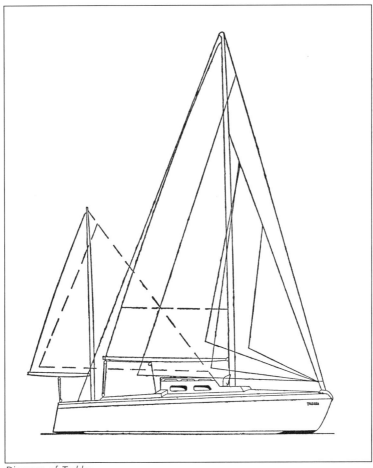

Diagram of *Trekka*

to take their shore-side conveniences with them. Most seem to want maintenance-free boats, yet load up on somewhat unnecessary equipment that needs constant attention to keep it working.

I would again use the portable containers to carry fresh water in as they can always be taken ashore and filled, whereas tanks frequently collect sediment and can be difficult to fill if there is no handy hose near by, and many of the places I would want to visit have no such thing as hoses.

As for the size of this little vessel, she would need to be no longer than 30 feet overall, and I think I would still go for a light displacement hull form, for one of the great joys of sailing *Trekka* was the feeling of sailing, of surfing off the waves, and the responsiveness of the steering. Although the yawl rig was very successful, the reason it was chosen was that in 1955 very little was known about vane gear self-steering systems. My boat would certainly have one of these units and be rigged as a masthead cutter with a good tall mast. One can always reduce sail, but there are many times when it would be nice to use the maximum sail area possible.

Probably for me the most important requirement of all would be that this little vessel be constructed with my own hands, for I would want to know her intimately no matter which material was used for her construction; perhaps then I would also know the confidence that *Trekka* gave me during her trek round the world.

Appendix II

What Happened to *Tzu Hang?*

One of the questions I was asked so many times during the second half of *Trekka*'s voyage and since is: What really happened to *Tzu Hang* down there in the Southern Ocean?

Miles Smeeton, in his book *Once is Enough*, described in detail how on two occasions *Tzu Hang* was turned completely over during storms in those high latitudes. Many people, in their ignorance of what conditions can be like down there, have criticized the boat, saying that there must have been something wrong with the design of the hull. Some of these armchair experts have done little coastwise sailing, let alone ocean crossings in small craft.

I do not say that it would be impossible to find a better boat, but anyone who knew her would agree that it would be hard to find a more seaworthy vessel than *Tzu Hang*. In no way was she an extreme design, her displacement was quite moderate for her size, and her seven tons of outside lead ballast with a draught of seven feet gave her excellent stability.

I have never doubted *Tzu Hang*'s ability, and her behavior during the 7,000 miles I sailed in her before that fateful day when she pitchpoled left me with nothing but praise for her sea-kindliness, design and excellent construction.

In my mind, the boat cannot in any way be blamed for what happened to her; the sea that was running at the time was in fact too much for her, as it would have been for any other yachts of similar size and displacement.

There was a time when I believed that a small, well-designed yacht in the open ocean would, if correctly handled, survive anything the sea had to offer, but since seeing with my own eyes the almost unbelievable state it can reach on rare occasions, my views have changed. I do not see how any yacht less than 50 feet overall could avoid being capsized in the extreme conditions it is possible to experience in the wastes of the Southern Ocean. If you have seen a child's toy bowled over in breakers at the seaside, you might be able to imagine what happened to *Tzu Hang.*

Many yachts have been capsized and have lived through the experience to bring their crews safely to port. Indeed many racing yachts are prepared with this kind of situation in mind, floorboards are fastened down, batteries are secured and storage bins are designed to retain their contents in the event of an unexpected capsize. This kind of preparation would have helped *Tzu Hang,* but would have made no difference to the initial forces which flung her forward and slammed her down onto her deck, smashing her doghouse and hatches and allowing the hull to flood.

My thoughts on the matter have not been in finding fault with the boat, but rather what could have caused the sea to reach such a staggering height on this one occasion. Remember, we were at sea for 50 days in Roaring Forties weather before the accident, and another month afterwards, without seeing the sea approach the state it did on 14 February 1957.

While in Honolulu toward the end of 1959, I had a most interesting discussion with William Albert Robinson who, it will be remembered, completed his excellent circumnavigation of the world in *Svaap* toward the end of 1931.

We talked about the more recent voyage he made down into the Roaring Forties in his lovely 70-foot brigantine-schooner, *Varua,* and on a chart compared her track with that of *Tzu Hang's.* During that voyage he encountered a storm of such severity that he called it "The Ultimate Storm." The scene of this storm and *Tzu Hang's* misadventure were a long way apart both in time and distance, though on similar latitudes. Robinson was quite emphatic that during that storm *Varua* passed over a shoal, though there is no evidence to show on charts of the area that a shoal exists.

The state of the sea when *Tzu Hang* pitchpoled was very similar to what would be encountered with a long swell passing over a shoal area—very steep seas, some of which toppled over and broke like surf on a beach.

I wrote to the Hydrographic Department in London seeking information on the depth of water in this part of the ocean. The reply I received is of sufficient interest to repeat an extract here.

> Admiralty Chart No. 789 shows only one line of soundings crossing the meridian of 98 degrees west longitude in about 50 degrees 42' south latitude.
>
> This line of soundings was taken by the United States ship *Enterprise* in 1883–86. The soundings nearest to your position are 2,383 fathoms and 2,291 fathoms. The only other soundings in this vicinity shown on the chart are 2,565 fathoms about 290 miles to the northeast and 2,555 fathoms about 310 miles to the south.

The closest soundings of 2,291 fathoms are in fact about 40 miles from the scene of *Tzu Hang*'s somersault.

In recent years, ships equipped with echo-sounders have discovered many "seamounts" in the North Pacific, shoals like mountain peaks that rise rapidly from the bed of the ocean to within a few hundred feet of the surface of the sea. These discoveries have been made largely by accident by shipping which crosses the North Pacific on the great circle course from the West Coast of North America to Far East ports.

I see no reason to doubt the existence of similar undiscovered "seamounts" in the South Pacific which have remained undetected solely because so little shipping uses the old sailing-ship route from Australia to Cape Horn.

If soundings taken in 1883 are to be taken seriously, what of other soundings that were also taken during the last century?

Take the case of the Maria Augustina Bank, the position of which *Trekka* passed 120 miles northward during the run from Thursday Island to Cocos. The Admiralty Pilot Book tells the history of this in these words:

> In 1856 the Captain of the Spanish frigate *Maria Augustina*, when cruising about 540 miles east-by-south of the Cocos Islands, perceived a change in the color of the water, and soundings taken immediately showed depths of 11, 9, 7, 5, and 13 fathoms, sand and mud; at the same time a black object on which the sea broke was observed about half a mile northward of the vessel. After sailing a further 7-1/2 miles on a course of 211 degrees, soundings of 6, 8, and 10 fathoms were obtained.
>
> From good observations taken at the time, and later verified at Java Head, the southern entrance point of the western end of Sunda Strait, the position of the rock was established at Lat 14 degrees 05' south and Long 105 degrees 56' east. Discolored water had been previously reported at approximately the same position, by the master of the *Helen Stuart* in 1845 who stated he ran over a

milk-white patch for about 50 miles in an east and west direction, no soundings, however were taken.

The existence of the above bank is considered doubtful.

What do you make of that one? The closest sounding to the bank other than those mentioned above is 2,825 fathoms, 120 miles to the northward.

Here is another one in the South Indian Ocean about 600 miles southeast of Durban:

Slot Van Capelle. The existence of this bank, as well as its position, is considered doubtful, but it is shown on the chart in latitude 36 degrees 34' south, longitude 41 degrees 20' east. It is named after the Dutch vessel by which it was reported in 1748, which vessel stated it to be of considerable dimensions and obtained soundings in 63 fathoms southwestward of it. The bank was again seen by the *Automatia* in 1801 and by Captain Viana of the *Jacques-Elizabeth* in 1856.

Perhaps some day when the oceans of the world have been accurately sounded we may be able to piece together some of the riddles of the sea, of the ships like *Tzu Hang* who survived a catastrophe, and of the many who didn't and left their bones rotting on the bed of the ocean or perhaps on some uncharted shoal.

In the early 1920s my father was invited as a guest to make a passage aboard a small trading schooner named *Southern Cross*, bound from Auckland, N.Z. to Tahiti. It was not until the vessel was at sea that he realised the reason for the invitation; he discovered that he was the only person aboard who could navigate! The recommended sailing-ship route for that particular passage is to run down the easting on much the same latitude as Auckland until a little east of Tahiti's longitude, at which point the course should be changed to the northward directly toward the island.

The prevailing conditions in this part of the ocean will usually allow a sailing vessel fair winds for the whole passage. Shortly before reaching the desired longitude, *Southern Cross* was almost becalmed on a peaceful ocean, the vessel's position on the chart was close to a notation which said "Breakers reported 1886," but due to the clear and calm conditions it was decided not to alter course. About mid-day with the sun high overhead, my father was on deck getting a latitude sight; glancing over the side into the depths below he was shocked to see the vessel was passing over a shoal and that the bottom was clearly visible. The entire crew witnessed the scene and all were much relieved when the vessel had reached deep water again.

While it is possible that *Tzu Hang* did in fact pass over a shoal, it seems more likely that she was the victim of a freak or rogue wave generated by the storm and possibly another separate disturbance, perhaps several hundred miles from us.

In recent years much more has been learned of these giant super waves in the open ocean. Observations from stable vantage points such as oil drilling rigs, lighthouses, and huge supertankers indicate that waves of abnormal height can form as a result of various factors—wind strength, and the duration of the gale, the amount of fetch (the distance of exposed water), the bottom topography, sea currents, sea and air temperature, and the effect of wave swells from other storm systems.

The Southern Ocean is an enormous expanse of open water undisturbed by land masses, so that a swell is ever present even when local conditions are calm. Although ocean swells appear to move in a regular pattern, there are subtle changes that are apparent to a careful observer. There will be a wave form dictated by the prevailing weather in the immediate surrounding area, but superimposed on this wave form may be the swell from a distant disturbance. The harmony of these waves may be quite different, with greater speed or longer distance from crest to trough, but it is possible for waves of each system to coincide at a critical moment, producing a freak wave often far bigger than the normal pattern.

A recent $1.8 million wind-and-wave study financed by 13 oil companies came up with some figures on what kind of storm waves could be generated in the Gulf of Alaska, an area attractive for oil producing but one that is noted for its bad weather. The experts' conclusion, based on the characteristics of the worst storms experienced in that area over a twenty year period, is that a wave measuring 198 feet in height is possible.

The sport of surf riding gives an understanding of the behaviour of wave systems in shallow water. Surfers know that every wave is slightly different from its predecessor. Waves arrive in groups called "sets," there being about seven to nine waves to a set. Each set has a variety of wave sizes, there being only one or two that are bigger than normal; but every once in a while a set arrives that is significantly above average size. This same phenomenon is experienced in the open sea, although it is more difficult to detect. For those of us that sail the oceans in small yachts. the chance of meeting rogue waves are slight, as the timing is critical, the odds of being in the right location at the moment a freak wave is generated make it a long shot at best. Also voyages are usually conducted over kinder and more forgiving seas than the Southern Ocean, but there will always be people with the spark of adventure in their souls who are prepared to accept the challenge of the elements, and those who have survived that confrontation know how easily the result could have been catastrophic.

Tzu Hang survived her baptismal in the Southern Ocean and Miles and Beryl Smeeton went on to make some splendid voyages in the high latitudes, including a circumnavigation of the world and an excellent rounding of Cape Horn the hard way, from east to west. *Tzu Hang* returned to Patagonian waters with her later owner, Bob Nance, who had been crew during her successful Cape Horn passage. I think she more than vindicated herself, confounding the critics who suggested that her design was to blame for the capsize.

Late in 1991, I received a copy of a newspaper article by Miles Clark, the Smeetons' biographer and godson. Published by the London *Daily Telegraph*, the story told of *Tzu Hang*'s last years spent in Caribbean waters, how she was sold to an American named Jerry Hart who used her to smuggle over 20,000 lbs. of marijuana from Colombia into the United States.

Tzu Hang was seized by Customs agents and a delivery crew sailed her

Tzu Hang in happy days, British Columbia, 1967   Hal Roth
Left to right: Raith Sykes, Vivienne Sykes, Miles Smeeton, Beryl Smeeton, Margaret Roth

to a holding dock in St. John, Puerto Rico, where other confiscated vessels were also being detained.

On September 16, 1989, nine months after *Tzu Hang*'s arrival, the worst hurricane in living memory swept through the region sinking all nine boats in custody. *Tzu Hang* was thrown back onto the jetty, smashing a five-foot hole in her quarter and she sank in 20 feet of water.

Seven weeks after the storm, a French diver hauled *Tzu Hang* to the surface, and for nearly a year she laid on an open piece of ground above the tide line. At this stage she was still repairable, but in August of 1991 the US Customs contracted a breaker named Pedro Ramos to destroy the six damaged boats held by them.

Ramos told Miles Clark that he wanted to rebuild *Tzu Hang* and had hired a truck to haul her the 80 miles over the mountains to his home in Mayaquez. Less than a mile from where she was lying, the truck was involved in an accident and was never able to collect her. *Tzu Hang*'s luck finally ran out and she ended up being demolished by a 10-ton bulldozer, with most of her remains being dumped at the city landfill on the hill above San Juan. Truly a sad ending for a gallant ship.

Author's Notes

Small boat sailing back in the 1950s was without many of the conveniences we take for granted today. Due mainly to long-distance ocean races like the Whitbread Round the World and the Around Alone (formerly the BOC Race), public interest and imagination have been captured. Sailing and ocean cruising have become an accepted form of recreation, even a lifestyle, as more people dream of breaking away from the rat race and running away to some tropical island over the horizon.

The ability to mass produce small craft using a material now known as fiberglass revolutionized the marine industry, making boating available to the general public at a cost similar to that of owning a family car.

With the growth of the sport came the demand for better equipment, and developments in synthetic fibers gave us superior sailcloth, ropes, and clothing. The technology of the "space race" spilled off into an expanding marine industry, and electronics and communications—formerly available only to the military—became available to the average man on the street.

As with the family car, today's boats are far more comfortable, easier to operate and faster, if not more reliable, than models of yesteryear. Though a few of us may feel a twinge of nostalgia for a simpler past, progress is inevitable.

Although many of the new products have diminished much of the discomfort, hard work and worry of ocean sailing, the offshore environment remains much the same as it was when man first ventured into the unknown. This may explain why many of us are attracted to an often bizarre existence. Anyone who chooses a small boat over modern transportation to get from A to B does so for the experience, rather than efficiency or cost. In small-boat voyaging it's the journey that counts rather than the destination.

In looking back over the years, *Trekka* was indeed a wonderful little boat from the drawing board of a brilliant and talented designer. J. Laurent (Jack) Giles was years ahead in his ideas and, even today, the *Trekka* design looks contemporary and would attract favorable attention in any company.

As mentioned in my Afterword, *Trekka* was presented to the Victoria, B.C. Maritime Museum in 1981 by a group of Victoria businessmen in the Thermopylae Club, an organization interested in maritime history and affairs. Since that time she has been exhibited at the Museum's Bastion Square location near the waterfront in downtown Victoria. I have made many visits to see her there and feel a bond rather like that of a first love, a love that—even though you may have had others during your lifetime— you never forget.

At this writing, because of changes at the Museum, *Trekka*'s future is uncertain. It is hoped that a new location will be found that will enable her to be preserved so that visitors to Victoria can again view the little boat—the first Canadian small yacht to circumnavigate the world and once listed in the *Guiness Book of World Records* as the smallest to do so.

One of the great examples *Trekka* has to offer is that it is possible to accomplish much with a little effort. With today's pressures from the media and advertising, it is easy to assume that many modern conveniences are necessary. Far too many people are discouraged from sailing and cruising by the cost and maintenance of all the gadgets associated with yachting. The old KISS acronym—Keep It Simple Stupid—makes a lot of sense when it comes to boating. Human nature being what it is tends to make things more complicated than they need to be, and unless you have the know-how and finances to maintain these conveniences, they cannot be relied upon and will fall victim to Murphy's Law.

In a past edition of this book I gave some thought to the type of boat I would choose if I were to make the voyage again singlehanded. It is interesting to note that I recently returned from competing in the Singlehanded TransPac Race in a new boat, *Endangered Species*, which I designed and built and which embodies much of the KISS philosophy and the thoughts I had when writing the original story in Russell, New Zealand nearly forty years ago.

Certainly my experience in sailing *Trekka* round the world has been one of my life's most treasured rewards. From it I gained a sense of confidence and patience, and I learned much from the people I met along the way and from the books I read. It was, to a large degree, the university education I never had and which would have condemned me to a certain class had I remained in Britain.

Perhaps because of this, I feel a strong sense of gratitude to the New World for allowing me the vision, energy, and freedom to pursue my dream without the need of some form of sponsorship which would have spoiled my sense of achievement and satisfaction in the venture.

About the Author

John Guzzwell, one of the world's great singlehanded sailors, was born in England and grew up in the Channel Islands where he spent most of his time on and around boats. John and his family were interned in Germany during World War II. Afterward, John learned the profession of boat joiner and then emigrated to British Columbia. At the age of 22, he began construction of *Trekka,* the boat in which he was to make his voyage around the world. John now makes his home in Seattle where he builds custom boats. He still sails, and recently completed the

Dorothy and John Guzzwell, just before the start of the 1998 Singlehanded TransPac Race

Singlehanded TransPac Race from San Francisco to Hawaii in *Endangered Species,* a half-scale model of a B.OC. racing sailboat which he built himself.

John Guzzwell with his twin sons, James and John Guzzwell

NAUTICAL TITLES FROM FINE EDGE PRODUCTIONS:

Cape Horn
One Man's Dream, One Woman's Nightmare
by Réanne Hemingway-Douglass

"This is the sea story to read if you read only one." —McGraw Hill, International
Marine Catalog   "The book grabbed me by the throat. . . . A true story about a couple
in a ketch that pitchpoled on the edge of the Screaming 50s off southern Chile, the book,
written by the wife, is easily the hairy-chested adventure yarn of the decade, if not the
half-century."—Peter H. Spectre, *Wooden Boat*   ISBN 0-938665-29-4

Sea Stories of the Inside Passage
by Iain Lawrence
A collection of first-person experiences about cruising the North Coast; entertaining and
insightful writing by the author of *Far-Away Places*.   ISBN 0-938665-47-2

GPS Instant Navigation
A Practical Guide from Basics to Advanced Techniques
by Kevin Monahan and Don Douglass
"If you want the greatest possible benefit from GPS, I strongly recommend this book.
The illustrated techniques will save you time and clearly explain the system."
—John Neal, Bluewater sailor, *Mahina Tiare*   This book introduces the novice to the
basics of instant navigation and carries him to advanced techniques of error reduction,
electronic charting, and navigation software.   ISBN 0-938665-48-0

Destination Cortes Island
By June Cameron
A well known Vancouver sailor recalls growing up on Cortes Island and exploring
Desolation Sound. A true story of island life as experienced by a pioneer family.
ISBN 0-938665-60-X

Final Voyage of Princess Sophia
by Betty O'Keefe and Ian Macdonald
The epic story of the tragic end of the steamer *Princess Sophia* as she founders in
Lynn Canal, Southeast Alaska. In October 1918, as she was southbound from Skagway,
carrying 353 prospectors, businessmen and crew on the last trip of the year, the *Sophia*
struck Vanderbilt Reef. It was Alaska's greatest maritime disaster. ISBN 0-938665-61-8

Exploring Vancouver Island's West Coast
All New Second Edition
By Don Douglass and Réanne Hemingway-Douglass
The complete cruising guide to the largest island on the west coast of North America.
Includes GPS waypoints and detailed anchor diagrams to the five great sounds, sixteen
major inlets. ISBN 0-938665-57-X

For other nautical titles visit our web site: **www.fineedge.com**

Exploring the San Juan and Gulf Islands
Cruising Paradise of the Pacific Northwest
by Don Douglass and Réanne Hemingway-Douglass
Contributions by Anne Vipond, Peter Fromm, and Warren Miller

The first publication to document all the anchor sites in the paradise of islands that straddles the U.S.-Canadian border, an area bounded by Deception Pass and Anacortes on the south, Nanaimo on the north, Victoria on the west, and Bellingham on the east.
ISBN 0-938665-51-0

Exploring the South Coast of British Columbia
Second Edition
By Don Douglass and Réanne Hemingway-Douglass
This new edition of a classic cruising and anchoring guide covers Victoria and Vancouver to the north end of Vancouver Island. Hundreds of inlets and islands are documented as never before in accurate detail based on the authors' personal research. Acclaimed as the most trusted guide available.
ISBN 0-938665-62-6

Exploring the North Coast of British Columbia
Blunden Harbour to Dixon Entrance — Including the Queen Charlotte Islands
by Don Douglass and Réanne Hemingway-Douglass

Describes previously uncharted Spiller Channel and Griffin Passage, the stunning scenery of Nakwakto Rapids and Seymour Inlet, Fish Egg Inlet, Queens Sound, and Hakai Recreation Area. It helps you plot a course for the beautiful South Moresby Island of the Queen Charlottes, with its rare flora and fauna and historical sites of native Haida culture.   ISBN 0-938665-45-6

Exploring Southeast Alaska
by Don Douglass and Réanne Hemingway-Douglass
A comprehensive cruising guide with routes to all the inlets and islands in S.E. Alaska, including detailed anchor diagrams from Dixon Entrance to Glacier Bay Park, Icy Point and Skagway.   ISBN 0-938665-58-8

Proven Cruising Routes for the Inside Passage to Alaska
By Don Douglass
Suggested itineraries, complete GPS waypoints for popular routes, detailed steering directions and anchor-diagrams for shelter along the route from Seattle to Glacier Bay. Almost completely protected, these routes give access to a pristine wilderness of breathtaking beauty, with thousands of islands, deeply-cut fjords, tidewater glaciers and icebergs.
ISBN 0-938665-49-9

For other nautical titles visit our web site: **www.fineedge.com**

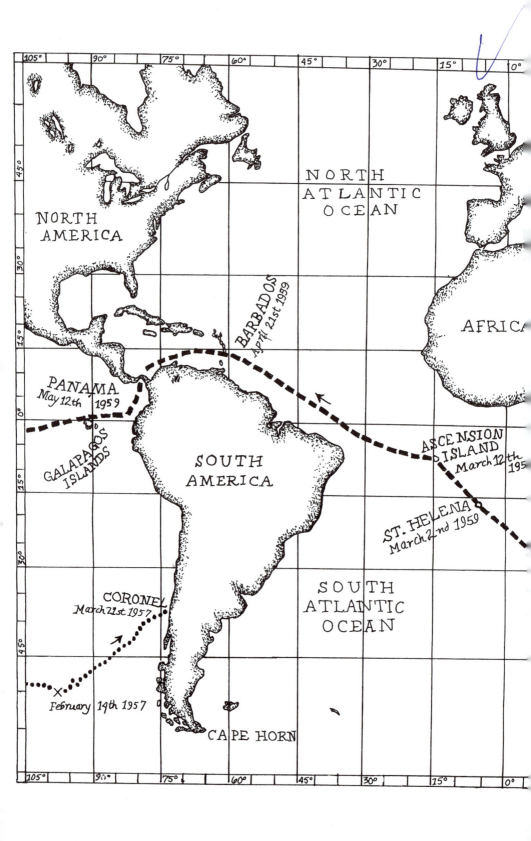

NORTH ATLANTIC OCEAN

NORTH AMERICA

BARBADOS
April 21st 1959

AFRICA

PANAMA
May 12th 1959

GALAPAGOS ISLANDS

SOUTH AMERICA

ASCENSION ISLAND
March 12th 195

ST. HELENA
March 2nd 1959

SOUTH ATLANTIC OCEAN

CORONEL
March 21st 1957

February 19th 1957

CAPE HORN